BEST
VERMONT
DRIVES

BEST VERMONT DRIVES

14 Tours
in the
Green Mountain State

Third Edition

Kay and Bill Scheller

Jasper Heights Press   Waterville, Vermont

The authors and publisher make no representation as to the safety
of any trails or bodies of water mentioned in this book. Hiking and
swimming, especially in unsupervised locations, are inherently
dangerous activities, and conditions can change without notice.
Readers assume all responsibility while engaging in recreational
activities at locations mentioned herein.

Cover design by Barbara Flack and Brian Heyliger
Cover photograph by Sheldon B. Korones, M.D.
Maps by Abigail Smith and Bill Scheller
Colophon design by Ben Grunow

Our thanks to Harry Orth for assistance with revisions

Special thanks to Green Mountain Technology and Career Center,
Hyde Park, VT

Printed in Canada
by Transcontinental Printing

10 9 8 7 6 5 4 3 2 1

Jasper Heights Press
438 Shipman Road
Waterville, Vermont 05492

Best
Vermont
Drives

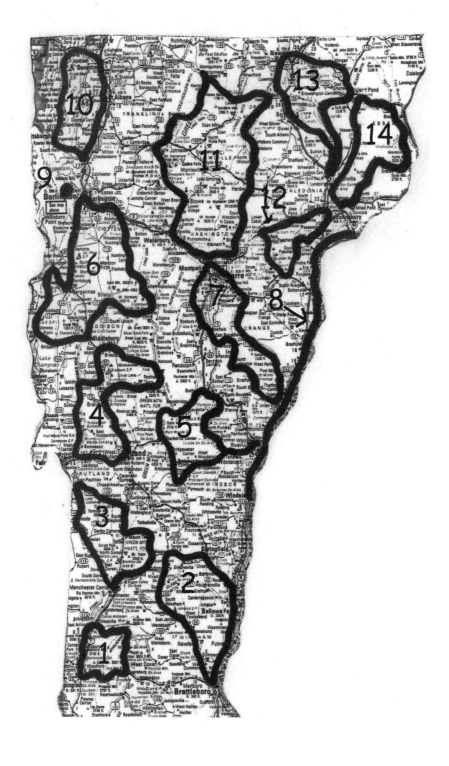

Contents

Introduction

Now in its third revised edition, *Best Vermont Drives* offers a unique approach to touring the Green Mountain State. We've divided Vermont into 14 drives, ranging from 60 to 140 miles in length and encompassing virtually all of the state's scenic highlights, historical touchstones, and recreational opportunities.

Our goal throughout Best Vermont Drives has been to offer an informal, conversational approach. But we haven't forgotten that along with anecdotes, most travelers want tips on where to stay, where to eat, and what attractions are worth their while. Within the drive narratives, numbers precede each new area or major point of interest. At the end of each drive, an "Information" section lists all of the lodgings, restaurants, attractions, activities, and shops that appear in boldface type in the text. Each listing is preceded by a number in parentheses, corresponding to the numbers that accompany places in the text. This makes it easy to tell if an inn or restaurant, for example, is close to the point where you've chosen to break up a drive with a meal or a night's stay.

For all lodgings in the"Information" sections, we've indicated rate categories keyed to dollar sign symbols. Rates are based upon double occupancy: $ = $75 or less; $$ = $76-$149; $$$ = over $150.

These rates are for low to high season: the former includes "shank" or off-season periods such as April and November; the latter includes summer, peak foliage season, and winter if there's a ski area nearby. Private bath is assumed, unless otherwise noted. We've also indicated where young children may not be welcome, but be sure to check. And book well ahead for foliage season -- just about every place fills up way in advance. Many lodgings require a two-night minimum stay during busy periods. All B&Bs listed serve a full breakfast unless otherwise indicated, and most lodgings that serve dinner offer an MAP (Modified American Plan) rate which includes dinner.

For restaurants and attractions, we've indicated only days closed--and they are subject to change. It's even more difficult to give hours as they change sesonally at many places. Always phone ahead to avoid disappointment. **All Area Codes are 802 except toll-free numbers as indicated.**

Dollar sign symbols for restaurants are based on the average cost of appetizer, entrée and dessert, before tax, tip or drinks (if dinner is not served, the signs are based on breakfast and/or lunch):
$ = less than $20; $$ = $21-$35; $$$ = $36 or more.

Lodgings that have highly-rated restaurants are indicated with an (R), and restaurants that offer lodgings with an (L).

Best Vermont Drives is not a mile-by-mile guide, and we have deliberately avoided instructions such as, "turn left 3.2 miles ahead" unless there is a chance of confusion. Before you head out on any of the drives, we recommend picking up a copy of Vermont's official road map, available free at information centers throughout the state. Hiking trail distances are for round trips, unless otherwise noted.

Happy driving!

Kay and Bill Scheller
May 2003

For a free Vermont Traveler's Guidebook call the Vermont Chamber of Commerce at 802-223-3443, e-mail them at: info@vtchamber.com, or check on-line at: www.vtchamber.com

For a free state guidebook, contact the Vermont Department of Tourism and Marketing (828-3237) , 6 Baldwin St., 4th floor, Drawer 33, Montpelier, VT 05633. For general information, call 1-800-Vermont. Website: www.travel-Vermont.com

Drive 1

Bennington, Arlington, and the Kelley Stand Road

60 miles

This drive begins in Bennington, a town steeped in early Vermont history, and passes through Arlington, one-time home of an illustrator whose depictions of his neighbors and everyday surroundings lent mythic proportions to up-country Yankee life. Before looping back to its starting place via the Molly Stark Trail, the drive follows a a little-used back road that meanders through one of the most secluded corners of the Green Mountain National Forest.

(1) **Bennington** looms large in Vermont's history as the locus of a battle that was actually fought somewhere else. The Battle of Bennington, an engagement fought between British and American forces on August 16, 1777, took place just across the border in Walloomsac, New York. But "Battle of Walloomsac" lacks that fine alliterative ring -- and besides, the Vermont town has the **Bennington Battle Monument**.

The monument, a granite obelisk erected in 1891 and at 306 feet still the tallest structure in the state, commemorates the American victory over a British force that was attempting to seize a cache of military supplies at Bennington. "There are the Redcoats. Today they are ours or Molly Stark's a widow" was the exhortation suppos-

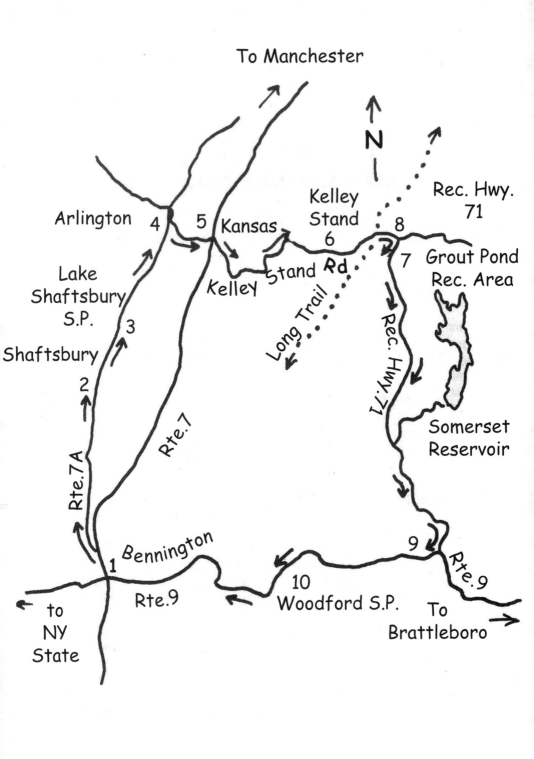

edly uttered by Colonel (later General) John Stark, who had led a detachment of New Hampshiremen to Bennington over what is now called the Molly Stark Trail (Route 9).

Among the American fighters facing the British that day were members of an informal local militia called the Green Mountain Boys, who had cut their teeth on the struggle to secure Vermont's independence from the would-be enforcers of New York land claims. Bennington's Catamount Tavern (no longer standing: a marker on Monument Avenue indicates the site) was a frequent meeting place of the Green Mountain Boys and their flamboyant leader, Ethan Allen. Allen, beloved by native Vermonters as the state's archetypal hero, was actually what today would be called a "flatlander" -- an emigrant from points south (in his case, Connecticut). Like a lot of flatlanders, Allen had made considerable investments in Vermont real estate. Needless to say, it was in his interest to keep out the "Yorkers" and their rival land claims.

The Battle Monument and Catamount Tavern site are in the part of town called Old Bennington, a National Register Historic District. This neighborhood's most architecturally distinctive structure is the Old First Church (First Congregational Church), built in 1806. It's a graceful, late-Georgian gem with exquisite Palladian windows and one of the two or three finest steeples in the state. Its adjacent burial ground contains the graves of five Vermont governors as well as that of Robert Frost, whose plain marker is inscribed with a line of his verse, "I had a lover's quarrel with the world."

In addition to its connections with the birth of Vermont and the struggle for American independence, Bennington has links to two other proud traditions: liberal education and hand-made pottery. Bennington College, founded in 1932, occupies a bucolic campus on the outskirts of town, and has long been noted for its writing, modern languages, and performing arts programs. And **Bennington Potters** represents the modern revival of an old-time local industry; its high-quality stoneware is renowned for its solid simplicity. The trigger mug -- two finger holes in the handle -- is a signature Bennington design.

Bennington pottery, along with many other examples of regional art and artisanship, make up the collection of the **Bennington Museum**. The museum possesses the largest public collection of Grandma Moses paintings; landscapes and portraits by lesser-known local artists; and local furniture and glassware. The "Grandma Moses schoolhouse" is the actual country school attended by Anna Mary Moses, nee Robertson, in the 1860s; it was moved here from its original site just over the border in New York State. Also among the exhibits are the Bennington-made Wasp, the only automobile ever produced in Vermont, and a flag carried at the Battle of Bennington that is believed to be the oldest surviving example of the Stars-and-Stripes design.

(2) Head north out of town on Route 7A to the **Shaftsburys**, which were settled in the 1760s by emigrants from Rhode Island and Connecticut. In 1920 Robert Frost bought the c. 1769 Stone House, on Route 7A in **South Shaftsbury**. It was here that he wrote the poem "New Hampshire," with its concluding line, "At present I am living in Vermont," as well as "Stopping by Woods on a Snowy Evening," referred to by the poet as "my best bid for remembrance." The Friends of Robert Frost bought the house and opened it as the **Robert Frost Stone House Museum**, with one floor dedicated to the poet, and another to changing exhibits. Daily poetry readings are scheduled for 2:00 P.M. in season. Woodcuts by J.J. Lanke, who did much of the art for Frost's books, are also on exhibit.

In **Center Shaftsbury** the 1846 Greek Revival **Baptist Meeting House**, still in use today, houses the Shaftsbury Historical Society's collection of more than 6,000 artifacts, including tools used by the the Eagle Square Manufacturing Company, makers of the first steel carpenters' tools. The village was home to Revolutionary War Captain Jonas Galusha, who served nine terms as governor of Vermont. His handsome white Colonial home, with its unique trinity window above the entrance, still stands in the village. Jacob Merritt Howard, who distilled Vermont's implacable abolitionist sentiment into his authorship of the Thirteenth Amendment to the Constitution, outlawing slavery, was born just east of town.

(3)   The beach at twenty-six-acre **Lake Shaftsbury State Park** is a delightful spot for cooling off on a hot summer day.   There are boat rentals and a picnic area.

(4)   **Arlington** stands alongside the Batten Kill, a legendary trout stream   ("kill" is Dutch for stream or small river; this is its only use in Vermont and shows the influence of nearby Dutch-settled New York).   Located between the Taconic Range and the Green Mountains, Arlington has been home to many of Vermont's most noteworthy -- and most notorious -- citizens.   The town's early history differed from other Vermont communities in that it was shaped not by the flinty Calvinism of the typical upcountry New England settlements, but by the more liberal precepts of the Anglican Church.   This religious anglophilia was, during Revolutionary days, accompanied by a Tory bent in politics -- the town was in fact known as Tory Hollow in the early 1770s.

Nevertheless, Arlington loomed large in the affairs of the 1777-1791 Independent Republic of Vermont, as it was the home of the first governor, Thomas Chittenden, who, after election, opened his office and conducted affairs of state from here.   Secretary of State Ira Allen (see Drive 9) was so taken with an Arlington vista that one of Chittenden's visitors had etched into his powder horn, that he incorporated a representation of the same scene into the state's seal.   Ira Allen's renovated 1759 home on the shores of the Batten Kill is a state historic site and now **The Ira Allen House** -- a lovely inn.

Arlington has been home to numerous artists and writers over the years.   Writer Dorothy Canfield Fisher's family lived in the red brick building that housed Vermont's first medical school, which opened in 1790 (corner of Route 7A and Fisher Road).   Mrs. Fisher lived in a home on Arlington's green for many years, and loved Vermont and its people.   Among her more than fifty books was *Vermont Tradition, The Biography of an Outlook of Life*.   Her friends included Robert Frost and composer Carl Ruggles, who lived in an old schoolhouse on School Street from 1924 to 1966.   Mrs. Fisher's home is now the Community House and Library.

Arlington was also home to two famous artists named Rockwell: Rockwell Kent and Norman Rockwell. Kent, whose work included illustrations for a now-prized edition of Herman Melville's *Moby-Dick*, drew inspiration for many of his works from the woods of nearby Red Mountain. Norman Rockwell lived here from 1939 to 1953, and used many of the townspeople as models for his illustrations. One of his most famous was of country doctor George A. Russell, an Arlington resident from 1879 to 1968. His extensive collection of books, letters, photographs and other mementos is preserved at the **Dr. George A. Russell Collection of Vermontiana** in the Martha Canfield Public Library. Many of Rockwell's Saturday Evening Post covers and other works are displayed in the **Norman Rockwell Exhibition and Gift Shop.**

Although the present St. James Episcopal Church dates to 1829, the first church was built here in 1787, and the walled cemetery is one of the state's oldest. Among those interred here is Ethan Allen's first wife, Mary Brownson (his second wife, Fanny, is buried in Elmwood Cemetery in Burlington, while Ethan himself lies in Burlington's Greenmount Cemetery; see Drive 9).

Turn left onto Rte. 313, which follows the Batten Kill to **West Arlington**, home to the 1852 West Arlington Covered Bridge (a great place for a dip) and the **Inn on Covered Bridge Green**, Mr. Rockwell's last Vermont home. The studio he built here in 1943 has been converted into a two-bedroom rental unit. Ethan Allen mustered his Green Mountain Boys on the Green across from the inn.

Back in Arlington, turn right off Route 7A onto East Arlington Road and right again after the second bridge onto Old Mill Road to **East Arlington**. The **East Arlington Antiques Center** on Main Street houses antiques and collectibles of more than 125 dealers. Daniel Shays, leader of Shays' Rebellion, a 1790s uprising of Western Massachusetts farmers against Federalist fiscal policies, lived in the village's Hard House after he left the Bay State.

(5) Continue to the end of Old Mill Road (which becomes Kansas Road at the Sunderland town line), cross a one-lane bridge, and then bear right at the "Y" onto Kelley Stand Road. Continue east through tiny Kansas, given its bittersweet name by a

group of pioneers with a sense of humor but not much stamina who were bound for Kansas during the mid-1800s and made it only this far before throwing in the towel. Dorothy Canfield Fisher was born here. (Kelley Stand Road, also shown on maps as the Arlington/West Wardsboro Road, is closed in winter).

Side Trip

Wilderness hiking enthusiasts will want to detour off the Kelley Stand Road to the north to visit Lye Brook Wilderness, 15,680 acres of lakes, streams, bogs and forest that is Vermont's second largest tract of federally-protected wilderness (the 21,480-acre Breadloaf Wilderness in the Rochester District -- on Drive 6 -- is the largest). The land was at one time heavily logged, and railroads crisscrossed these woods hauling material to and from Manchester. Forest Road 70 dead-ends at one trailhead, and several other trails begin at points along the Kelley Stand Road. Contact the Green Mountain National Forest for more information.

(6) Continue through the abandoned, all but vanished community of **Kelley Stand** and past the right-hand turnoff for Recreation Highway 71, to where the Appalachian/Long Trail intersects the road. It was near here, in 1909, that James P. Taylor dreamed up his idea of a "footpath in the wilderness" -- today's Long Trail. A bit further, at a picnic area, a rough stone monument marks the spot where, in 1840, Senator Daniel Webster, stumping for Presidential Candidate William Henry Harrison, addressed 15,000 Whigs and sympathizers.

(7) A short distance up, turn right onto Grout Pond Road to visit **Grout Pond Recreation Area**, a 1,600-acre portion of the Green Mountain National Forest which offers fine opportunities for remote camping, swimming in spring-fed Grout Pond, and more than twelve miles of hiking trails. Several of the hikes -- rated "easy" -- make loops around the pond; others connect with the north end of nearby **Somerset Reservoir**, formed by the damming of the East Branch of the Deerfield River.

The town of Somerset was "disorganized" by an Act of the 1937 Vermont Legislature. (Its 2000 population was five.) The neighboring town of Glastenbury was also disorganized by the '37 legislature. Until then it had three voters, who always elected whoever happened to be the head of the Mattison family as their state representative.

(8) If you continue straight ahead, you'll soon reach one of the access roads to Stratton Mountain Ski Area. Our drive requires that you backtrack to Recreation Highway 71 (also known as the Arlington Road; closed in winter) and turn left to head south through the valley of the Deerfield River. Several roads along Highway 71 lead off toward the east (left) to Somerset Reservoir. At the intersection with Route 9 turn right (west) onto Route 9, also known as the Molly Stark Trail, a 46-mile scenic road that winds from Brattleboro, through the Green Mountain National Forest and over Hogback Mt. (with its '100-mile view') to Bennington.

(9) In **Searsburg**, eleven wind turbines on the top of Waldo Mountain are researching how well wind power can work in cold climates. The 132-foot towers with sixty-foot ro- tor blades, built at a cost of $11 million, comprise the largest wind power installation east of the Mississippi River. To see the installation, detour south (left) on Route 8.

(10) Four-hundred acre **Woodford State Park**, on a mountain plateau above Adams Reser- voir, is surrounded by

Side Trip

Detour seven miles east on Rte. 9 to Wilmington. The tiny village near Mount Snow Ski Area offers some of the region's finest lodging and dining. The White House of Wilmington, in a turn-of- the-century mansion, has elegant accommodations; Le Petit Chef, four mi. north of town on Rte. 100, specializes in lovingly-prepared classic French cuisine. The sixth- generation, working Adams Farm, with a myriad of activities including hay jumps, farm animals, and afternoon tea, is a wonderful place for a family outing.

the Green Mountain National Forest. The park has a small beach, picnic area, and rowboat, canoe and paddleboat rentals (motor boats are not permitted on the reservoir). Hiking trails include a pleasant 2.7-mile loop around the lake.

Large iron deposits were discovered in **Woodford**, Vermont's highest village, in the early 1800s, and forges manufactured bar iron and hammered out anchors for the fledgling country's gunboats. The spire of the Union Church has been judged to be the "closest to God" in the state. Industrialist Franklin W. Olin (1860-1954), who with his sons founded Olin Mathieson Chemical Corporation, forerunner to Olin Industries, was born here.

(11) Approximately 1 1/2 mi. past Woodford, the Appalachian/Long Trail intersects. The Glastenbury Mountain and West Ridge Loop trail, a strenuous 21.8-mile loop, begins here.

Return to Bennington on Route 9.

Information

Bennington Area Chamber of Commerce (800-229-0252 or 447-3311), 100 Veterans Memorial Drive, Bennington 05201. www.bennington.com

Green Mountain National Forest (747-6700), 231 North Main St., Rutland 05701. www.fs.fed.us/r9/gmfl.

Manchester and the Mountains Regional Chamber of Commerce (362-2100), Historic Rte. 7A N., Manchester Center 05255. www.manchestervermont.net.

Lodging

(1)(R) The Four Chimneys Inn (800-649-3503 or 447-3500), 21 West Rd. (Rte. 9), Old Bennington. Beautifully restored, 1910 Colonial Revival home has 11 elegant rooms with some fireplaces and/or jacuzzis. Continental fare in the elegant dining room ($$$),

with entrees such as pan seared duck breast and leg confit, and chicken Florentine. D. www.fourchimneys.com $$-$$$

(1) Paradise Motor Inn (442-8351), 141 W. Main St., Bennington 05201. 76 rooms and suites, some with private balconies, saunas and jacuzzis. Heated pool, spa, sauna, tennis courts, restaurant. www.theparadisemotorinn.com $-$$

(1) Vermonter Motor Lodge and Sugar Maple Inn (442-2529), Rte. 9, West Rd., Bennington 05201. 10 cottages sleep 2-4, and a 22-unit motel, all with house-keeping facilities. Restaurant. $-$$

(1) Molly Stark Inn (800-356-3076 or 442-9631), 1067 E. Main St. (Rte. 9), Bennington 05201. Lovely 1890 Queen Anne Victorian B & B has 6 guest rooms and 3 cottage suites with jacuzzis. Champagne dinner packages. www.mollystarkinn.com. $-$$

(2) Hillbrook Motel (447-7201), Rte. 7A, Shaftsbury. 17 units, 4 efficiencies on 5 acres set well back from highway; pool, picnic area. $

(3)(R) The Arlington Inn (800-443-9442 or 375-6532), Rte. 7A, Arlington 05250. Antiques-filled 1848 Greek Revival mansion has 12 rooms and 6 suites and 6 rooms in adjacent building. Full breakfast. Dinner ($$$) in the elegant dining room might include grilled filet mignon or roasted Atlantic salmon. www.arlingtoninn.com. $$-$$$

(3) Arlington Manor House B & B (375-6784), Buck Hill Rd., R2, Box 420, Arlington 05250. Hilltop Dutch Colonial a short walk from town has 5 rooms (4 with private bath) and 2 fireplace suites; tennis court. $-$$

(3) The Inn on Covered Bridge Green (800-726-9480 or 375-9489), off Rte. 313, 3587 River Rd., West Arlington 05250. C. 1792 farmstead has 6 guest rooms with whirlpool baths and some fireplaces, and two cottages. www.coveredbridgegreen.com. $$-$$$

(3) The Ira Allen House (362-2284), Rte. 7A, Arlington 05250. Located just across from the Batten Kill, with 9 guest rooms (several are perfect for families). $-$$

(3)(R) Arlington's West Mountain Inn (375-6516), River Rd., Rte. 313, Arlington 05250. 150-acre inn/ B&B/llama ranch has 18 rooms, 6 suites, and prix-fixe ($38) dining by candlelight, with entrees such as lamb medallions and pan-seared scallops. Hiking trails and bird sanctuary. www.westmountaininn.com. $$$

(10) Greenwood Lodge and Campsites (442-2547), Rte. 9, Woodford (PO Box 246, Bennington 05201). Lodge/hostel; dorm, private and family rooms; kitchen privileges. Late May-mid-Oct. $

Side Trip

The White House of Wilmington (800-541-2135 or 464-2135), 178 Rte. 9 East, Wilmington 05363. www.whitehouseinn.com $$-$$$

Off the Drive

(R) The Inn at Saw Mill Farm (800-493-1133 or 464-8131), Rte. 100 & Crosstown Rd., Box 367, West Dover 05356. One of Vermont's most elegant inns, this Relais & Chateaux property with 30 rooms offers an adult environment, superb dining ($$$), and an award-winning wine list. www.vermontdirect.com/sawmill. $$$

Restaurants

(1) Alldays & Onions (447-0043), 519 Main St., Bennington. Create your own luncheon sandwich at this restaurant/deli; dinner menu features creative fish and pasta dishes. Breakfast and lunch daily. D, Thur.-Sat. except nightly in foliage season. $-$$

(1) Bennington Station (447-1080), Depot St., Bennington. American favorites including chili, prime rib, chicken pot pie, and a salad bar served in an authentic 1897 railroad station. L, D, Sun. brunch. $-$$

(1) Blue Benn Diner (442-5140), Rte. 7N, Bennington. Breakfast and sandwiches are served all day in this 1940s Silk City diner; long weekend waits possible. B, L, Mon.,Tues., Sat. and Sun.; B, L, D Wed.-Fri. $

(4) Jonathon's Table (375-1021), Rte. 7A, Arlington. Ask for a riverview table at this casual but romantic spot behind the Sugar Shack. House specialties include prime rib, veal, and seafood. D. $$-$$$

Side Trip

Le Petit Chef (464-8437), Rt. 100, Wilmington. Wed.-Sun., D. $$-$$$

Attractions

(1) Old First Church, Church St. and Monument Ave., Bennington.

(1) Bennington Battle Monument (447-0550), 15 Monument Ave., Bennington. Elevator. Mid-April-late Oct. $

(1) Bennington Museum (447-1571), W. Main St. (Rte. 9), Bennington. $

(1) Hemmings Motor News Garage (442-3101), 216 Main St., Bennington. The company that publishes the bible of classic car aficionados operates an old-fashioned filling station/vintage vehicle display/gift shop.

(1) Park-McCullough House (442-5441), Cor. Park and West sts., North Bennington. Open late May-late Oct. Tours on the hour 10-3. $

(2) Baptist Meeting House, Shaftsbury Historical Society Museum (447-7488), Center Shaftsbury. Mid-June-mid-Oct. Closed Mon.

(2) Lake Shaftsbury State Park (375-9978), Rte. 7A. Swimming, nature trail, boat and canoe rental. Late May-Labor Day. $

(2) Robert Frost Stone House Museum (447-6200), Historic Rte. 7A, Shaftsbury. Open Tues.-Sun. 10-5, May-Dec. $

(3) The Dr. George A. Russell Collection of Vermontiana (375-6307), Martha Canfield Public Library, Arlington. Tues. and by appt.

(3) Norman Rockwell Exhibition (375-6423), Rte. 7A, Arlington. In an 1800s church. $

(5) Lye Brook Wilderness, Green Mountain National Forest (see Information).

(7) Grout Pond Recreation Area, Green Mountain National Forest (see Information).

(7) Somerset Reservoir, Green Mountain National Forest (see Information).

(10) Woodford State Park (447-7169), 142 State Park Rd., Woodford. Mid-May-Columbus Day. $

Shopping and Activities

(1) Bennington Potters Yard (800-205-8033 or 447-7531),324 County St., Bennington. First-quality and seconds; walking tour of factory and Potters Yard at 10 and 2.

(1) Camelot Village (447-0228), Rte. 9W, Bennington. More than 120 antiques dealers and a craft center selling work by more than 250 regional artisans.

(1) Cutting Edge (442-8664), 160 Benmont Ave., Bennington. Bike rentals and skateboard park (no rentals). Adm. to park.

(1) Hawkins House Craftsmarket (447-0488), 262 North St. (Rte. 7), Bennington. The works of approximately 450 craftspeople are exhibited and for sale.

(1) Oldcastle Theatre Company (447-0564), Rte. 9 & Gypsy Lane, Bennington. Professional theater troupe performs at the Bennington Center for the Arts Theatre from June-Oct.

(2) The Chocolate Barn (375-6928), Rte. 7A N, Shaftsbury. Antiques and 65 varieties of hand-dipped chocolate and fudge; more than 600 antique chocolate molds.

(2)(L) Kimberly Farms Riding Stables (442-4354), Myers Rd., Shaftsbury. Trail rides, hayrides, pony rides, and inn-to-inn tours.

(4) Battenkill Canoe Ltd. (800-421-5268 or 362-2800), River Rd., Arlington. Day trips, rentals, instruction, and inn-to-inn tours.

(4) East Arlington Antiques Center (375-9607), Old Mill Rd., East Arlington. More than 125 dealers display their wares in two historic buildings.

Side Trip

Adams Family Farm (464-3762), 15 Higley Hill Rd., Wilmington. Call for hours.

Quaigh Design Centre (464-2780), Main St., Wilmington. Vermont crafts and imported Scottish woolens.

Drive 2

Brattleboro and the West River Valley

96 miles

Start out in Brattleboro, a focus for the great countercultural migration of thirty years ago -- and the home, many years earlier, of one very high profile arch-imperialist. The drive then follows the valley of the West River through a skein of inviting villages, before winding back to the Connecticut Valley via Weston and Grafton, two once-forgotten towns now emblematic of Vermont's calendar-photo image.

(1) **Brattleboro**, nicknamed "Brat" (pronounced like the errant tot, not the German sausage) is a melting pot for native Vermonters, aging hippies who arrived in the 60s and put down roots, "swamp yuppies" attracted by relatively low real estate costs compared to the nearby Berkshires, and artists who have converted old brick factories into airy lofts.

The magic of the town (in spite of its size and population, Brattleboro is not a city: its populace conducts their affairs through representative town meetings) is that it all works: it's a thriving mini-metropolis packed with first-rate book stores, galleries, ethnic restaurants, and shops. The downtown Latchis Building, which houses the **Latchis Hotel**, was built in 1938

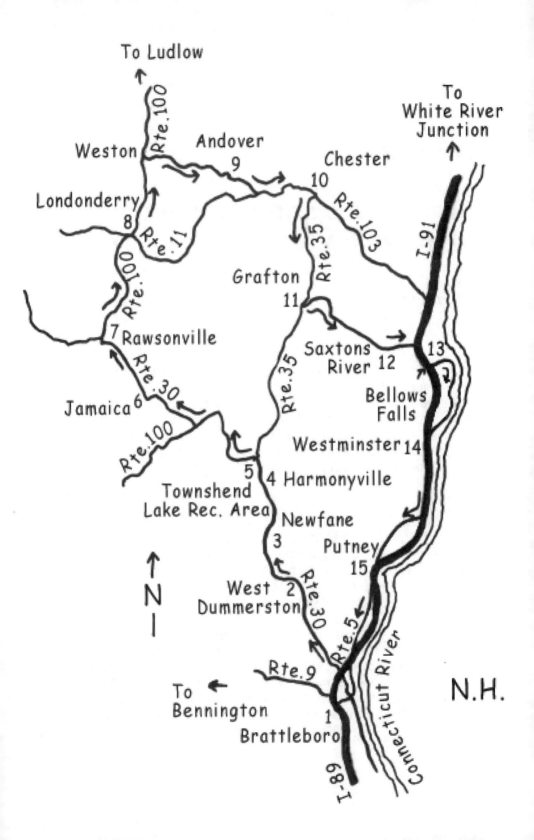

by four sons of Demetrius P. Latchis, a Greek immigrant whose fruit stand grew into a chain of fifteen movie houses and three hotels. In 1940 the Latchis Theater screened Gone With the Wind , making Brattleboro the first small town in America to see the film. (Fans of art deco should note that this is one of only two large commercial buildings in the state built in this style. The other is in Rutland; see Drive 4.)

One of the state's earliest white settlements was located near Brattleboro at Fort Dummer, which was completed in 1724 and served as a defense against hostile Indians as well as a scouting post and trading center. For its first two years the fort was under the command of Capt.Timothy Dwight. His son Timothy, the first white child born in Vermont, later became an accomplished poet and president of Yale College. The fort was dismantled in 1763, and the land it stood on was later flooded by Vernon Dam on the Connecticut River. A granite marker about 1 1/2 mi. south of town on Rte. 30 marks the approximate site.

In the 1840s, springs were discovered along Whetstone Brook in West Brattleboro, and the Brattleboro Hydropathic Establishment opened its doors a few years later. For more than thirty years it catered to wealthy patrons who flocked here to take the " water cure" -- a plunge into the generally icy waters. Today the brookside area is the site of the Saturday **Brattleboro Area Farmers Market**.

The J. Estey Organ Company began production in Brattleboro during the 1850s, and eventually employed more than 500 people. In the days when families made their own evening entertainment, Estey spread Brattleboro's fame as the "organ capital of America," and manufactured parlor organs until the ascent of radio and phonographs in the 1920s. Several Estey organs are on exhibit at the **Brattleboro Historical Society** .

The Robert H. Gibson River Garden on Main Street in Brattleboro is filled with plants and light, and has several restaurants and food carts. The outdoor terrace is a delightful spot to have lunch and enjoy one of the free summer concerts. Call the Chamber of Commerce (see Information below) for a schedule.

In 1892, flush with his early success as a journalist and chronicler in fiction of Britain's colonial adventures in India, 26-year-old Rudyard Kipling began building a handsome shingle-style home called Naulakha on a hillside in Dummerston, just over the town line from Brattleboro. Kipling had recently married an American woman, Caroline Balestier, whose family had long summered in the area, and the young writer quickly fell under the spell of rural Vermont. "The sun and the air and the light are good in this place and have made me healthy as I never was in my life," he wrote, and his literary output reflected this new invigoration: while living at Naulakha, Kipling wrote The Jungle Book, The Day's Work, The Seven Seas, *and* Captains Courageous *. But the idyll was short lived: Kipling became caught up in a bitter feud with his eccentric brother-in-law, Beatty Balestier, and left Vermont for good in 1896. His beautifully preserved house, together with much of its original furnishings, remains -- it's the property of a British organization, The Landmark Trust, which rents it out for periods of a week or more. Once a year, there's an open house with guided tours for day visitors. For information, contact The Landmark Trust, Shottesbrooke, Maidenhead, Berkshire, Great Britain SL6 3SW; 44-1628-825925. If you want to just drive by for a look, head north out of Brattleboro on Rte. 5 for 2 1/2 mi., make a left at the sign for the School for International Training (there's a Kipling marker here too), then turn right on Kipling Road. The house is up ahead on the left.*

Head northwest out of Brattleboro on Rte. 30. The Brattleboro Retreat, on the outskirts of town, opened in 1836 as the Vermont Lunatic Asylum, and was one of the first hospitals in the country designed exclusively for the treatment of mental illness (it's now a drug and alcohol abuse rehabilitation center).

(2)   Rte. 30 follows the West River. Just north of the village of **West Dummerston** is the West Dummerston Covered Bridge. Built in 1872 at a cost of $7,777.08, this is the state's longest two-span covered bridge still used by

cars (at 280 feet, it requires a central stone pier for support). In December 1994 townspeople voted to spend up to $621,000 to do major repairs on the single-lane span. There's a good swimming hole alongside the bridge.

(3) The entire village of **Newfane**, one of Vermont's prettiest, is on the National Register of Historic Places. It has two elegant town greens and several noteworthy Federal and Greek Revival buildings, including the magnificent County Courthouse, built in 1825. Across the street is the Windham County Jail (now part of the **Old Newfane Inn**), once the most famous county jail in the country. For many years it served as both a jail and a hotel, lodging prisoners awaiting trial along with travelers who had business at the court. Seeing no reason to provide separate dining facilities for the two groups when the jail was already serving up "fair to middlin' vittles", the authorities gave travelers their meals in the jail's dining hall. The hotel's stationery was marked "Windham County Jail, Newfane, Vt."

Among Newfane natives was children's poet Eugene Field, who wrote "Wynken,Blynken,and Nod," and his father Roswell, who defended Dred Scott before the United States Supreme Court in 1856-1857. Economist John Kenneth Galbraith summered here.

Newfane is the home of several antiques shops, as well as the by-appointment-only shop of antiquarian horologist Ray Bates, "The British Clockmaker." Bates, who qualified as a master clockmaker under Britain's centuries-old apprentice system, specializes in the restoration and sale of antique timepieces. On his website (www.thebritishclockmaker.com) he lists clocks he does not work on. Among these: "cuckoo clocks, anniversary clocks, usually described as 'the one George brought back from Germany 40 years ago, has little balls that go around a glass dome!', clocks made by your uncle, [and] clocks repaired by your uncle." At the more pedestrian end of the antiques business, visitors pack the Newfane flea market -- one of the state's biggest -- held just north of town on Rte. 30 on Sundays May-October.

(4) Continue north through the once-thriving community of **Harmonyville**, nicknamed "Tin Pot" by the citizens of nearby

Townshend circa 1830. In turn, Harmonyville-ites dubbed their neighbor to the north "Flyburg." Sticks and stones ...

Alphonso Taft, the father of President William Howard Taft, was born in **Townshend**, a charming village with a two-acre common. The Congregational Church was built in 1790. Townshend's Leland and Gray Union High School began as a seminary in 1834. The **Mary Meyer Stuffed Toys Factory Store**, Vermont's largest and oldest stuffed toy maker, began here as a family business more than sixty years ago. Their toys are sold at the **Big Black Bear Shop** there. It's just north of town on Rte. 30.

(5)   A bit further north is **Scott Bridge**, Vermont's longest single-span covered bridge ("single-span" means it isn't supported by a central pier, like the West Dummerston bridge, above). Built in 1870, the 277-foot Town lattice (see Drive 11) structure was closed to traffic when engineers couldn't shore it up properly. Townspeople back in the 1950s -- the Dark Ages of preservationism --didn't want to spend $20,000 for repairs and were prepared to put the bridge to the torch, but the chairman of the Townshend select board worked with the state to have ownership transferred, and in 1955 it was made a State Historic Site.

Ready for a swim? Just past the bridge is the entrance to **Townshend Lake Recreation Area**. Turn left and drive across the dam (built by the Army Corps of Engineers in 1961) and then turn right to the beach /recreation area. Much of the infrastructure here was built in the 1930s by the Civilian Conservation Corps; the headquarters lodge was constructed from stone quarried in the forest, and the handcrafted stone arch bridges were crafted by local masons. A steep trail with a vertical climb of 1,100 feet winds for 2.7 mi. past waterfalls, chutes, and pools to the top of Bald Mountain.

(6) The West River wraps around **Jamaica**, nestling in the shadow of the granite, 1,745-ft.-high Ball Mountain to the north. The local Congregational minister, John Stoddard, never got to preach in the fine church built here in 1808. In 1799 he was fired after selling his wife to another man (local

legend has it that she was delighted with the transaction). Turn right off Rte. 30 onto Depot Street to 756-acre **Jamaica State Park**. The West River Railroad once ran through the park, and today the old railbed is a trail that leads along the West River to **Ball Mountain Dam**. Twice a year, in late April and late September, kayakers flock to the dam in anticipation of the U.S. Army Corps of Engineers' controlled release of water, which creates conditions for terrific whitewater paddling. A hiking trail leads to 120-foot Hamilton Falls, about a mile up Cobb Brook. (Note: Hamilton Falls are pretty to look at, but the pools and flumes are dangerous for swimmers.)

(7) In **Rawsonville**, before turning off Rte. 30 onto Rte. 100 North, pause at the fenced-in Rawson Monument to pay homage to Bailey Rawson, who founded the town in 1810-12. Before he fetched up here he made a name for himself selling sorrel seed to hopeful -- if naive -- farmers as "not clover seed." When disappointed planters brought him to court he said, "I sold the stuff for 'not clover seed'. If you can prove they are clover seed, I will pay the damage."

(8) Continue north on Rte. 100 along the West River through South Londonderry and **Londonderry**, a major service area for nearby ski areas. If you're passing through on Saturday between 10 A.M. and noon, be sure to stop at the lively and copiously stocked **farmers' market** in the parking lot of The Mill restaurant.

At Londonderry, Rte. 100 jogs north to one of the first Vermont towns to trade on its beautiful location, serene atmosphere, and architectural harmony -- the hill village of **Weston** at the northern end of the West River Valley. Writer Vrest Orton, a Vermont native who fondly recalled the general stores of his youth, helped put the town on the map in the late 1940s when he opened the **Vermont Country Store**, although by that time outsiders had been drawn here for more than a decade to attend performances at the **Weston Playhouse**, one of America's oldest summer theaters. Today the town -- with its cast-iron-fenced green, Victorian bandstand, historic homes, and interesting assortment of shops, is one of Vermont's most popular tourist destinations. With murals (done by WPA artists) and artfully arranged exhibits, curators at the restored **Farrar-Mansur House**, built as a tavern in 1797, recapture what life was like in a Vermont community like Weston two centuries ago. The **Kinhaven Music School**, perched on a hill outside of town, offers free concerts on summer weekends. Ask in town for directions.

(9) Just north of Weston, turn right off Rte. 100 onto Andover Road (which turns into Weston Road), and continue east through **Andover**, a stopover on what was called the "Ideal Tour" between Manchester and the White Mountains during the early days of automobile touring. Today, to quote an internet source (www.linkvermont.com), "Except for a very large and heavily wooded RV Campground, and an inn high upon a mountain (**Inn at High View**), there is absolutely nothing here." How's that for succinct?

(10) The Andover-Weston road ends at its intersection with Rte. 11: turn left and continue on Rte. 11 to **Chester**. It was here, on November 10, 1774 -- twenty months before the issue was taken up by the Continental Congress in Philadelphia -- that local citizens issued a Declaration of Independence stating that "all the acts of the British Parliament tending to take away Rights of Freedom ought not to be obeyed."

Chester is another one of those Vermont towns where an abundance of local materials, skilled housewrights, and plain good taste combined to create an admirable architectural display. Gingerbread Victorian homes and stately public buildings such as the 1871 Gothic Revival St. Luke's Episcopal Church line both sides of the long, narrow green which splits Main Street. A drive up North Street (Rte. 103) through the Historic District will explain Chester's nickname,

Stone Village. Here are thirty houses faced with gneiss and rough-hewn mica schist quarried from nearby Mt. Flamstead. The homes, built before the Civil War by two brothers, were used as safe houses on the Underground Railroad.

The Victorian Chester Depot between Main and North streets, once used by the Rutland Railway, is now the northernmost stop for the **Green Mountain Flyer**, an excursion train with turn-of-the-century cars (see below). Admirers of expert cartography should stop in at **The National Survey**: the company, founded in 1912 by sons of the town's Baptist minister, is a major map publisher, and sells maps and books in its store at 75 School Street.

(11) From Chester, turn south onto Rte. 35 to **Grafton**, a Vermont village deliberately plucked from obscurity and reborn as a picture-perfect rural community. Before the Civil War Grafton was a thriving agricultural center, shepherding 10,000 merino sheep and supporting a large woolen mill. One of the country's largest soapstone quarries added to the town's prosperity. But one of every three of the town's menfolk went to war, and many who weren't killed in battle headed west when peace came, triggering Grafton's economic and physical decline. It wasn't until 1963 that New York businessman Matthew Hall, with the help of a legacy left by his aunt, formed the nonprofit Windham Foundation with his cousin and co-heir, Dean Mathey. They began the monumental task of totally renovating an entire nineteenth-century village, and restoring its economic vitality.

Today's Grafton is testimony to the cousins' success. The Foundation owns fifty buildings and 3,000 acres in town, and its centerpiece is **The Old Tavern at Grafton**, which opened in 1801. In addition to the inn, Windham operates three museums, gives sheep-shearing demonstrations, and runs the Grafton Village Cheese Company, which manufactures award-winning cheddar using traditional methods (the original Grafton Cooperative Cheese Company was founded in 1890). The popular Grafton Coronet Band performs on weekends throughout the summer.

(12) Follow Rte. 121 east out of Grafton through **Cambridgeport** (named, like a lot of Connecticut Valley settlements, by emigrants honoring their home town in Massachusetts) and **Saxtons River**. The latter is the home of the private Vermont Academy, founded in 1876. In 1910 the school's associate principal, James P. Taylor, a New York City transplant, hatched the idea for a state-wide Green Mountain Club "to make Vermont mountains play a larger part in the life of the people." The Long Trail is an outgrowth of his efforts. (To visit Green Mountain Club headquarters, see Drive 11.)

(13) Continuing on Rte. 121, cross under I-91 and head into **Bellows Falls**, settled in the 1780s. Like a lot of Vermont towns its size (small cities, by local standards), Bellows Falls is a place that has spent the past few decades coming to grips with its transition from an industrial community to a market town and tourist gateway. At one time, it was home to the nation's principal paper mill, and it was one of Vermont's first important rail centers. In 1802, work was completed here on one of America's first canals, designed to carry boat and barge traffic around the biggest natural falls on the Connecticut River. (Harking back to an even earlier era, there are Indian petroglyphs visible on the rocks along the river downstream from the Vilas Bridge.)

Hetty Howland Green (1834-1916) was heiress to a New Bedford whaling fortune who married a Bellows Falls man, Edward Green, and lived in town for part of her life. She was one of America's richest individuals, and was known as the "Witch of Wall Street" -- although to be fair, she was no more a practitioner of the financial black arts than many male nabobs who were never accused of necromancy. She was, however, a legendary penny pincher. Her father had advised her, "never owe anyone anything, not even a kindness." When her son's leg became infected, she dressed as a beggar and brought him to the charity ward at Bellevue Hospital, where surgeons had to amputate. The same son later became adept at spending his late mother's fortune; her daughter married the great-grandson of John Jacob Astor.

The canal's importance waned when the railroad arrived at Bellows Falls in 1849. When the first train pulled into town, the Weekly Times reported, "The engine came up in Grand Style and when opposite our village the Monster gave one of the most savage yells, frightening men, women and children considerable, and bringing forth deafening howls from all the dogs in the Neighborhood."

The **Green Mountain Flyer** is carrying on the local railroad tradition, without causing quite as much fear and commotion. The restored, vintage 1930s train carries passengers alongside the Connecticut and Williams rivers between Bellows Falls and Chester.

(14)   As you drive into **Westminster**, one of the state's earliest settlements, note the wide main street (US 5). Originally 10 rods (165 feet) wide and still a healthy six rods (nearly 100 feet) across, it was designed so militia could use it as a training ground. In an action which came to be known as the "Westminster Massacre," what may have been the first shots of the Revolution were fired here in 1775 when a group of local dissidents launched a guerrilla campaign against New York land grabbers. When the government attempted to gain back control after the insurrectionists seized the local courthouse, twenty-two-year-old William French and another defender were killed. A replica of French's headstone, bemoaning his death at the hands of "Cruel Ministereal Tools of Georg ye 3rd; in the Courthouse at a

Side Trip

Head north on Rte. 5 to Rte. 103 north and follow signs to the National Historic Landmark Rockingham Meeting House. One of Vermont's earliest public buildings, built in 1787 and restored in 1907, the 2 1/2 story, white clapboard building perched on a hilltop is magnificent in its stark simplicity. The adjacent graveyard has some wonderful old stones.

Continue on Rte. 103, just past the turn-off for the Meeting House, to visit the Vermont Country Store's Rockingham location.

11 a Clock at Night..." is in Westminster burying ground. On January 15, 1777, Vermonters issued their own declaration of independence at Westminster, thus inaugurating the 14-year existence of the sovereign Republic of Vermont. Later that year, the Republic's constitution was ratified at Windsor (see Drive 8).

(15) As you continue south on Rte. 5, you might want to divert the kids' attention unless you're planning a stop at **Santa's Land**, a charming and low-key theme park with kiddie rides, a train, petting zoo, restaurant, and lots of shops.

Putney is the home of Ines and Eric Bass' **Sandglass Theater** and of Jody Williams, the 1997 Nobel Peace Prize winner. The late George Aiken, Vermont governor and later long-time senator, operated a fruit tree and flower nursery here. Along with his famously inexpensive Senate campaigns, championing of publicly-owned electric utilities, and suggestion that the U.S. "declare victory in Vietnam and get out," Vermont's most revered modern politician is remembered for his book Pioneering With Wildflowers.

Over the past few decades, Putney has been known for its counterculture flavor. But alternative lifestyles go back a lot further hereabouts. In 1847 John Humphrey Noyes, leader of a group who espoused "Bible Communism," set up a Putney commune whose members shared property, work, and wives. Noyes was eventually charged with adultery and escaped to Oneida, New York, where his group founded the silverware company. Today, Putney is the home of the Putney School and of Landmark College, the nation's first college for dyslexic students.

Just off Rte. 5, chef Curtis Tuff bastes pork ribs with his own secret sauce on an outdoor, wood pit barbecue at **Curtis Barbecue**. Diners place their orders at an old blue bus and chow down at picnic tables. The last time we were there, Curtis's pet hog was supervising the operation. The menu also includes chicken, homemade baked beans, potato salad and coleslaw.

Return to Brattleboro on Rte. 5.

Information

Brattleboro Area Chamber of Commerce (254-4565). 180 Main St., Brattleboro 05301. www.brattleboro.com

Okemo Valley Regional Chamber of Commerce (228-5830), P.O. Box 333, Ludlow, VT 05149 www.vacationinvermont.com

Grafton Information Center (843-2255), Townshend Rd., P.O. Box 9, Grafton 05146. Closed April. www.theoldtavern.com

Great Falls Regional Chamber of Commerce (463-4280), 55 Village Square, P.O. Box 554, Bellows Falls 05101. Mon.-Fri. 10-3. www.gfrcc.org

Londonderry Area Chamber of Commerce (824-8178), Mountain Marketplace Box 58, Londonderry 05148. www.londonderryvt.com

Lodging

(1) Forty Putney Road B & B (800- 941-2413 or 254-6268), 192 Putney Rd., Brattleboro 05301. French Provincial, 1930s estate with 4 guest rooms and a 2-room suite, all with TV and A/C; elegant gardens; pub. www.putney.net/40putneyrd/ $$-$$$

(1) Latchis Hotel (254-6300), 50 Main St., Brattleboro 05301. A rare find, this downtown hotel has nicely-furnished and comfortable rooms at a bargain price. Rooms facing street can be noisy. Continental breakfast. www.brattleboro.com/latchis $-$$

(3)(R) Four Columns Inn (800-787-6633 or 365-7713), On the green, Newfane 05345. 1832 classic Greek Revival has 16 rooms and suites, some with gas-log fireplaces, two-person jacuzzis and/or decks. Pool. The restaurant ($$-$$$) fuses New American, Asian and French cuisines to offer dishes such as

Peking duck breast, and seared venison loin. Children $25. www.fourcolumnsinn.com $$- $$$

(3)(R) Old Newfane Inn (800-784-4427 or 365-4427), Rte. 30, Village Common, Newfane. Chef-owned and operated since 1970, this 1787 inn has 10 antiques-filled rooms and a highly-acclaimed restaurant ($$ - $$$) specializing in classic French-Swiss cuisine, with specialties such as cream of garlic soup and breast of capon Cordon Rouge. Closed Nov. & April; no credit cards. www.oldnewfaneinn.com $$

(3) West River Lodge (365-7745), 117 Hill Rd., Newfane 05345. Horse lovers and families feel particularly welcome at this farmhouse with 8 guest rooms (some with shared bath) adjacent to an English riding stable (trail rides and lessons available). Private beach. www.westriverlodge.com $- $$

(4) Boardman House B & B (365-4086), Village Green, Townshend 05353. 19th-century farmhouse with 6 guest rooms and a 2-bedroom suite. $-$$

(4)(R) Windham Hill Inn, (800-944-4080 or 874-4702),311 Lawrence Drive, W. Townshend 05359. "Upscale country" lodgings at an 1825 house on 160 acres. 21 guest rooms, some with soaking tubs, jacuzzis, and fireplaces. Pool and tennis. The menu ($$-$$$) might include an appetizer of grilled quail with pineapple-kiwi salsa and entree of roasted free range chicken. www.windhamhill.com $$$

(6)(R) Three Mountain Inn (800-532-9399 or 874-4140), Rte. 30, Jamaica . Small, romantic 1790's country inn on the edge of Jamaica State Park has 15 guest rooms in the main and adjacent houses, and 2 cottages. Dinner ($$-$$$) blends various cuisines and might include Vermont cheddar ale soup and pan seared gulf shrimp. www.threemountaininn.com $$

(8) Colonial House Inn & Motel (800-639-5033 or 824-6286), 287 Rte. 100, Dept. VG, Weston 05161. Comfortable, family-friendly property has 9 motel

units and 6 rooms with shared baths in the inn. Game room. Full breakfast; restaurant. Pets welcome in motel. www.cohoinn.com $-$$

(8)(R) Inn at Weston (824-6789), Rte. 100, Weston 05161. Romantic hideaway offers 13 guest rooms and 2 suites with some balconies, fireplaces, and two-person whirlpools. Imaginative, contemporary regional fare ($$$) might feature an appetizer of baked sea scallops atop a Maine lobster cake, and an entree of hempseed encrusted striped bass. Extensive wine list. Children over 12. www.innweston.com $$-$$$

(8) Londonderry Inn (824-5226), Rte. 100, South Londonderry 05155. Rambling 1826 homestead with 25 guest rooms (5 with shared bath) has been a haven for families for more than 50 years. Game room, pool, and tavern.   Breakfast buffet; light dinners served at busy times. www.londonderryinn.com $-$$

(9) Inn at High View (875-2724), E. Hill Rd., Andover 05143. Secluded inn on 72 acres has 6 rooms and 2 suites, great views, and a pool and hot tub. Gourmet dinners available to guests on Saturdays. www.innathighview.com $$-$$$

(10) The Chester House (888-875-2205 or 875-2205), Town Green, Chester 05143. www.ChesterHouseInn.com. All 7 rooms at this c. 1790 National Register Historic Inn have phones, private baths and AC; some have whirlpool baths and gas fireplaces. Breakfast and dinner served in the Keeping Room. www.chesterhouseinn.com $$-$$$

(10) Stone Cottage Collectables (875-6211), 196 North St., Rte.103, Chester 05143. 1840, antiques-filled stone house in the historic district has two guest rooms including one with fireplace. $$

(11) Inn at Woodchuck Hill Farm (843-2398), 347 Woodchuck Hill Rd., Grafton 05146. 6 guest rooms/ suites (4 with private bath) in a 1780s farmhouse

on 200 hilltop acres west of town. Cottages and efficiencies available. Hiking, swimming pond, and sauna. www.woodchuckhill.com $$-$$$

(11)(R) Old Tavern at Grafton (800-843-1801 or 843-2231), Main St. at Townshend Rd., Grafton 05146. The historic, 1801 lodging has more than 60 rooms and suites in the inn and nearby buildings. Upscale New England fare ($$-$$$) is served in the formal dining room as well as a more casual restaurant. Sun. brunch and afternoon tea. X/C ski center, tennis, pub. Closed April. www.old-tavern.com $$-$$$

(12)(R) Inn at Saxtons River (869-2110), Main St., Rte. 121, Saxtons River 05154. 16 rooms in a handsome "downtown" 1903 inn. Tea (in the garden when weather permits) and fireside cocktail hour. Dishes with a Continental flair are served in the lovely dining room at lunch and dinner ($$-$$$) Tues.-Sun. Victorian pub. www.InnSaxtonsRiver.com $$

(15) Hickory Ridge House (800-380-9218 or 387-5709), 53 Hickory Ridge Rd. So., Putney 05346. 6 luxurious guest rooms (5 with fireplaces) in the main house -- an 1808 Federal brick manor on 8 acres; 2-bedroom cottage. $$-$$$

(15)(R) Putney Inn (800-653-5517 or 387-5517), PO Box 181, Depot Rd., Putney 05346. www.putneyinn.com. Great care has been taken to preserve the charm and integrity of this 1790s farmhouse. The 25 guest rooms, all in a less historic adjacent building, are well-appointed. The restaurant ($$-$$$), in the inn, earns accolades for its Classic New England fare. Pets welcome. www.putneyinn.com $$-$$$

Restaurants

(1) Common Ground (257-0855), 25 Eliot St., Brattleboro. One of the country's oldest natural food eateries serves up non-meat dishes, homemade

desserts (without white flour), and yogurt shakes. Beer and wine. Thurs., D; Fri.-Sun., L, D; Sun. brunch. $

(1) Peter Haven's (257-3333), 32 Elliot St., Brattleboro. Filet mignon with Roquefort walnut butter and house-cured gravlax are specialties of this chic bistro with an upscale, imaginative menu. D Tues.-Sat. $$-$$$

(1) Sarkis Market (258-4906), 50 Elliot St., Brattleboro. Lebanese and Middle Eastern specialties. $

(1) T. J. Buckley's (257-4922), 132 Elliot St., Brattleboro. Gourmet fare in a tiny, 1920's, fire-engine red diner. Appetizers such as a smoked trout tartlet followed by a choice of 4 entrees such as pan-seared halibut or Black Angus beef tenderloin.   D Wed.-Sun. No credit cards. Reservations a must. $$

(4) Townshend Country Inn (365-4141), Rte. 30, Townshend.   Traditional favorites including the house-special roast turkey dinner served in the former summer home of Grandma Moses.   D nightly except Wed., Sun. brunch buffet May-Oct. $$

(8) The Bryant House Restaurant (824-6287), next to Vermont Country Store, Rte. 100. Traditional New England dishes, afternoon tea, and homemade pies. L; closed Sun. $

(8) Downstairs at the Playhouse (824-5288), Weston Playhouse, Weston. From 5:30 P.M. on theater nights (5:00 P.M. Sunday). Reservations suggested. $$

(8)(L) Three Clock Inn (824-6327), off Rte. 100, So. Londonderry. The chef -- from Provence -- creates marvelous French dishes; desserts are homemade. D; closed Mon. $$-$$$

(10) Country Girl Diner, jct. Rtes. 11/103, Chester. The crowds pack in for tasty, traditional diner eats. $

(15) Curtis' BBQ (387-5474),40 Old Depot Rd., Putney. April-Oct., Tues.-Sun., 10 'till dark. $

Attractions

(1) Brattleboro Historical Society (258-4957), Municipal Building, 230 Main St., Brattleboro. A fine collection of Estey organs, historic photographs, and a walking tour brochure. Thurs. 1-4, Sat. 9-noon.

(1) Brattleboro Music Center (257-4523), 38 Walnut St., Brattleboro. New England Bach Festival, held Sept.-Oct. at Marlboro College, as well as concerts and festivals throughout the year.

(1) Brattleboro Area Farmers Market, Rte. 9, West Brattleboro (west of exit 2 off I-91). May-Oct, Saturdays 9-2. Wednesday: Merchants Bank, Main Street, mid-June through mid-Sept., 10-2.

(1) Brattleboro Museum & Art Center (257-0124), Union Railroad Station, Vernon St., Brattleboro. Mid-May-mid-Dec., Tues.-Sun. 12-6; closed holidays. $

(1) Marlboro Music Festival, Parsons Auditorium, Marlboro College, Marlboro (summer: 254-2394). Musicians from around the world perform a 5-week chamber music concert series. Fri.-Sun. mid-July - mid-Aug. Advance tickets: 135 South 18th St., Philadelphia, Pa. 19103 (215) 569-4690). Tickets often available at door.

(3) Historical Society of Windham County (365-4148), Rte. 30, Newfane. Memorial Day-Oct., Wed., Sun. and holidays, 12-5. $

(5) Townshend Lake Recreation Area (874-4881), off Rte. 30, Townshend.

(5) Townshend State Park (365-7500), off Rte. 30, Townshend. Mid May-Columbus Day. Camping, swimming, day use area. Late May-Columbus Day. $

(6) Ball Mountain Dam (874-4881), off Rte. 30, Ball Mountain Lane, Jamaica.

(6) D&K's Little Farm (874-4160), 3417 Rte. 30, Jamaica. 11-acre complex includes a children's petting farm, perennial and display gardens, a butterfly pavilion and bird aviary, a lizard house, a quail farm, and llamas. $

(6) Jamaica State Park (874-4600), Rte. 30, Jamaica. Camping, picnicking, tubing, swimming. Late April-Columbus Day. $

(8) Farrar-Mansur House (824-5294), Village Green, Weston. Mid-June-Sept., Wed.-Sun., Sept.-mid-Oct., weekends, 10-4. $

(8) Kinhaven Music School (824-4332), 354 Lawrence Hill Rd., Weston. Free student concerts early July through mid-August: Fri. at 4 P.M.; faculty concerts Sat. at 8 P.M. Picnics welcome.

(8) Vermont Country Store (824-3184), Rte. 100, Weston. Closed Sun.

(8) Weston Priory (824-5409), Rte. 100, Weston.

(12) Grafton Village Cheese Co. (843-2221), Grafton Village. Mon.-Fri., 8:30-4:30, Sat. and Sun. 10-4.

(13) Adams Grist Mill Museum (463-3374), Mill St., Bellows Falls. Original machinery, tools, and memorabilia left when grist mill closed in the 1960s. July and Aug., Sat. and Sun. 1-4.

(13) Green Mountain Flyer (800-707-3530), 54 Depot St., P.O. Box 498, Bellows Falls. runs daily except Mon. in summer; daily in fall; special excursions. $

(13) Rockingham Meeting House (463-3941), off Rte. 103, Rockingham. July and August, 10-5. Donation.

(13) Vermont Country Store (463-2224), Rte. 103, Rockingham. Open daily.

(15) Harlow's Sugar House(387-5852), Rte. 5, Putney. Sugar house has pick-your-own fruit, spring horse-drawn sleigh/wagon rides, winter sleigh rides.

(15) Sandglass Theater (387-4051), Kimball Hill Rd., Putney. October-Xmas, April, and May. Live theater and puppets join together in original performances. The troupe also performs in other locations. $

(15) Santa's Land (800-726-8299 or 387-5550), Rte. 5, Putney. May-Christmas. $

Activities and Shopping

(1) Belle of Brattleboro (254-1263). Scenic cruises on the Connecticut River.

(1) The Book Cellar (254-6026), 120 Main St., Brattleboro. Full-service bookstore.

(1) Brattleboro Bicycle Shop (800-272-8245), 178 Main St., Brattleboro. Bike rentals.

(1) Le Tagge Sale (254-9224), Rollerdrome, next to the marina, Putney Rd., Brattleboro. Antiques, furniture, books, etc. Mon.-Sat.

(1) Twice Upon a Time (254-2261), 63 Main St., Brattleboro. 103 dealers in 10,000 sq. ft. of space.

(1) Robb Family Farm (888-318-9087 or 254-7664), 827 Ames Hill Rd., W. Brattleboro. Dairy farm offers "A Day on the Farm", maple sugaring, a Country Shop, and barn tours.

(1) Sam's Outdoor Outfitters (254-2933), Main St., Brattleboro. Clothing, footwear and sporting goods; fishing and hunting licenses.

(1) Tom and Sally's Handmade Chocolates (258-3065), 55 Elliott St., Brattleboro. Fabulous candy, chocolate cow pies.

(1) Vermont Artisan Designs (257-7044), 106 Main St., Brattleboro. The state's largest contemporary American crafts gallery.

(1) Vermont Canoe (257-5008), Veterans Memorial Bridge, Rte. 5, Brattleboro. Canoe and kayak rental; guided river trips.

(1) Vermont Jazz Center (254-9088), 72 Cotton Mill Hill,Brattleboro. Concerts and weekly jams.

(3) Ray Bates, The British Clockmaker (365-7770), 49 West St., Newfane.

(4) Lawrence's Smokehouse (365-7751), Rte. 30, Townshend. Smoked meats and cheeses.

(4) Big Black Bear Shop at Mary Meyer Stuffed Toys (888-758-2327 or 365-4160), 1 Teddy Bear Lane, Rte. 30, Townshend.

(6) West River Canoe Sailboard Center (869-6209), Rte. 100, East Jamaica. Canoes, sailboards, and paddleboat rentals by hour or longer.

(7) Horses for Hire (297-1468), Diers Rd., Rte. 30, Rawsonville. 1 hr. and half-day trail rides.

(8) Weston Antiques Barn (824-4097), Rte. 100N, Weston. Multi-dealer shop. Closed Wed.

(8) Weston Playhouse (824-5288), Village Green, P.O. Box 216, Weston. Late June - Labor Day, nightly except Mon.; Wed. and Sat. matinees.

(10) The National Survey (875-2121), 75 School St., Chester. Closed Sun.

(11) Gallery North Star (843-2465), Grafton Village. Six rooms of fine art. Closed Tues.

(12) Saxtons River Playhouse (869-2030), Westminster West Rd., Saxtons River. Musicals, plays, children's theater (Friday). and after-show cabaret.

(14) Harlow Farmstand (722-3515), Rte. 5, Westminster. Vermont's largest organic farmstand, in the family since 1918, sells syrup, honey, baked goods, crafts, flowers, and produce. Open year-round.

(14) Putney General Store (387-5842), Rte. 5 and Kimball Hill, Putney. Historic store with old-fashioned soda fountain, deli-café, scoop shop, and gifts.

(15) Heartstone Books (387-2100), jct. Rte. 5 and West Hill Rd., Putney. Full-service bookstore in a restored tavern; adjacent café; readings.

(15) Major Farm (387-4473), 875 Patch Rd., Putney. Award-winning sheep's milk cheese goes on sale mid-August; cave open for tour and tastings. Call for directions. Aug.-Oct., Thurs. & Sat. 10-noon.

(15) Yellow Barn Music Festival (800-639-3819 or 387-6637), Behind Public Library, Putney. Summer chamber music concerts.

Drive 3

Manchester, the Mettawee, and the Mount Tabor Road

92 miles

This drive starts with a look at the twin personalities of Manchester, then follows a northwesterly course along one of Vermont's most bucolic valleys. After a visit to a one-time spa town, the route continues south between two distinct mountain ranges, finally veering east on a loop through the silent, solemn heart of the Green Mountain National Forest.

Note: on the official Vermont State map, Manchester Center has been mistakenly labeled "Manchester Depot." The actual Manchester Depot is the one identified directly to the east.

(1)   Begin the drive in **Manchester Village**, one of Vermont's earliest summer resort towns.   (Note: the sites described here are all located within a four-mile stretch extending south from the intersection of Rte. 7A and West Street. We haven't put them in any particular order, since the drive's main route extends north from the village.)

Manchester Village, tucked into the shadow of 3,816-foot **Mt. Equinox**, is an architectural gem: beautifully-preserved colonial and early Federal period buildings line the shade-dappled main street (Rte. 7A), which

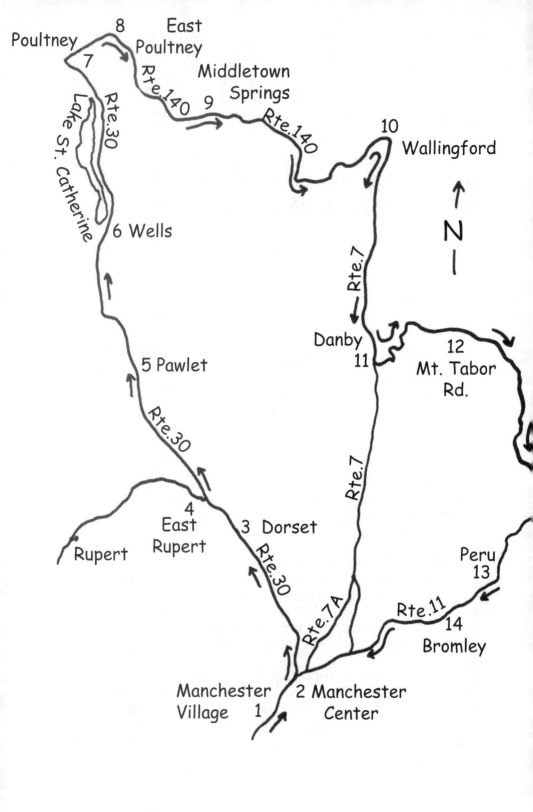

is flanked by sidewalks made of marble slabs. Manchester Village's premier resort, **The Equinox**, has in its various permutations been the town's main focal point for the past 230 years. It's a bastion of Yankee hospitality with a British tinge. Since Guinness Enterprises purchased the inn in the 1980s, management has completely refurbished the landmark hostelry, which is characterized by a long, colonnaded veranda that lends an older meaning to the term "Rock On." The new regime has also renovated the Equinox's golf course, and introduced programs such as The British School of Falconry and the Land Rover Driving School.

In 1993 The Equinox bequeathed 850 acres of land on Mount Equinox to the Vermont Land Trust, so the tract could be kept "forever green." The preserve, which abuts the resort (park in the Equinox lot), is a wonderful spot for taking a short walk or a vigorous hike. It's supervised by the Vermont Institute of Natural Science, which offers natural history programs. If you've only time for a quick stroll, the gentle 1.2-mile loop around Equinox Pond is ideal.

Much of the rest of Mt. Equinox is owned by an order of Carthusian monks. Their monastery is visible from the top of Skyline Drive, which begins on Rte. 7A just south of Manchester Village and winds about 5 mi. to the summit. There are also hiking trails to the summit, and a web of short and scenic trails to follow once you get up there.

The **Charles F. Orvis Company**, which began making bamboo fishing rods in Manchester Village in 1856 and became the country's first mail order company, has a strong presence in the area to this day. In 2002 it opened a new, 23,000-sq.-ft. flagship store billed as "Vermont's largest retail attraction". The $7 million facility overlooks two trout ponds and houses the world's largest rod shop. It's the place to outfit yourself for a stylish safari -- or to splurge on a superbly balanced fly rod crafted of the finest Tonkin cane, which you can try out on Orvis's own casting pond. If you want to learn from the folks who wrote the book, the **Orvis Fly Fishing School** runs 2 1/2-day schools twice a week from April through early October. An upland game shooting course is also offered. Many Orvis artifacts, along with a huge collection of other memorabilia, are on exhibit at the relocated and expanded **American Museum of**

Fly Fishing. If you've eaten Kellogg Company's Country Inn Specialties Cereal, you might recognize the **Inn at Ormsby Hill**, featured on the box in a recent promotion by the company.

Just south of the village is the turnoff from Rte. 7A (on the left, if you're heading south) to **Hildene**. In the summer of 1863 Abraham Lincoln's only son, Robert Todd, visited The Equinox with his mother. Forty years later, after he had made his money in the railroad business, he purchased land on the outskirts of Manchester Village and built a summer home. Robert Todd Lincoln, and afterwards his descendants, lived in the twenty-four-room Georgian Revival mansion until 1975. Since then the home has been preserved, complete with many of the Lincoln family's furnishings and possessions. Visitors are treated to a concert played on the 1,000-pipe Aeolian organ, installed in 1908. The formal gardens, with many of their original plantings, are a favorite part of the tour. Guests are invited to enjoy a picnic and/or take a walk on one of the trails that crisscross the 412-acre estate. Hildene is sumptuously decorated for Christmas, and the cross-country ski trails are open all winter.

Before continuing north on Rte. 7A, take West Road out of the center of Manchester Village and follow signs up the long, winding drive to the **Southern Vermont Art Center**. The twenty-eight-room Georgian revival mansion on a slope of Mt. Equinox was built in 1917 as a summer home, and has been an art center since the 1950s. Contemporary and near-contemporary works (many are for sale) by local artists are displayed in ten galleries and in an outdoor sculpture garden. The 400-seat Arkell Pavilion hosts concerts, lectures and theatrical performances. The Café serves lunch, Sun. brunch and dinner on performance nights. **Manchester Music Festival** performs here Thursday evenings in season.

(2) Return to Manchester Village and take Rte. 7A north to **Manchester Center**. In its early days, the Center was a bustling mill town called Factory Point. Today the mills are gone, replaced by a sprawl of discount outlets for big-name retailers including Giorgio Armani, Brooks Brothers, Cole Haan, Timberland, Christian Dior, Anne Klein, and Godiva Chocolatier. Take time, though, to look beyond the outlets:

Manchester's Main Street looks much as it did 100 years ago, except for the names of the businesses. There are some handsome old buildings: the mansard-roofed **Northshire Bookstore** occupies the 1872 Colburn House, once Manchester Center's main hotel. Norman Rockwell used the **Quality Restaurant**, where he often ate, as the setting for his painting, "War News." The original canvas, a gift from Rockwell to the Quality's late owners, hung in the restaurant as recently as the 1970s; it has since been replaced by a copy.

(3) As you head north on Rte. 30 -- also called the Seth-Warner Highway, after the Green Mountain Boy who helped slow down the British at the Battle of Hubbardton (see Drive 4) -- designer outlets quickly give way to rolling farmland. About three miles north of Manchester Center, watch for the **Dorset Antiques Center**; dealers display their wares in the 200-year-old blue farmhouse. If you miss it, there are a number of other antique shops along the way.

The venerable town of **Dorset**, which received its charter in 1761, was at one time a major trading place for farmers throughout this corner of Vermont. Today's population, though, is more likely to meet on the golf course, or at the local coffee shop to trade stock tips. The entire village is on the National Register of Historic Places. The country's first marble quarry was opened here in 1785, and supplied marble for New York City's Public Library. In 1776, at the first convention of the New Hampshire Grants in the now-defunct Cephas Kent's Tavern on the main street (Rte. 30), the Green Mountain Boys declared Vermont an independent state. The **Dorset Inn**, a National Historic Site on the town's trim little green, opened its door to travelers just twenty years later, and is the state's oldest continuously operating hostelry.

Be sure to stop at the United Church of Dorset, constructed of Dorset marble. The stained glass windows portray scenes of the surrounding valley. A professional acting troupe performs in two prerevolutionary barns at the **Dorset Playhouse**, one of Vermont's oldest summer theaters.

(4) Continue north on Rte. 30 to **East Rupert**. It was near here, in 1785, that Reuben Harmon minted the first cop-

Side Trip

Take Rte. 315 west out of East Rupert to Rupert and the New York border for a classic country drive through meadow and forest. You'll know when you're in Rupert: it's the serene little village with no businesses except the long-closed but still partly stocked Sheldon General Store, whose window displays the sign, "This Building and Its Contents Are Not for Sale. Please Do Not Inquire." On the way back to Rte. 30, there are panoramic views of Dorset Peak in the Green Mountains to the east, and Mount Equinox in the Taconic Mountains to the south. Although Vermont's Taconic peaks are often

per coins for the Republic of Vermont. If you ever see a coin with the inscription, Vermontensium Res Publica 1786, snap it up: Reuben isn't making them any more.

Between East Rupert and Pawlet, Rte. 30 follows the Mettawee River. The river, which first comes into view at a state-maintained access area about a mile north of East Rupert (right) and dodges back and forth from one side of the road to the other, drains a valley that is home to some of Vermont's most picturesque dairy farms. Much of this agricultural land is legally preserved -- many local farmers have arranged conservation easements through the Vermont Land Trust, assuring that their acres will never be developed.

(5) **Pawlet** is a quiet village with memories of an industrial past; the Mettawee and its tributary, Flower Brook, once turned the wheels of local commerce. Over the years, once-workaday Pawlet has metamorphosed into one of Vermont's prettiest hamlets. The main street (Rte. 30) is lined with art galleries and craft studios. But don't let their allure keep you from stopping in at **Machs' Market and Brick-Oven Bakery**, the Fallingwater of general stores. The rambling old emporium (it carries everything from eye drops to eye bolts) extends out over Flower Brook, and that gave original owner Johnny Mach an idea. He installed a viewing window in an elevated platform in one of the store aisles, and to this day visitors can look down at water raging through a dramatic rock formation some fifty feet below.

Restaurateur Charles Shinn bought a 1905 railroad depot from the town of Wallingford, eleven mi. to the northeast, dismantled it, and had it moved in pieces to its present Pawlet location on a bank alongside Flower Brook. Today the **Station Restaurant**, it's a popular and scenic spot for breakfast, lunch and ice cream.

Side Trip

For one last look at the Mettawee River (it's bound for New York State, where it empties into the Champlain Canal), turn left onto Button Falls Road between North Pawlet and Wells. Go down a few hundred yards and park at the bridge, a lovely spot where the river plunges through a series of rapids in a deep, stone-walled gorge.

(6) Continue north on Rte. 30 through tiny **Wells**, in the shadow of the Taconic Mountains. Little Pond at the south end of town is actually the southernmost portion of Lake St. Catherine. A few miles ahead is the entrance to **Lake St. Catherine State Park**, on the 930-acre lake. There's a pleasant little sand beach here, as well as rowboat rentals. A boat rental might be just the ticket for anglers, as the lake teems with large- and smallmouth bass, yellow perch, and lake and rainbow trout.

(7) **Poultney** was settled in 1771 by Ethan Allen's cousins and his brother Heber. For many years the town's primary industry was slate, and today many of the quarries are once again open for business.

Take a stroll down Main Street, a National Register business district. If you're ready for a sandwich, stop in at **Perry's Main Street Eatery**; the turkey is real roasted breast, and the cole slaw homemade. The **Poultney Perk** is a please-'em-all little bistro; in addition to its regular coffee house fare, it hosts both poetry readings and cigar dinners. The street ends at the campus lawns and trim brick buildings of Green Mountain College, founded in 1836 by the Methodist Episcopal Church, but today a secular institution.

(8)   From Poultney, take Rte. 140 east to **East Poultney**, a tiny crossroads with a big history. During the late 1820s, New York Tribune founder Horace Greeley learned how to set type when he worked as a printer's devil at the Poultney Gazette , behind the elegant, 1805 Old Baptist Church on the town green. The fellow who apprenticed with him, a Poultney-born man named George Jones, went on to found the New York Times with Henry J. Raymond in 1851.

Greeley boarded for several years at the Eagle Tavern (don't stop in for a drink; it's a private home), built circa 1790 as a stagecoach stop. The tavern is forty feet square, but is saved from having anything like a blunt, blocky appearance by the two-story columns that support the gently hipped roof and create a graceful portico on two sides. In his 1940 book *Old Vermont Houses*, Herbert Wheaton Congdon tells us that "When the frame of the building was raised the usual keg of rum was provided to refresh the workers, and there are hints in the architecture that it was frequently refilled." Among the evidence Congdon cites for his whimsical conclusion is the fact that of the twelve columns, "... no two are the same distance apart." You can't miss the place -- it's yellow, and stands right on the green. Right nearby is the **East Poultney General Store**, as genuine as its name and a good place to stock up on picnic provisions. Also near the green is the Old Cemetery, where Heber Allen is buried.

(9)   Continue east on Rte. 140, following the Poultney River, past Burnham Hollow Orchard and on to **Middletown Springs**. It was in the 1770s that Native Americans first told settlers that mineral springs here had restorative powers. More than 100 years later, hordes of health-conscious tourists were flocking to the springs to partake of the iron- and sulfur-laden waters. A family of local entrepreneurs named Gray built an ornate hotel --the Montvert -- near the springs to accommodate 250 guests, and then began to bottle and sell their natural elixir. They eventually sold the operation to an out-of-state group, which dismantled the hotel in 1906 when people lost interest in "taking the waters."

The Grays were more than hotel keepers and bottlers. A.W. Gray invented "horsepowers," treadmills on which horses walked to run machines that cut corn and sawed wood (smaller animals were hitched up to accomplish smaller jobs). The invention was ingenious for its era and put the Gray Company, and Middletown Springs, on the map.

But the arrival of gasoline engines meant the demise of horsepowers, and the factory closed just before World War I. This, followed by a devastating flood in 1927 that covered the springs under a mound of gravel and dirt, signaled the end of the golden age of Middletown Springs.

Today, a core group of Middletown boosters is working hard to breathe new life into the old resort. Visitors can once again sample the waters at a replica of a Victorian spring house at Mineral Springs Park. The town's fascinating history is recounted at the **Historical Society Museum** on the green. And two beautifully restored B & Bs, **Priscilla's Victorian Inn** and the **Middletown Springs Inn**, once again offer tourists overnight lodging.

(10) Continue east on Rte. 140 through Tinmouth, where, in the early 1800s, furnaces and forges processed iron, to **Wallingford**, at the junction with Rte. 7. From here to Danby, the route follows the floor of the Valley of Vermont, which separates the Green Mountains from the Taconics.

Wallingford was the childhood home of Paul Harris, the founder of Rotary International. It also has a long history in the hand tool business: Lyman Batcheller started a garden tool factory here in 1836; its modern out growth is a branch manufacturing plant of True-Temper.

(11) Head south on Rte. 7 through South Wallingford to **Danby**, home to what may be the world's largest underground marble quarry. (If you want to bring home a little piece of town, stop in at the **Danby Marble Company**, just north of town on Rte. 7.)

Quakers were among Danby's first settlers. Among its most prominent early citizens was Thomas Rowley, described by his biographer Walter Coates as "the pioneer minstrel of Vermont," who helped Ethan Allen organize the Green Mountain Boys.

Danby was also the home of novelist Pearl S. Buck, who restored several buildings in town and spent her last years here. There are unsubstantiated rumors that the Second-Empire Victorian with the shingled tower and widow's walk on Raymond Road (turn at the end of North Main Street) was used as the model for the Bates homestead in Alfred Hitchcock's "Psycho."

Vermont's first millionaire, lumber baron Silas Griffith, carved his wealth out of Danby's forest lands in the mid-1800s. Danby's library is named after him, and each Christmas the children in town receive presents from his legacy. Griffith's mansion is now the Silas Griffith Inn.

(12)   Take Recreation Highway #10, the Mount Tabor Road, east out of Danby.   Paved for only the first few of its fourteen miles, and not kept open during the winter, the Mt. Tabor Road plunges through the heart of the Green Mountain National Forest. After a sharp climb, the road levels near its intersection with the Long and Appalachian trails (they're one and the same between the Vermont / Massachusetts border and Killington, Vermont) at the Big Branch Picnic Area, approximately 3 1/2 mi. from Danby.   Contact the Green Mountain National Forest, either at its Rutland headquarters or at the Ranger Station on Rte. 11 east of Manchester, for maps of the Long / AT and other other trails in this area.

Even if you don't get out on the trail, these woods are a fine place to stop the car, turn off the engine, and get outside to savor an atmosphere of gorgeous desolation. Don't expect broad, scenic vistas -- this isn't that sort of backcountry experience. Instead, expect the sounds and sights of the deep woods -- scant sunlight reaching the ground even at midday; ambient bird song attributable to no single source; drying, abandoned beaver ponds studded with dead trees, slowly being reclaimed by the earliest stages of forest floor vegetation.

(13) Continue on Forest Road 10 to the first T intersection and bear left here; at the second intersection, bear right; and at the third intersection, bear right on Hapgood Pond Road to **Hapgood Pond Recreation Area**. The little pond has a fine

sandy beach; there are also tent sites and a nature trail just under a mile in length. (14) Continue on Hapgood Pond Road past the recreation area entrance (if you've stopped here, turn right as you leave) and continue into the village of Peru, immortalized in the movie "Baby Boom", with Diane Keaton. At the village green (church on your right; general store straight ahead), turn right to reach Rte. 11 and bear right (west) on 11 to return to Manchester. Rte. 11 passes **Bromley Mountain**, one of Vermont's oldest ski areas. Gravity also works here in the summer: At the **Thrill Zone**, there's America's longest alpine slide, the Northeast's only Parabounce, The Trampoline Thing, scenic chairlift rides, miniature golf, and a climbing wall.

The loosely-strung-together village that lies between the end of the Mt. Tabor Road and Hapgood Pond is called Landgrove, and if it looks like a particularly plummy little place, that's because someone planned it that way. Landgrove was a typical busy hill town of the nineteenth century, surrounded by small farms; by the 1930s, though, it was all but a ghost town. Enter Sam Ogden, who in the depths of the Depression bought most of the houses in the core village for about $6,000, and began a one-man restoration program. Ogden sold off the houses as he fixed them up, and Landgrove was reborn. It's stayed that way, and today $6,000 might buy you a Landgrove horse.

Return to Manchester on Rte. 11.

Information

Dorset Area Chamber of Commerce (867-2450), P.O. Box 121, Rte. 30, Dorset 05251. www.dorsetvt.com

Green Mountain Club (244-7037), Rte. 100, Waterbury Center 05677. www.greenmountainclub.org

Green Mountain National Forest (362-2307), Manchester Ranger District, Rtes. 11/30, Manchester Center 05255. www.fs.fed.us./r9/gmfl

Manchester & the Mountains Regional Chamber of Commerce (362-2100),Rte. 7A North, Manchester Center 05255. www.manchestervermont.net

Poultney Area Chamber of Commerce (287-2010), P.O. Box 151, 63 Main St., Poultney 05764. www.poultney-vermont.com

Vermont Institute of Natural Science (362-4374). Adm. for programs.

Lodging

(1)(R) The Equinox & The Charles Orvis Inn (800-362-4700 or 362-1595), Rte. 7A, Manchester Village 05254. Landmark historic resort with 136 rooms and 47 suites in the main inn, and 9 luxury suites in the inn next door is a popular choice for meetings and conventions. Fitness center and spa, indoor and outdoor pools, stocked trout pond, tennis court, and 18-hole golf course. Fixed-price Sun. brunch ($21; $25 with champagne) in the formal Colonnade dining room is a local tradition. Marsh Tavern, with hearty American fare, offers a more casual option. www.equinoxresort.com $$$

(1)(R) Reluctant Panther Inn & Restaurant (800-822-2331 or 362-2568), West Rd., Manchester Village. 05254. Superb accommodations and gourmet fare make the inn and adjacent Porter House one of the area's most popular. Many of the 21 rooms and suites have fireplaces; the suites, in an adjacent building, have whirlpool tubs and fireplaced bathrooms ad bedrooms. The fireplaced dining room serves Swiss specialties including raclette and Veal Zurich and offers a fixed price menu ($35.95). Call for hrs. Children 14+. www.reluctantpanther.com $$$

(2) Aspen Motel (362-2450), Rte. 7A N, PO Box 548, Manchester Center 05255. Modern, clean, and comfortable motel set well back from busy highway. 22 units and cottage with kitchen and fireplace. $-$$

(2)(R) The Inn at Ormsby Hill (800-670-2841 or 362-1163), 1842 Main St. (Rte. 7A), Manchester Center 05255. 10 guest rooms with canopy beds, fireplaces and 2-person jacuzzis. www.ormsbyhill.com $$$

(2) River Meadow Farm (362-1602), Sugarhouse Lane, Manchester Center 05255. Secluded farmhouse on 90 acres bordering the Batten Kill has 5 bedrooms which share 2 1/2 baths. Large country kitchen with fireplace. $

(2) Palmer House Resort (800-917-6245 or 362-3600), Rte. 7A, Manchester Center 05255. 22-acre resort has large, comfortable rooms; 9-hole golf course. www.palmerhouse.com $-$$$

(3)(R) Barrows House (800-639-1620 or 867-4455), Rte. 30, Dorset 05251. Small resort on 12 acres has 28 rooms in 1804 main inn and 8 historic outer buildings. Tennis courts, outdoor pool, sauna, bicycles. Families welcome; limited pet accommodations. www.barrows-house.com $$$

(3) Cornucopia of Dorset (800-566-5751 or 867-5751), Rte. 30, Dorset 05251. Each of the 4 luxurious guest rooms in the restored 1880 colonial Main House has a sitting area; 3 have corner fireplaces. 1 housekeeping cottage suite with fireplace. Young adults welcome. www.cornucopiaof dorset.com $$$

(3)(R) Dorset Inn (877-367-7389 or 867-5500), Church St., Dorset 05251. Country charm and sophistication mesh nicely at this inn with 30 antiques-filled guest rooms (two suites have TVs) and a porch perfect for lounging. The dining room ($$) serves American comfort food, with specialties including turkey croquettes and grilled lamb chops. www.dorsetinn.com $$-$$$

(3)(R) Inn at West View Farm (800-769-4903 or 867-5715), Rte. 30, Dorset 05251. Romantic getaway has 10 guest rooms with 4-poster beds and sitting rooms (some fireplaces). The restaurant ($$$), open Thurs.-

Mon., serves continental American cuisine with French influences, with appetizers such as arborio crusted sweetbreads, and entrees including short ribs and sauteed skate. A tavern menu is available. www.innat westviewfarm.com $$-$$$

 (7) The Bentley House (800-894-4004 or 287-4004), 399 Bentley Ave., Poultney 05764. Century-old Queen Anne Victorian across from Green Mountain College has 5 guest rooms (one with private bath) and a guest kitchen. $-$$

(9) Priscilla's Victorian Inn (235-2299), 52 South St., Middletown Springs 05757. 6 rooms in a Classic gingerbread Victorian on 13 acres of gardens and farmlands bordering the Poultney River. $$

(10) White Rocks Inn (866-446-2077 or 446-2077), Rte. 7, Wallingford 05773. National Register of Historic Places property has 5 antiques-filled guest rooms and a private housekeeping cottage. Children over 12 in inn. www.whiterocksinn.com $$-$$$.

(11)(R) Silas Griffith Inn (800-545-1509 or 293-5567), 178 Main St., Danby 05739. The lumber baron knew how to live: there are 15 rooms and suites with fireplaces and Victorian period furnishings in this handsome mansion perched on 11 acres. The dinner menu features French country cuisine; Saturday nights in summer, lobster is the specialty. By reservation Thurs.-Sun. www.silasgriffithinn.com $-$$
(13)(R) Landgrove Inn (800-669-8466 or 824-6673), Landgrove 05158. Red clapboard, family-oriented country inn has 16 rooms with antique Colonial furnishings, a heated pool, tennis, trout pond, and horse-drawn sleigh and hay rides. Specialties in the candlelit dining room ($$) include grilled pork tenderloin and rack of lamb. www.landgroveinn.com $$-$$$

(14) Bromley Mountain Resort (800-865-4786 or 824-5522), Box 1130, Manchester Center 05255.

www.bromley.com. Fully-equipped slopeside condominiums.

Restaurants

(2) Bistro Henry (362-4982), Chalet Motel, Rte. 11/30, Manchester. Mediterranean-style restaurant serves bistro and trattoria specialties. D; closed Mon. $-$$

(2) Chantecleer (362-1616), Rte. 7A, East Dorset. Classic continental cuisine with an accent on Swiss specialties and table side service in a renovated dairy barn. Reservations. D, closed Mon. and Tues. $$-$$$

(2) Laney's Restaurant (362-4456), Rte. 11/30, Manchester Center.   Family-friendly dining: wood-fired pizza, ribs, steaks, and draft beer. D. $-$$

(2) Up for Breakfast (362-4204), 710 Main St., Rte. 7A, Manchester Center. Creative omelettes, homemade hash, baked goodies, and lots more. B, L. $

(5) The Barn Restaurant & Tavern (325-3088), Rte. 30, Pawlet. Hand cut steaks, burgers, fresh fish, and a terrific salad bar. June-Oct. D. $-$$

(5) The Station Restaurant (325-3041), Rte. 30, Pawlet. Open 6 A.M.-3 P.M. winter; later in summer. $-$$

(7) Perry's Main Street Eatery (287-5188), 18 Main St., Poultney. Sandwiches (try the Perry burger), daily specials, and Sat. prime rib. B, L, D (closes at 2 PM on Sun.) $-$$

Attractions

(1) American Museum of Fly Fishing (362-3300), 4104 Main St, Manchester Village.
World's largest collection of angling artifacts and the tackle of famous fishing celebrities.

(1) Hildene (362-1788), Rte. 7A South, Manchester Village. Mid-May-Oct. Guided tours every half hour. $

(1) Skyline Drive (362-1114), Rte. 7 South, Manchester Village. May-Nov. $

(1) Southern Vermont Art Center (362-1405), West Rd., Manchester Village. Botany trail. Closed Mon. $

(2) Manchester Music Festival (800-639-5868 or 362-1956), West Rd., Manchester Center. Tickets sold at Northshire Bookstore (see below).

(2) Vermont Valley Flyer (800-707-3530 or 463-3069), cor. rtes. 11/30, Manchester Center. Vintage passenger coaches travel along the Battenkill River, through Arlington, to North Bennington's 1880 Victorian station. July-August, Fri.-Sun, Mid-Sept.-mid-Oct. daily except Tues. $

(3) Emerald Lake State Park (362-1655), 374 Emerald Lake Lane, East Dorset. 430-acre park with swimming, boating, fishing, nature and hiking trails, and canoe and boat rental (no motors allowed). Mid-May-Columbus Day. $

(6) Lake St. Catherine State Park (287-9158), Poultney. Swimming, fishing, camping, boat rental. Mid- May- Columbus Day. $

(9) Middletown Springs Historical Society Museum, on the green, Middletown Springs. Memorial Day-Oct. Sunday 2 -4 PM.

(10) White Rocks Recreation Area (362-2307), Manchester Ranger District. Hiking trails.

(12) Big Branch Recreation Area (362-2307), Danby. Picnicking, swimming, hiking trails. $

(13) Hapgood Recreation Area (362-2307) Mt. Tabor Rd., Peru. Camping, swimming, boating, foot trails. $

(14) Bromley Mountain Thrill Zone (824-5522), Rte. 11, Peru. Late May-mid-June, weekends; mid-June-Labor Day, daily; after Labor Day-Columbus Day, weekends.

Activities and Shopping

(1) Gallery Northstar (362-4541), Rte. 7A, Manchester Village. Regional artists' works are exhibited in one of Vermont's oldest art galleries.

(1) Vermont State Craft Center/Frog Hollow (362-3321), Across from the Equinox, Manchester Village. More than 200 juried Vermont artisans.

(2) Battenkill Sports Cycle Shop (800-340-2734 or 362-2734), jct. Rte.7/ 30, Manchester Center. Mountain, hybrid and road bike rentals.

(2) Battenkill Anglers (362-3184), Rte .7A, Manchester. Thomas & Thomas sponsored fly fishing school; guide, instruction, and outfitter.

(2) The Carriage Trade Antiques Center (362-1125), Rte. 7 N, Manchester Center. 15 dealers. Closed Wed.

(2) Gremlin Animation (800-541-2278), 646 Richville Rd., Manchester Center. 25,000 pieces of animation artwork from major studios.

(1) Eqinox Valley Nursery (362-2610), Rte. 7A, Manchester. Complex includes 17 greenhouses with 1,000 perennial varieties, display gardens, annuals, and a gift shop with homemade jams and jellies.

(2) Mother Myrick's Confectionery and Ice Cream Parlor (362-1560), Rte. 7A, Manchester Center. Homemade candy (try the butter crunch) and fudge, soda fountain specialties, fresh baked goodies, and specialty coffees. Open late in summer.

(2) Northshire Bookstore (362-2200), Main St., Manchester Center. Independent store with a large collection of books, music, and, in The Next Chapter, used and antiquarian volumes.

(2) The Orvis Store (362-3750), Rte. 7A, Manchester Center. Orvis Fly Fishing School (362-3622).

(2) Tilting at Windmills Gallery (362-3022), Rtes. 11/ 30, Manchester Center. Vermont's largest fine art gallery includes works by Wyeth, Korus, and Flackman.

(3) Dorset Antiques Center, Rte. 30, Dorset.

(3) Dorset Playhouse (867-5777), Rte. 30, Dorset.

(5) Machs' Market and Brick Oven Bakery (325-3405), Rte. 30, Pawlet.

(5) The Pawlet Potter (325-3100), School St., Pawlet. Visit "The Pawlet Potter" in her studio where she creates contemporary porcelain in pastel glazes and a unique specialty, "Roadkill Impressionism".

(6) Sailing Winds Marina, Inc. (287-9411), Rte. 30, Lake St. Catherine. Sailboat, motorboat, bass boat, paddle boat, sailboards, and kayaks. rentals. Late June-Labor Day and by appointment.

(7) Poultney Perk (287-4155), 61 Main St., Poultney.

(8) East Poultney General Store (287-4042), On the green, East Poultney.

(10) Tinmouth Hunting Preserve & Sporting Clays (446-2337), Northeast Rd., Tinmouth. One of the country's top courses. Catch and release fishing. Gun rentals. Beginners welcome.

(11) Danby Antiques Center (293-5990), Main St., Danby. 11 rooms and barn packed with folk art, pottery, furniture and other stuff.

(11) Danby Marble Co. (293-5425), Rte. 7N, Danby.

(11) Peel Gallery (293-5230), Rte. 7 N, Danby.
**The works of 50 well-known American artists in a
beautifully-restored 18th-century barn. Closed Tues.
in winter.**

Drive 4

Rutland, the Western Lakes, and the Green Mountain Gaps

105 miles

Start out in Vermont's "second city," then head west through the architecturally interesting college town of Castleton before driving up the east shore of Lake Bomoseen. By way of lakes Hortonia and Dunmore, swing north and east to reach the Green Mountain National forest and a pair of roller-coaster roads through natural "gaps" in the steep, forested hills. At Brandon, turn south and return to Rutland via the heart of Vermont's marble country.

(1) If things had worked out differently -- if it weren't for Burlington's fine lakeside location and the presence of the University of Vermont -- **Rutland** might well have become the state's largest city. Actually, it did briefly claim that title, when an economic and population boom in the 1880s sent it into the number one spot. Rutland's location on Otter Creek, at the crossroads of central Vermont, was in those days mightily reinforced by the rise of the marble industry and the Rutland Railroad.

Although a number of smaller operators still take marble from the surrounding hills, the monolithic Vermont Marble Company is no more; as for the Rutland Railroad, it became part of the Vermont Railway some forty years ago. But Rutland is still an industrial center, and its location has given it a new life as a service

threshold for the massive Killington / Pico ski resort complex just east of the city.

A curious symbol of central Rutland's determination to stay afloat in the face of suburban development is the fact that Wal-Mart was persuaded to move into the city's big downtown shopping mall, which itself was a symbol of an earlier stab at urban renewal -- the mall was once the site of the Rutland railroad's grand terminal. Although the giant retailer prefers the wide open spaces of suburbia, the company was persuaded to locate downtown as a way of placating opponents of its entry into Vermont (by the mid-90s, the last state in the Union without a Wal-Mart). So there stands the Arkansas giant, with the old shopping precincts of Merchants Row and Center Street fanning out from the mall.

Wal-Mart notwithstanding, there are still plenty of distinctive home-grown nuances to downtown Rutland. Local businesses occupy premises with a midcentury, Edward Hopperesque cast about them; one edifice, the Service Building on Merchants Row, is a squat mini-skyscraper that has the honor of being one of only two sizable art deco buildings in the state (the other is the Latchis Hotel in Brattleboro; see Drive 2). Just up the street, on Strongs Avenue, is the **Palms Restaurant**, where the first pizza ever served in Vermont popped out of the oven more than sixty years ago (there were plenty of Italian immigrants in this old marble-and-railroad town). There's the Vermont State Fair, held at the fairgrounds on the south side of the city each September. And, of course, Rutland has the Rutland Herald, a proudly independent, Pulitzer-winning daily newspaper that has been printed continuously since 1794.

One of the best ways to get acquainted with the history and architectural heritage of Rutland is to take a walk with the Crossroad Arts Council's guided walking tour, "Views through Time". The $2.00 brochure is available at their headquarters.

Any walk through Rutland should take in not only the downtown commercial blocks, but the extremely handsome array of Victorian homes that stretches along North Main Street (Rte. 7), and speaks volumes about where marble money liked to settle back before this broad thoroughfare was taken over by cars.

(2)   Head west out of Rutland on Rte. 4A (note -- this is "old" Rte. 4; don't get confused with the new one, which is a limited-access road on the outskirts of town).   Just past the junction with Rte. 3, turn right onto West Proctor Road and follow signs to **Wilson Castle**, a thirty-two-room mansion   complete with towers, turrets, balconies, stained glass, and thirteen fireplaces.   It was built by a doctor for his wife, an English noblewoman, in 1888, and there is no Gilded Age monument quite like it in Vermont.

(3) Back on Rte. 4, follow signs for Rte. 4A (which parallels Rte. 4) toward **Castleton**. To the left is Bird Mountain, named for Castleton's first settler, Colonel Bird, who died so soon after building a sawmill that the first boards were used to make his coffin. A marker on the outskirts of town commemorates the **Battle of Hubbardton** (see below), the only Revolutionary War engagement actually fought in Vermont (see Drive 1 regarding the Battle of Bennington, which was fought in New York); and Fort Warren, built in 1779 to defend the northern frontier.

Castleton's Main Street is lined with a series of elegant, pillared houses designed by Thomas Royal Dake, who arrived here in 1807 and stayed for fifty years, following the trade of an architect-builder.   Among the finest are the Ransom-Rehlem mansion;   the   much-photographed   1833 Langdon-Cole House with its unusual inverted portico; and the 1833 Federated Church, with its Greek Revival Manse, at the east end of the village. Dake used his own money to build the church's magnificent pulpit, after the congregation's building committee put a cap on expenses. Another historic marker, just past the handsomely restored **Birdseye Diner**, proclaims that Castleton State College, Vermont's first college and the eighteenth oldest in the nation, opened here in 1787.   In its early days, the college boasted the largest and best equipped medical school in New England. It moved to its present location, just off Main Street, in 1833.

(4) Turn right from Rte. 4A onto Rte. 30 at Castleton Corners, and head north as the road hugs the eastern shore of **Lake Bomoseen**. The territory surrounding the one-and-a-half-mile-wide, eight-mile long lake was once the home of a

small band of Algonkian Indians called the Obom Sawin. In the 1920s and 30s, the lake's Neshobe Island sheltered a more exotic band: critic Alexander Woollcott bought the island and made it a summer outpost of New York City's legendary Algonquin Hotel Round Table. Woollcott and his friends -- among them Harpo Marx, who was known to paint himself blue with crayon and walk along the shore naked to frighten picnickers -- used Neshobe for their own special brand of R & R, including martini-fueled cutthroat croquet matches the likes of which staid old Vermont hasn't seen since.

Side Trip

In Hubbardton, at the northern end of Lake Bomoseen, turn off onto Monument Hill Road and follow signs for six mi. to Hubbardton Battle Monument and Museum. A granite shaft marks the spot where, on July 7, 1777, Colonel Seth Warner and his Green Mountain Boys -- the ragtag assemblage of farmers and backwoodsmen who had formerly battled land surveyors from the colony of New York -- were camped while protecting the retreat of American General Arthur St. Clair from nearby Mount Independence. Early in the morning they were attacked by a superior British force. The British won the battle, but Warner and his men, aided by Massachusetts militiamen and a regiment from New Hampshire, inflicted such heavy losses that the enemy had to give up their pursuit of St. Clair.

Lake Bomoseen also attracted a more sedate tourist clientele to a string of rambling Victorian waterfront hotels, all vanished now. The bass fishing those old-time sojourners enjoyed is still excellent, although fishermen and others who care about Bomoseen are attempting to fight off an invasion of Eurasian milfoil that threatens to choke its waters. Down near the lake's southern end, you may see one or more of the floating machines that rip up and haul away the fast-growing aquatic weed.

(5)   Continue north on Rte. 30 through Hubbardton Gulf and past the eastern shores of **Lake Hortonia** (note: Bee-

be Pond, not Hortonia, is the first body of water to appear on your left after Lake Bomoseen). Hortonia is a popular anglers' lake, as the camp dwellers along its shores well know; bass as well as rainbow and lake trout are prime quarry. There is a paucity of accommodations in these parts, although boat access points can be reached by turning left (west) onto Rte. 144 at the northern tip of the lake.

The next community along Rte. 30 northbound is **Sudbury**, which overlooks the Lemon Fair River valley. There are several stories that venture to explain how the river got its name. One of the most popular tells of a massacre of settlers by Indians along the banks of the river. The event was described as a lamentable affair, which over the years evolved into "Lemon Fair." Another version offers the same etymology, but bases the description on the somewhat less lamentable loss of a horse in quicksand. More prosaic, but probably more reliable, is the suggestion that the river's name is a derivation of "limon faire", French for "making silt". Whatever the history of its pleasantly-scented name, the Lemon Fair is esteemed by canoeists partial to bird watching along pokey, meandering streams rather than rocketing through torrents.

Side Trip

Turn west on Rte.73 and continue for approximately 12 mi. (follow the signs) to Mount Independence State Historic Site, on a headland overlooking Lake Champlain. The defensive fort, connected to New York State's Fort Ticonderoga by a floating bridge, garrisoned 12,000 American troops during the brutal winter of 1776-77. From here they marched to battle and defeated the British at Saratoga. Exhibits here recount their grueling winter and the battle that helped win the Revolution.

(6) Back on Rte. 30, as you drive into **Whiting**, take a look at the tiny elementary school on the outskirts. This is the school attended, just a few years back, by then-sixth-grader Amanda Brigham, on whose behalf a lawsuit was filed contending that since public elementary education in Vermont was financed by town property taxes, radical differences in the grand lists of taxable properties from one town to another led to inequali-

ties in facilities and programs that constituted a violation of the right of all students, under the Vermont constitution, to an equal education. Much to the surprise of nearly everyone on both sides of the issue, the Vermont Supreme Court agreed. The ruling sent the state legislature scrambling to come up with a way to equalize funding between towns lush with ski areas, hotels, and big manufacturing or retail establishments, with towns like Whiting, where there isn't an awful lot to tax. The result was 1997's controversial Act 60, with its statewide property tax. If you pick up a local newspaper while traveling in Vermont, odds are you'll get to listen in on the continuing dust-up over fine-tuning this Byzantine piece of legislation. And you can say that you saw where little Amanda started it all.

When Ethan Allen wanted to round up his Green Mountain Boys for the attack on Fort Ticonderoga, he sent as his courier Whiting native Samuel Beach, who ran sixty-four miles through the countryside with the news. There's an interesting old cemetery in back of the 1811 Whiting Community Church.

Turn right in the center of town by Bulwagga Books and Gallery onto the Leicester-Whiting Road, one of Vermont's prettiest country byways. The mountains straight ahead are part of the Green Mountain National Forest and include Hogback (2,285 ft.), Romance Mountain (3,140 ft.), Cape Lookoff Mountain (3,360), and Mt. Horrid (3,216). When the road ends at a T intersection, turn left and then bear right for Leicester, cross Rte. 7, and continue onto East Road / Fern Lake Road. Continue to the intersection of Fern Lake and Lake Dunmore roads, and turn left (north) onto Rte. 53.

(7) You'll now be riding along the edge of a tiny portion of the 350,000-acre (almost 550 square miles) **Green Mountain National Forest**, which stretches over two-thirds the length of the state and is laced by more than 500 miles of trails. The road here also follows the eastern shore of Lake Dunmore.

While following Lake Dunmore's east shore, watch for signs for the Green Mountain National Forest's **Silver Lake/Falls of Lana Recreation Area**. Follow the moderately difficult (some steep sections) Silver Lake Trail about a half-mile to the falls (there are rumored to be some good swimming holes below the cataract). Several trails branch off from the falls, including the Silver Lake rail to remote Silver Lake. There's good swimming at the north end of the lake, near the foundation stones of a grand hotel that burned in the 1940s. The lake is classified by the state as a semi-primitive site, and camping is allowed. Campers are strongly cautioned not to leave their cars in the recreation area parking lot overnight -- there's a big problem with vandalism -- but to pay the entrance fee to **Branbury State Park**, just past the Silver Lake parking lot, and leave their cars there.

Lake Dunmore was named for the Earl of Dunmore, described in one account as "a rapacious Scottish peer." History notes that "Lord Dunmore and his party came up the Leicester River to the site of Salisbury village, and from thence on foot over to the lake where the Earl waded into the water a few steps, and pouring upon the waves a libation of wine, proclaimed, 'Ever after, this body of water shall be called Lake Dunmore, in honor of the Earl of Dunmore'." Two Indians spread the branches of a small tree and stuck the empty bottle in it, making the naming official (all the while, we imagine, rolling their eyes at each other). The Lord, "as proof of his industry ... in the short space of eight months granted to speculators four hundred and fifty thousand acres of Vermont lands and received fees for the same, and also had granted to himself in the name of others fifty-one thousand acres more."

Fortunately, not everyone involved in the history of these parts was as greedy as Lord Dunmore. In 1945 multimillionaire philanthropist Shirley Farr donated land to the state for this sixty-four-acre park at the base of Mount Moosalamoo on Lake Dunmore. The facility has a sandy beach, boat rentals, a nature museum, and trails, include one that passes the Falls of Lana.

(8) At the end of Rte. 53, turn right (north) onto Rte. 7 for a few miles to the junction of Rte. 125 and then right (east) to **East Middlebury**. The Waybury Inn, a short distance from the turn, was the setting for the outdoor shots of the inn on television's "Newhart." To take a dip in

East Middlebury Gorge, turn right about 1.5 mi. after turning onto Rte. 125, cross a small bridge, park, and walk back across the bridge. A ten-foot waterfall feeds a narrow channel below the bridge, making it a delightful spot for cooling off.

(9) Follow Rte. 125 (one of Vermont's two official Scenic Routes (the other is Rte. 108 through Smuggler's Notch,; see Drive 11), designated as the Robert Frost Memorial Highway, to **Ripton**. Vermont's favorite adopted son, Robert Frost, bought a summer home here in 1939; ten years later he made Ripton his legal address. The **Chipman Inn** was built in 1833 for Middlebury College co-founder Daniel Chipman.

(10) Continue east on Rte. 125 to the **Robert Frost Wayside Area and Trails**. A marker honors Frost, a "Vermonter by preference, poet laureate of Vermont, first citizen of the town of Ripton ..." Poems by Frost line the gentle, mile-long trail that winds through woods and meadows to the Middlebury River. The first three-tenths of a mile is a barrier-free boardwalk. There's an interesting old cemetery on the right just past the rest area.

The **Spirit in Nature Interfaith Path Center**, adjacent to the Robert Frost Trails, is a work in progress spear-

Side Trip

Just east of Ripton, take a right onto Forest Rte. 32, the access road for Moosalamoo Recreation Area, a 20,000-acre semi-wilderness of mountains, lakes, forests, valleys, and streams. Moosalamoo, an Abenaki word believed to mean "the moose departs" or "he trails the moose", was used as a winter encampment by the Missisquoi band of the Abenaki more than 300 years ago. This is also the turnoff for Blueberry Hill Inn and Cross Country Ski Area.

headed by Unitarian Universalist minister Rev. Paul Bortz. A web of 11 different faith paths totaling six miles--each representing various religions' ideas about the environment -- wind through ninety acres of woods, apple orchard, and along 6,000 feet of river frontage and meet in a clearing known as the "sacred circle." Signs en route quote philosophy, bits of scripture, and poetry from the spiritual traditions represented.

(11) Further east, perched high on a hill overlooking the vast Moosalamoo tract, is Middlebury College's Bread Loaf campus, long famous as the site of the **Bread Loaf Writers' Conference** held each August. The complex was originally developed as an inn by Colonel Joseph Battell, a Middlebury newspaper editor and horse lover who established the national headquarters for developing purebred Morgan horses here (see Drive 6 for the Morgan's current Middlebury-area connections).

(12) Continue east past the Middlebury College Snow Bowl and Middlebury Gap (elevation 2149 ft.), which marks the divide between the Lake Champlain and Connecticut River watersheds. The Long Trail crosses here, then climbs to the **Breadloaf Wilderness**, a 21,480 acre tract that is the largest wilderness in the Green Mountain National Forest (the area takes its name from 3,835-foot Bread Loaf Mountain). The road wends its way down through a scenic valley, past the turn-off for **Texas Falls**, a dramatic cascade complete with flumes and potholes. A boardwalk and stone steps descend to the falls, where there are wonderful views into the ravine. To continue on the easy, 1.2 mile interpretive Texas Falls Trail loop, cross over Texas Brook and follow the signs. Pick up a brochure at the registration box.

Joseph Battell loved horses, and he loved the tranquil pace of a vanishing way of life. Not surprisingly, he hated automobiles. Each week he offered the readers of his weekly newspaper, the Middlebury Register, a generous sampling of grisly auto accident reports. Nor would he let visitors drive to his farm: they had to leave their cars at Ripton Hollow and come by horse the rest of the way.

(13) In Hancock, at the end of Rte. 125, turn right (south) onto Rte. 100 and follow alongside the White River to **Rochester**. Stop at the Green Mountain National Forest District Ranger Office just north of town for information on camping and / or hiking in the area. The community voted "Model Town of the United States" at the 1907 Jamestown Exhibition is home to the Quarry Hill Community, the state's longest-lasting commune, founded in the late 1940s by Irving and Barbara Fisk. Today "The Commune" is one of the town's top taxpayers.

(14) Just south of Rochester, turn right and head west on Rte. 73 toward Goshen. As the road climbs up Goshen Mountain to **Brandon Gap** (elevation 2,170 ft.), there will be numerous turnoffs for National Forest roads and trails. Among them are Forest Road 42 (Bingo Road), right, which meanders along a stream leading past a trove of cellar holes, nineteenth-century cemeteries, and swimming holes; Forest Road 45 (Chittenden Brook Road), left, which leads to the difficult, 7 1/2 mile Chittenden Brook Trail and its intersection with the Long Trail; and the Mt. Horrid Great Cliff Trail, right, a steep 1 4/10 mile route from Brandon Gap to the top of the "Great Cliff" on 3,216-ft. Mt. Horrid. (Note: This trail is closed when peregrine falcons, which disappeared in the 1950s and were reintroduced by the state in the 1980s, are nesting in the cliffs.)

(15) The turnoff for Recreation Rte. 32 and **Goshen** -- once famous for Goshen potatoes -- is on the right as you descend the Gap (if you follow this road to its end, you'll head past the Blueberry Hill Inn and through Moosalamoo Recreation Area, ending up back on Rte. 125 in Ripton). Continue on Rte. 73 for Forest Dale, where a plaque commemorates the iron works which thrived here from 1810 until 1865.

(16) As you head toward downtown **Brandon** on Rte. 73, keep an eye out for Country Club Road on the left across from Neshobe Country Club: the house on the corner is the home, studio, and shop of folk artist **Warren Kimble**, whose delightful animals and rural scenes are known throughout the world.   A bit further up, turn right onto Park Street. This broad avenue lined with maple trees and early American homes was once a military parade ground. At the end of Park Street, by the granite Civil War Monument, there's a well-stocked information booth. Be sure to pick up the brochure, "Map & Guide for Brandon & Pittsford." You're now in the town center, whose entire core of 243 buildings is listed on the National Register of Historic Places. Even if you're not staying at the 1786, **Brandon Inn**, stop for a look at the comfortably elegant lobby, which seems to have been frozen in time.

At the small shopping plaza on the left, just before Rte. 7 heads off to the north, turn left on Pearl Street for 1.3 mi.

(bear right at the fork after the railroad tracks) to the 132-ft. Sanderson Bridge, built c. 1840. This bridge over Otter Creek was closed to vehicles in 1987, and was slated for renovations to make it passable for pedestrians. But because the creek was a known Indian route, and the state requires an archaeological investigation of any possibly sensitive area before construction begins, the University of Vermont conducted a dig in 1993. To the west of the bridge they found remains dating back 5,000 years; to the east, Woodland Indian remains approximately 1,600 years old. It is believed that there may have been a permanent Woodland settlement here -- the only one ever found in Vermont.

Head back into Brandon and drive north a short distance on Rte. 7 to the white cottage next to the Baptist Church. It's the birthplace of **Stephen A. Douglas**, "The Little Giant" of Lincoln-Douglas Debate fame.

(17) Turn around and continue south on Rte. 7 into **Pittsford**. A marble monument on the right marks the site where Caleb Houghton was killed by Indians in 1780, and where Fort Vengeance, named by his friends, was erected. The **New England Maple Museum**, "the world's largest maple museum" (and a mighty big gift shop, too), tells the story of maple sugaring from sap to syrup.

Pittsford is home to four covered bridges, including the 139-foot **Hammond Covered Bridge**, now a State Historic Site. To get to the bridge, turn right onto Kendall Hill Road approximately 1.1 mi. north of town (follow signs for "truck route") and continue for 0.3 mi. If you're at the bridge in late April or May, look for fiddlehead ferns, one of Vermont's most popular native delicacies. Refer to the "Map & Guide for Brandon & Pittsford" if you want to tour all four bridges.

The Hammond Covered Bridge is one of Vermont's better-traveled historic spans, having taken a mile-long journey down Otter Creek during the Great Flood of 1927. It was brought back to its proper site by the clever means of floating it on empty steel barrels and hauling it upstream with a team of horses.

Salmon and trout for stocking in streams are hatched at the Fish and Wildlife Service's **Pittsford National Fish Hatchery**, on Furnace Road just south of town off Rte. 7.

(18) At the junction of Rte. 7 and Rte. 3, turn south onto Rte. 3 to **Proctor**, "Marble Center of the World." Marble was first quarried here in 1836, and for more than 100 years the town was home to the Vermont Marble Company, established by Redfield Proctor, one-time state senator, governor, and secretary of war. In its heyday, in addition to its home state, Vermont Marble had quarries in Colorado, Tennessee, and Alaska. Proctor marble (and some from nearby Danby) went into Washington D.C.'s U.S. Supreme Court building and the Lincoln Monument.

In 1991 a Swiss company which was operating the quarry closed operations. But the town's product is in evidence everywhere -- at the bridge into town, in public buildings, on signs, and in cemeteries. Exhibits at the **Vermont Marble Exhibi**t, the world's largest marble museum, include geological displays, demonstrations by "Dr. Rock", and a giant mural.

Before leaving town, be sure to stop at the roaring, 128-ft. Sutherland Falls, named for an early settler who harnessed the falls' cascade to power a sawmill and gristmill.

Back on Rte. 3, continue south to Rte. 4 and Rutland.

Information

**Brandon Area Chamber of Commerce (247-6401),
Franklin St., P.O. Box 267G, Brandon 05733.
www.brandon.org**

**Green Mountain National Forest, USDA Forest Service.
Manchester Ranger District (362-2307), Rtes. 11/
30, R.R. #1, Box 1940, Manchester Center 05255.
Rochester Ranger District (767-4261), RR 2, Box 35,
Rochester 05767. www.fs.fed.us/r9/gmfl**

Rutland Region Chamber of Commerce (800-756-8880 or 773-2747), 256 N. Main St., Rutland 05701. Info. booth: Memorial Day weekend - Columbus Day weekend, Main St. Park, cor. Rte. 4/ 7. www.rutlandvermont.com/ www.rutlanddowntown.com

Lodging

Note: There are numerous chain and independent motels on Rtes. 4 & 7 on the outskirts of Rutland.

(1) The Inn at Rutland (800-808-0575 or 773-0575), 70 N. Main St., Rte. 7, Rutland 05701. 1889 Victorian mansion has 10 individually decorated rooms and TV and some A/C. www.innatrutland.com $$-$$$

(1) Harvest Moon B&B (773-0889), 1659 North Grove St., Rutland 05701. Vt. State Register of Historic Places, 1835 farmhouse overlooking the Green Mountains has two guest rooms--one with a four-poster bed, another with a claw-foot tub. Heirloom gardens. www.harvestmoonvt.com $$

(1) Motel at Mendon Mountain Orchards (775-5477), Rte. 4 E, Rutland. 12 pleasant non-housekeeping cabins with cable TV and AC nestled in Vermont's oldest working apple orchard. Pool. Pets welcome. Also, a farm store with gifts and homemade pies. www.mendonorchards.com $

(4) Edgewater Resort (888-475-6664 or 468-5251), Rte. 30 N, Lake Bomoseen 05732. 50 motel rooms with A/C, color TV, and fridges; 24 housekeeping units and cottages. Many units on lake. Pool, game room, restaurant, golf course next door. Weekly rates available. www.edgewatervermont.com $-$$

(10) The Chipman Inn (800-890-2390 or 802-388-2390), Rte. 125, Ripton. Traditional 1828 inn with 8 rooms and "fine food, wine & spirits for guests." Closed April and Nov. www.chipmaninn.com $$

(11)(R) Blueberry Hill Inn (800-448-0707 or 247-6735), off Rte. 32, Goshen 05733. Antiques, quilts and--in winter--hot water bottles to warm the beds are trademarks of this lovely 112-room inn in the Green Mountain National Forest. Activities include hiking and mountain biking, and x-country skiing. The chef prepares creative fare such as garlic fish soup with mussels, and venison fillet with cherry sauce (BYOB). www.blueberryhillinn.com $$

(18)(R) Brandon Inn (800-639-8685 or 247-5766), Village Green, Brandon 05733. Spacious rooms with period furnishings and colonial wallpaper. Secluded pool. The dining room ($-$$) is elegant, and the chef-owner prepares entrees such as shellfish linguini, roast duck, and barbecue ribs and game hen. www.historicbrandoninn.com B, L, D. $$-$$$

(18) Brandon Motor Lodge (800-675-7614), Rte. 7, Brandon 05733. 25 units. Pets welcome. $-$$

(18)(R) Lilac Inn (800-221-0720 or 247-5463), 53 Park St., Brandon 05733. Handsome 1909 National Register mansion on two landscaped acres has nine elegantly-furnished guest rooms ideal for a romantic interlude. Fabulous honeymoon suite, and a cottage sleeps 4.   Dinner, served Wed.-Sat., might include a lobster ravioli appetizer and entreé of peppercorn breast of duck or wood-grilled yellow fin tuna. www.lilacinn.com $$-$$$

Restaurants

(1) Coffee Exchange (775-3337), 101-3 Merchants Row, Rutland. "Jazz, java and jabber" are served up along with wine, pastries,salads and sandwiches. Patio. Light B, L, D. $

(1) The Palms (773-2367), 36 Strongs Ave., Rutland. This Italian restaurant has been chef-owned and family-operated for more than 65 years. D; closed Sun. $-$$

(1) Panda Pavilion (775-6682), Rte. 4E, Rutland. Highly-regarded Chinese restaurant serves authentic Szechuan, Hunan and Mandarin specialties. L, D. $

(1) Royal's 121 Hearthside (775-0856), 37 North Main St., Rutland. The restaurant that Ernie Royal built lives on and still serves classic American specialties such as prime rib and seafood. L, D. $$

(1) Seward Family Restaurant (773-2738), 224 N. Main St., Rte. 7N, Rutland. The former dairy bar, in operation since 1946, serves up 34 flavors of homemade ice cream as well as sandwiches and dinner platters. The sharp cheddar the family has been making since the Civil War is on sale. B, L, D. $

(3) Birdseye Diner (468-5817), Main St., Castleton. Restored 1949 Silk City diner features homemade muffins and pastries; daily specials. B, L, D. $

(16) Patricia's Restaurant (247-3223), Center St., Brandon. Traditional country fare includes pork chops and fried haddock ; daily specials. L, D, and Sun. brunch. $

Attractions

(1) Chaffee Center for the Visual Arts (775-0356), 16 S. Main St., Rutland. Work of 250 member artists are displayed in a 7-room Victorian mansion. Closed Tues. Donation.

(1) Crossroads Art Council (775-5413), 39 East Center St., Rutland. "Views through Time" walking brochure; concerts, theater and ballet performances.

(1) Norman Rockwell Museum of Vermont (773-6095), Rte. 4E, Rutland. Magazine covers, advertisements and other published illustrations document the artists' career from 1912 to 1978. $

(2) Wilson Castle (773-3284). West Proctor Rd., Proctor. Late May-late Oct. $

(4) Hubbardton Battle Monument and Museum (759-2412), Rte. 30, E. Hubbardton. Late May-Columbus Day, Wed.-Sun.

(5) Mount Independence State Historic Site (759-2412), 6 mi. W. of Rte. 22A, Orwell. Memorial Day-Columbus Day. Visitors Center, hiking trails.

(7) Branbury State Park (247-5925), Lake Dunmore. Campground. Late May - mid-Oct. $

(9) Moosalamoo Recreation Area (800-448-0707).

(10) Robert Frost Wayside Area and Trails (388-4362), Rte. 125, Ripton.

(10) Spirit in Nature Interfaith Path Center (388-7244), Rte. 125, Ripton; (mailing address: P.O. Box 253, East Middlebury 05740.

(12) Breadloaf Wilderness: see Green Mountain National Forest in "Information" above.

(16) Stephen A. Douglas Birthplace, Rte. 7N, Brandon. For information: the Nelsons (247-6569) or the Martins (247-6332).

(17) New England Maple Museum (483-9414), Rte. 7, Pittsford. Closed Jan.-mid-March. $ (exhibit).

(17) Pittsford National Fish Hatchery (483-6618), Furnace Rd., Pittsford.

(18) Vermont Marble Exhibit. (800-427-1396 or 459-2300), 52 Main St., Proctor. Mid-May-late Oct.; gift shop open year-round. $

Activities and Shopping

(1) Annie's Book Stop (775-6993), Trolley Square, 120 S. Main St., Rutland. Comprehensive selection of new and used books; children's books and cassettes; educational puzzles and games.

(1) Costantino's Italian Imports (747-0777), 10 Terrill St., Rutland. Stock up on provolone, prosciutto, sandwiches, and picnic supplies. Closed Sun.

(1) Great Outdoors Trading Company (775-6531), Woodstock Ave., Rutland. One-stop, sporting goods store.

(1) Rocking Horse Country Store (773-7882), Rte. 4 E, Rutland. Three floors of Vermont foods, homemade wine, antiques, and gifts.

(1) Tuttle Antiquarian Books (773-8930), 28 S. Main St., Rutland. One of New England's major vendors of used and rare books, specializing in Oriental art and Asian works.

(3) Farrow Gallery & Studio (468-5683), Old Yellow Church, Main St., Castleton. Bronze and steel sculptures by Mr. Farrow, and the works of several other artists are dramatically displayed in a century-old converted church. May-Dec., closed Tues.; Jan-April, call ahead.

(3) Pond Hill Ranch (468-2449), Pond Hill Rd., Castleton. Trail rides; winter hay rides.

(6) Bulwagga Books and Gallery (623-6800), cor. of Rte. 30 and Leicester-Whiting Rd., Whiting. New and used books, crafts, local products, and tea, coffee and scones.

(16) Warren Kimble Gallery (247-3026), just off Rte. 73E, Brandon (mailing address: RR 3, Box 3038, Brandon 05733) . July-Oct., daily; Nov.-June weekdays, and weekends by appt.

(17) Fred's Dollhouse & Miniature Center (483-6362), Rte. 7, Pittsford. Vermont-made dollhouses, furniture, and accessory kits.

Drive 5

Woodstock, Route 100, and the White River Valley

80 miles

From the depths of Vermont's deepest gorge and the streets of its poshest small town, this drive ventures into the little town that forged the character of a president forever associated with the dry, plain-spoken style of rural Yankeedom. After skirting the boundaries of the Green Mountain National Forest in the shadow of lofty Killington Peak, this route follows the fresh-from-the-mountains White River before dropping south through gently rolling farmland where a great American novelist once played squire. (Note: If you're heading to the beginning of this drive from I-89, take exit #1 and head west on Rte. 4 toward Quechee and Woodstock.)

(1)   More than 13,000 years ago, **Quechee** was covered by an ice-age glacier.   As the glacier receded, meltwater ate away at the bedrock, eventually carving out **Quechee Gorge**, Vermont's Little Grand Canyon. Today, the river that runs through the gorge is called the Ottauquechee, a Native American word meaning "swift mountain stream" or "cattails or rushes near a swift current."   The highway bridge over the gorge, built on the site of a former railroad bridge which was at one time the highest in the East, spans the river at a height of 165 feet.   An easy 1 1/2 mile round-trip

12 Bethel

Rte.107

11 Gaysville

10 Pittsfield

Rte.100

Rte.12

13 Barnard

Rte.12

N

To I-8

Taftsville

9 Gifford Woods S.P.

Killington

2

1

Quech Gorg

3 Woodstock

Rte.4

W. Bridgewater

Bridgewater Corner

8

Rte.100

5

Rte.100A

4 Bridgewater

6 Plymouth

7 Junction Rte.100 & Rte.100A

hike into the gorge on a stone-and bark-covered trail be-gins behind the gift shop near the **Quechee Gorge Rec-reation Area**. Maps are available at the Chamber of Commerce information booth on Rte. 4, near the gorge. If you're ready for a dip, this is the place to ask for directions to the great swimming hole at the west end of the bridge.

Follow signs to **Quechee Village**, where, throughout the nine-teenth and well into the twentieth century, the Ottauquechee supplied power for the large woolen mills that lined its banks. One of the mills, J.C. Parker & Co., produced some of the coun-try's finest white baby flannel. Today the mill houses **Simon Pearce Glass**, which is using the river's power to keep its glass furnace roaring. Pearce, a glassmaker from Ireland, converted the abandoned mills into an attractive studio, retail operation and restaurant. Visitors can watch glass being blown daily.

(2) Back on Rte. 4, continue west past Quechee Village and **Quechee Gorge State Park** to **Taftsville**, home of the 1840 **Taftsville Country Store** and the Taftsville Covered Bridge. The 1836 bridge, built at a cost of $1800 to link the villages of Quechee and Taftsville with outlying communities and farms, measures 189' and is one the state's oldest and longest. A bike path parallels River Road from the bridge to Woodstock village.

(3) From Taftsville, stay on Rte. 4 for four miles to **Wood-stock**, one of the handful of towns most frequently taken by outsiders -- rightly or wrongly -- to be emblematic of Ver-mont. What began as an unassuming village on the banks of the Ottauquechee has been a popular tourist destination since mineral springs first brought summer visitors in the late 1800s. Woodstock's next big boost came in 1934, when a group of skiers hobnobbing at a local inn started lamenting the fact that every run had to be preceded by an exhausting uphill climb. They pitched in $500, and built Vermont's first ski lift -- a rope tow powered by an old Model T. Woodstock soon became a chic ski capital -- a role in which it has long since been eclipsed by Killington and Stowe, but which is nice-ly commemorated in the final few feet of a mural in the post office downtown. The painting goes from Indians to settlers to schussboomers, in one neat WPA sweep. It could be updat-

ed, if the post office had a bit more blank plaster, to portray a posh and immaculate little town filled with snazzy boutiques, appealing bistros, and splendidly restored Georgian and Federalist homes. But that's all right outside the door, anyway.

Woodstock boasts a disproportionate number of famous native sons. Sculptor Hiram Powers (1805-1873) garnered immense Victorian-era popularity via works such as The Greek Slave. George Perkins Marsh (1801-1882) was a congressman and diplomat whose landmark book *Man and Nature* was a founding text of the conservation movement; he also helped make the Smithsonian Institution a reality. Marsh's great admirer Frederick Billings, who made his fortune with the Northern Pacific Railroad, put the conservationist's principles to work in the reforestation of his Woodstock estate and the 1871 founding of his model farm, now the **Billings Farm and Museum**. Billings' operation continues as a working farm, as well as a museum of agriculture and rural life.

The skein of influence that began with Marsh continues into our own time with the recent establishment of **Marsh-Billings-Rockefeller National Historical Park**, a 500-acre-plus tract on the outskirts of town. The property, Vermont's first and only national park and the only park in the system to concentrate specifically on conservation, was the recent gift of Laurance Rockefeller, one of the two currently-surviving grandsons of John D. the First. Rockefeller's late wife, Mary, was Frederick Billings' granddaughter. For years a part-time Woodstock resident, the conservationist and resort developer counts among his properties the luxurious **Woodstock Inn**. Visitors to the park can tour the mansion, which houses personal effects of former residents Billings and Rockefeller as well as paintings by Thomas Cole and Albert Bierstadt; take a guided walk on the carriage roads; and explore the professionally-managed forest stands and hiking trails of Mt. Tom.

Other Woodstock attractions include the **Vermont Institute of Natural Science** (VINS) and its Raptor Center devoted to birds of prey. Bald eagles, peregrine falcons, snowy owls, and more than 20 other raptor species live at the 78-acre nature preserve. Visitors to the Woodstock Historical Society's 1807 **Dana House** are offered a view of village life in the days before rope tows and Rockefellers.

The Woodstock Historical Society publishes several excellent publications to help visitors exploring the area, including "Woodstock: A Walking Guide." It's available at the Dana House, Chamber of Commerce, and at local bookstores. Highlights include the 1809 Georgian Colonial Johnson House; the Richardson Romanesque 1885 Norman Williams Public Library, and the 1808 Old White Meeting House, with a Bulfinch tower and a Paul Revere bell. Revere bells also grace the Universalist, Christian and Episcopal churches. As you head west through the village on Rte. 4, watch on the right for Middle Bridge, a handsome Town lattice design covered bridge erected in 1969 by Milton Graton, the self-described "last of the covered bridge builders." Lincoln Bridge, three miles further west on Rte. 4, was built in 1877 and is the only covered bridge in the country which incorporates the wood-and-iron truss designed by T. Willis Pratt.

> *The Dana Brothers, who published The Elm Tree Monthly in Woodstock in the early 1900s, wrote, "Woodstock Village is the best village in Vermont. Few doubt this and none can prove it isn't true. ... Woodstock has more good people in more comfortable homes than any village of its size in the world. ... The library is better than we need, but not above our tastes. The natives are of good old Yankee stock, with enough Canadians, Italians, and Negroes to give a little zest."*

(4) Continue west on Rte. 4 to **Bridgewater**, where one of the vast, rambling woolen mills that manufactured the popular "Vermont Tweeds" in the 1800s now houses the **Bridgewater Mill**. Bridgewater was the birthplace of geologist and naturalist Zadock Thompson (1796-1856), who wrote an almanac of flora and fauna to raise tuition money to attend the University of Vermont. His later works included the 700-page *Civil, Natural History, Gazetteer, Botany and Geology of Vermont*.

(5) At **Bridgewater Corners**, take a tour of one of the state's first craft breweries, the **Long Trail Brewing Company**. It's also housed in one of the Ottauquechee valley's old textile mills.

(6) Turn left onto Rte. 100A and continue past the entrance to Coolidge State Park and Forest to **President Calvin Coolidge State Historic Site** in **Plymouth**. Looking like nothing so much as Vermont's version of Brigadoon, the Broadway-musical Scottish village lost in the mists of time, Plymouth Notch is the birthplace and boyhood home of Calvin Coolidge, thirtieth president of the United States. It has remained virtually unchanged since 1923, when, at 2:47 A.M. on August 3, Coolidge's father, a justice of the peace, administered the oath to the then-vice-president when word arrived of the death of President Warren G. Harding.

Alone among America's presidential birthplaces, the Plymouth Notch site preserves not only an individual home, but an entire village. Among the hill town's Coolidge-related sites are the birthplace home itself; the house in which the oath was administered (the parlor the Coolidges stood in still contains the kerosene lantern that lit it that night); the general store Coolidge's father ran (above which was the mail room and office that served the Coolidge summer White House); the village church; and a recently-restored building which once housed the cheese factory formerly run by the president's father and son. A number of Vermont cheeses are for sale, and the second floor houses the Vermont Cheese Museum, where visitors can access computer information on cheesemakers throughout the state. Current plans call for a resumption of artisan cheese manufacture on the premises. There's also a carriage barn, filled with antique horse-drawn vehicles (we like the postman's snug, stove-heated sleigh), and a modern visitor center with exhibits interpreting the Coolidge era. "Silent Cal" himself now lies with the rest of the silent majority in the village cemetery.

Side Trip

Orchid lovers will want to make an appointment with owner Darrin Norton and detour south on Rte. 100 for about 8 mi. to Tyson, home to Mountain Orchids, a thriving nursery with more than 3,000 exotic blooms. Watch for his small sign, between Echo Lake and Lake Rescue.

(7) Continue south on Rte. 100A to the junction with Rte. 100. The **Salt Ash Inn and Brew Pub** at the junction, which served as a stagecoach in the 1800s, is an English-style establishment

that turns out its own beers and ales. The pub is in the old general store which housed the post office boxes where Calvin Coolidge used to pick up his mail (the boxes are still here).

(8) Turn north on Rte. 100 through West Bridgewater into **Killington** country. The largest ski area in the East is also a major summer resort: it boasts two championship golf courses, forty-two miles of mountain biking trails, fifty miles of hiking trails, water and skate parks, and a bungee jump. Both the **Killington Skyeship** and the **K1 Express Gondola** whisk visitors to the top of Vermont's second-highest peak (4,241 feet), where, in 1763, the Rev. Samuel Peters is said to have stood when he dubbed the state "Verd-Mont."

It was at Buffalo Brook in nearby Ludlow, in 1855, that Matthew Kennedy's discovery of a gold nugget launched Vermont's short-lived, and mostly non-lucrative, gold rush. If you want to try your luck, at the intersection of routes 100A and 100, detour south on Rte. 100 to Camp Plymouth State Park. Prospectors have also plucked gold nuggets and dust from streams near the abandoned town of Five Corners in Coolidge State Park. Ask at the park office for directions.

Almost 200 years later, in 1946, more than 3,000 acres of forest were purchased by the state for less than $7 an acre, and surveyed as a possible ski area. Connecticut resident Preston Smith leased land from the state and opened Killington in 1958. The resort, along with neighboring Pico Peak, is now part of the American Skiing Company's multi-state empire.

After years of confusion, Killington and the town in which it is located now share the same name. At their 1999 town meeting, Sherburne residents voted to change the name of their municipality back to Killington, the original name under which it was chartered in 1761.

(9) Continue north on Rte. 100 to **Gifford Woods State Park**. The 2,100-mile Appalachian Trail passes through

the park (it meets up with the Long Trail about 1 1/2 miles from the campground; the two become one between here and the Massachusetts border) and provides access to several rewarding hikes, including a trek up Deer Leap Mountain, and to a waterfall along the Thundering Brook Trail. The seven-acre old-growth natural hardwood stand at **Gifford Woods Natural Area**, across from the campground, is a National Natural Landmark and a State Fragile Area. (There's a closer trailhead to the top of Deer Leap Mountain at the **Inn at Long Trail**, on Rte. 4 in Sherburne Pass).

Anglers may want to try their luck at hooking bass, sunfish -- and stocked rainbow and brown trout early in the season -- from the man-made, 71-acre Kent Pond, just off Rte. 100 on the right. There's a Fish and Wildlife Department public launch site here. The Appalachian Trail crosses Rte. 100 near the pond, and offers day hikers a pleasant ramble along its south shore. Golfers can opt for a round at the the award-winning **Green Mountain National Golf Course**.

(10) Follow Rte. 100 north along the Tweed River through tiny Pittsfield (settled by pioneers from Pittsfield, Massachusetts) to the junction with Rte. 107. Head east (right) on 107: soon you'll be paralleling the White River, which along with its many tributaries forms one of the major watersheds of eastern Vermont. With its primary source on the eastern slope of Battell Mountain in Ripton, the White has its outlet at the Connecticut River near White River Junction. It thus forms part of the drainage system which ultimately empties into Long island Sound -- as opposed to the system on the western slope of the Green Mountains, which drains into the Atlantic Ocean via Lake Champlain and the St. Lawrence River. (There's also a watershed in southwestern Vermont emptying into the Hudson, and thence into New York harbor.)

(11) Some of the state's best swimming holes are along the White River. One is right by Twin Bridges, just across the road from Gaysville Trading Post. You can turn the simple act of getting wet into a mini-excursion: just rent an inner tube ($10.70 adults; $7 for kids 12 and under) or a sit-on style kayak ($25/ hr., $5 additional hours) at Vermont River Adventures. The fee

includes equipment and a shuttle service. River trips generally take 2-4 hours, and cover 2-10 miles. At present Vermont River Adventures is in the White River Valley Campground on Route 107, but call ahead to make sure they're there before you go.

(12) Continue east on Rte. 107 to **Bethel**. As you come into town, watch for the **White River National Fish Hatchery**. Each year it produces about 400,000 newly hatched salmon fry as part of the Atlantic Salmon Restoration Program, which aims to reintroduce the fish which thrived in the White River before dams built on the Connecticut blocked their route to the sea.

Side Trip

At the intersection with Rte. 107, detour north on Rte. 100 for a short distance to Peavine State Forest. The White River valley has been used as a travelway for almost 12,000 years: there is evidence that nomadic Paleoindians passed through as early as 10,000 B.C. Today the area hosts transients of a different sort -- it's on the migration path for many bird species. For details, stop at the interpretive site in Peavine, so nicknamed because of the short, crooked route of the defunct White River Railroad.

Bethel, which bills itself as "A Real Vermont Town" (where does this leave all the others?), was in 1779 the first town to be chartered by the newly formed Republic of Vermont. At the turn of the century, the town's economy was firmly based on granite: it supplied two million dollars worth of "Bethel White" for buildings such as Washington, D.C.'s Union Station and the Western Union Building in New York City. Today, the town's tiny Main Street is lined with antique shops, and only its handsome public buildings and banks hearken back to its glory days. Before leaving town, head north over the bridge on Rte. 12 to see the fine 1816 United Church, originally called the Old Brick Church.

Backtrack to the junction of Rte. 12 and head south. Approximately six miles out of town, look on the right (by a white house with green trim) for a small plaque mounted on a large rock. This marks the site of Fort Defiance, built in 1780 after an Indian raid.

(13) Continue south to **Barnard**, whose "downtown" at the outlet of Silver Lake consists of little more than the **Barnard General Store** (well-stocked with necessities and treats, and boasting a genuine old-time soda fountain). The "beach" across from the store is a popular swimming spot, and the dam makes a great diving board. **Silver Lake State Park**, just beyond the village center, has a beach and boat rental.

Barnard has long been popular among summer visitors, including writers Sinclair Lewis (1885-1951) and his wife, journalist Dorothy Thompson (1894-1961), who liked the area so much they settled here at a property called **Twin Farms** during the 1930s. Another visitor had a less pleasant stay: the last panther killed in the state was shot here in 1881, and is now in the collection of the State Historical Society museum in Montpelier (see Drive 11). Mrs. Thompson and her third husband, Czech artist Maxim Kopf, have a more private resting place; they're buried in the Barnard cemetery.

Side Trip

About four miles south on Rte. 12, turn right onto Lakota Road, park in the lot, and hike for 45 minutes to Lucy's Lookout on the Appalachian Trail. There's a house with an exterior widow's walk; the views from the top are outstanding. (Note: this area can be tricky. Best ask at the Barnard General Store for a map.)

Back on Rte. 12, continue south to return to Woodstock. An historic marker on the outskirts of town commemorates the site where those far-sighted and forgivably lazy weekenders built that primordial rope tow. For better and for worse, it did more than anything else to pull Vermont into the twentieth century.

Information

Green Mountain National Forest (747-6700), U.S. Forest Service, 231 North Main St., Rutland 05701. Rochester Ranger District (767-4261), Rte. 100, Rochester 05767. www.fs.fed.us/r9/gmfl

Killington Chamber of Commerce (773-4181), Rte. 4, (P.O. Box 114), Killington 05751. www.killington-chamber.org

Hartford Area Chamber of Commerce (800-295-5451 or 295-7900), 1789 Quechee Main St., Quechee 05059. Gorge Information booth mid-May-mid-Oct. www.quechee.com

Woodstock Area Chamber of Commerce (888-496-6378 or 457-3555), 18 Central St., PO Box 486, Woodstock 05091. Information booth on the Green. www.woodstockvt.com

Lodging

(1)(R) Quechee Inn at Marshland Farm (800-235-3133 or 295-3133), Clubhouse Rd., Quechee 05059. The 18th-century restored farmhouse of the state's first lieutenant governor has 22 handsomely-furnished guest rooms with TV and A/C. Guests have access to Quechee Lakes Country Club. Dinner ($$-$$$), featuring country cuisine, might include an appetizer of New England crab cakes, followed by pancetta-wrapped Angus tenderloin. A lighter menu is also offered. Home to Wilderness Trails (see "Activities and Shopping" below). www.quecheeinn.com $$-$$$

(3)(R) Jackson House Inn (800-448-1890 or 457-2065), 37 Old Rte. 4 W, Woodstock 05091. 1890 landmark estate furnished with fine period antiques has 15 luxuriously-furnished rooms, including 4 suites. The award-winning restaurant serves New American cuisine, with a choice of fixed-price menus: a two-course + dessert; a 6-course vegetable tasting menu;

and a 6-course chef's tasting menu. Prices range from $49-$58. Spa & steam room; 5 acres of gardens. www.jacksonhouse.com $$$

(3)(R) Kedron Valley Inn (800-836-1193 or 457-1473), Rte. 106, South Woodstock 05071. Elegant inn has rooms with fireplaces, jacuzzis, canopy beds, and patios. The fireplaced, candlelit dining room ($$$) offers dishes such as salmon stuffed with a shrimp, scallop, and salmon mousse; and pan-sauteed medallions of prosciutto-wrapped pork. A tavern menu is also offered. Trail rides (see 'Activities and Shopping' below). www.kedronvalleyinn.com $$-$$$

(3) Shire Motel (457-2211), 46 Pleasant St., Woodstock. Comfortable in-town motel with 36 nicely furnished rooms and suites overlooking the Ottauquechee River. $-$$$

(3) Three Church Street B & B (457-1925), Woodstock 05091. Federal home just off the green has 11 guest rooms (6 with private baths) on 2 landscaped acres; swimming pool, tennis court. Pets welcome. www.scenesofvermont.com/3church $$-$$

(3)(R) The Woodstock Inn and Resort (800-448-7900 or 457-1100), the green, Woodstock. 144 elegantly-appointed rooms and suites. 3 restaurants include the formal dining room, serving an "innovative interpretation of classic American and New England fare," with offerings such as oysters Rockefeller (Laurance's favorite), and grilled sea scallops with Maine lobster risotto. Sunday brunch is a standout. Full resort activities, including championship golf course, indoor/outdoor tennis, and health and fitness center. www.woodstockinn.com $$-$$$

(3) Ottauquechee Motor Lodge (800-253-8861 outside VT, or 672-3404), Rte. 4 W, West Woodstock 05091. 15 comfortable units with refrigerators, color TV and A/C; and a 3-room fireplaced suite overlooking the Ottauquechee River. www.ottauquechee.com $-$$$

(5) The October Country Inn (800-648-8421 or 672-3412), Upper Rd., jct. Rte. 4 and 100A, Bridgewater Corners 05035. 10 guest rooms (8 with private baths), a swimming pool, and meals featuring ethnic specialties from around the world make this farmhouse a popular overnight retreat. MAP or B & B. www.octobercountryinn.com $$-$$$

(6) Farmbrook Motel (672-3621), Rte. 100A, P.O. Box 320, Plymouth 05056. Tidy 12-unit lodging by a brook 3 miles from the Historic District. www.motel-vt-farmbrook.com $

(7) Salt Ash Inn (800-725-8274 or 672-3748), Jct. rtes. 100 & 100A, Plymouth 05056. 1830s inn and restored horse barn has 18 country-style rooms with TVs and phones; deluxe rooms and suites have gas fireplaces. Dinner is served family style to guests. The pub has the oldest bar in Vermont. Heated outdoor pool and hot tub. Pets permitted in some rooms. www.saltashinn.com $$-$$$

(8) Inn at Long Trail (800-325-2540 or 775-7181), Rte. 4, Sherburne Pass, P.O Box 267, Killington 05751. Historic country inn with 14 guest rooms and 6 fireplaced suites. Fieldstone fireplace, hot tub, restaurant, and Irish pub. MAP during foliage. www.innatlongtrail.com $-$$$

(8) Grey Bonnet Inn and Restaurant (800-342-2086 or 775-2537), 831 Rte. 100, Killington. 41-room inn on 25 wooded acres, with indoor and outdoor pools, tennis, jacuzzi, sauna, exercise and game rooms. Hiking trails. www.greybonnetinn.com $-$$$

(8)(R) Red Clover Inn (800-752-0571 or 775-2290), Box 7450, Woodward Rd., Mendon 05701. 1840s country inn on 13 acres has 14 handsomely-furnished rooms and suites, some with fireplaces, whirlpools for two, and views. 2 of the 3 dining rooms ($$$; open Mon.-Sat., Sun in foliage and holidays) are fireplaced, and the 4-course menu changes daily, with appetizers such as balsamic, goat cheese and onion tart; and an entree of beef Wellington with foie gras. Pets welcome in carriage house. www.redcloverinn.com $$$

(12) Greenhurst Inn (800-510-2553 or 234-9474), Rte. 12, Box 60, Bethel 05032. National Register of Historic Places Queen Anne Victorian mansion overlooking the White River has 13 guest rooms (7 with private bath). Friendly dogs welcome. Continental breakfast. www.greenhurstinn.com $-$$

(13) Maple Leaf Inn (800-516-2753 or 234-5342), Rte. 12, P.O. Box 273, Barnard 05031. The "pillow library", where guests choose their own, best sums up the lengths the owners go to please guests at this reproduction Victorian-style farmhouse on 16 acres. Each of the 7 guest rooms has a sitting area and king-size bed with handmade quilts; most have fireplaces and whirlpool tubs. www.mapleleafinn.com $$-$$$

(13) Twin Farms (800-894-6327 or 234-9999), Barnard 05031. The state's most exclusive lodging, on 300 acres, features opulent accommodations, round-the-clock meals, an open bar, and a host of activities, including a ski lift, fitness center, and mountain bikes. www.twinfarms.com $$$

Restaurants

(1) Simon Pearce Restaurant (295-1470), The Mill, Quechee. Hearty yet sophisticated American and British Isles served in contemporary surroundings overlooking the Ottauquechee River and falls. House specialties include Irish soda bread and Ballymaloe brown bread. L, D. $$-$$$

(3) Bentley's Restaurant & Cafe (457-3232), 3 Elm St., Woodstock. Good, solid American fare amidst comfortable Victorian surroundings. Lighter menu in cafe. L, D and Sun. brunch (with jazz from Thanksgiving -April). $$

(3) Pane é Salute (457-4882), 61 Central St., Woodstock. An extensive selection of fresh baked regional Italian breads, homemade pizzas, sandwiches, and soups, and, in summer, pasta specials. B, L daily; D Fri. and Sat. in summer. $

(3) The Prince and the Pauper (457-1818), 24 Elm St., Woodstock. A Woodstock institution for more than 20 years, the owner-chef serves gourmet Continental cuisine. A selection of appetizers for the 3-course, $39 prix-fixe menu might begin with lobster gazpacho and include an entree of carre d'Angneau "Royale" (boneless grilled rack of lamb baked in puff pastry). A lighter bistro menu ($) includes Maine crab cakes pulled pork, and hearth-baked pizza. D. $$-$$$

(3) Woodstock Farmers' Market (457-3658), Rte. 4 W, Woodstock. Home baked goodies, deli, soups, lattes, and sandwiches to go. $

(5) Blanche and Bill's Pancake House (422-3816), Rte. 4, Bridgewater Corners. Breakfasts are legendary at this popular restaurant, which also serves up great burgers and sandwiches. B (served all day), L, 7A.M.-2 P.M.; closed Mon. and Tues. $

(8) Casey's Caboose (422-3795), Killington Rd., Killington. A popular family restaurant (in a real caboose) with an extensive menu including burgers, taco salad, Italian specialties, and free buffalo wings at Happy Hour. Closed early May. D; L weekends and holidays. $

(8) Hemingway's Restaurant (422-3886), Rte. 4, Killington. Consistently rated one of Vermont's finest, the restaurant in an 1860 country house features fireside dining, handcrafted American cuisine, and a wine tasting menu. D; closed most Mon. and Tues.; closed early Nov. and mid-April to mid-May. $$$

(8) Mother Shapiro's Restaurant (422-9933), Killington Rd., Killington. Family-style eatery

features great breakfasts, giant burgers, overstuffed sandwiches, and homemade soups. Game room. B, L, D.

(12) Tozier's (234-9400), Rte. 107, Bethel. Light meals, sandwiches, and ice cream. $$

(13) Barnard Inn Restaurant (234-9961), Rte. 12, Barnard. Duck and cognac pâte or lobster risotto might precede quail wrapped in bacon or Black Angus fillet mignon with Bordelaise sauce at this elegant 1796 inn with several fireplaced dining rooms. A lighter tavern menu is available. D Wed.-Sun. $$-$$$

Attractions

(1) Quechee Gorge State Park (295-2990), Rte. 4, Quechee. Mid-May-Columbus Day. Camping on 611 acres perched above the gorge. Late May-Columbus Day. $.

(3) Billings Farm and Museum (457-2355), Rte. 12, 7 River Rd., Woodstock. May- late Oct., daily. Limited winter hours. $

(3) The Dana House (457-1822), Woodstock Historical Society, 26 Elm St., Woodstock. Late May- Oct. $

(3) Marsh-Billings-Rockefeller National Historical Park (457-3368), Rte. 12, Woodstock. Early June-mid Oct. Advance reservation for tours; grounds open year-round. $

(3) The Vermont Institute of Natural Science (VINS) (457-2779,2723 Church Hill Rd., Woodstock. Self-guided nature trails. Closed Sun. $

(6)(L) Camp Plymouth State Park (228-2025), 2008 Scout Camp Rd., Ludlow. Off Rte. 100 on the shores of Echo Lake. Popular day-use park. Swimming, boat and canoe rental; hiking trails. Two housekeeping cottages; Late May-Labor Day. $

(6) Coolidge State Park and Forest (672-3612), Rte. 100A, Plymouth. The 16,166-acre preserve stretches through seven towns; the park has hiking trails, a campground, and picnic area. $

(6) President Calvin Coolidge State Historic Site (672-3773) off Rte. 100A, Plymouth. Mid-May-mid-Oct. daily. $

(8) Killington K1 Express Gondola/Mountain Bike Center (422-6232), Rte. 100, Killington. Chairlift transports bicyclists and bikes to top of Killington, where there's 50 miles of marked trails. For rentals: (800-372-2007). Memorial Day-Columbus Day. $

(8) Pico Peak Alpine Slide and Mountain Resort Attractions (866-677-7426), Rte. 4, Killington. Memorial Day-Columbus Day. Take the triple chairlift up 3,410 ft, and the slide down (you control the speed) "Bungee Thing" ride. Mountain bike rentals.

(9) Gifford Woods State Park (775-5354), Rte. 100, Killington. Late May-Columbus Day. Camping, trails. $

(10) Peavine State Forest, Rte. 100, Stockbridge: see Green Mountain National Forest in "Information". Interpretive site, wildlife viewing site, picnic area, hiking trails, and fishing.

(12) White River National Fish Hatchery (234-5400), Rte. 107, Bethel.

(13) Silver Lake State Park (234-9451 or 773-2657), Barnard. Picnicking, camping, swimming, fishing, boat rental. Late May-Labor Day. $

Off the Drive

Fort at Number 4 (603-826-5700), Rte. 11, Charlestown. Living history museum at a reconstructed 1740s frontier village. Reenactments. Memorial Day weekend-Columbus Day, Wed.-Mon. Closed Mon.-Fri. first 2 weeks of September. $

Activities and Shopping

(1) Antiques Collaborative (296-5858), Rte. 4, Quechee. 90 dealers.

(1) Timber Village (295-1550), Rte. 4, Quechee. Antique mall with more than 300 dealers; country store, restaurant.

(1) Ottauquechee Valley Winery (295-9463), 5967 Woodstock Rd., Rte.4, Dewey Barn Complex, Quechee. Free tastings of wine made from locally grown fruit.

(1) Quechee Gorge Gifts (295-2075), Rte. 4, Quechee Gorge. Vermont maple products, souvenirs, light fare. May-Nov.

(1)(R) Quechee Gorge Village (800-438-5565 or 295-1550), Rte. 4, Quechee. Country store, arts & crafts center, 1946 Worcester Diner, and large antiques mall. $ for carousel and train ride.

(1) Quechee Outdoor Adventures (800-438-5565, ext. 114), Quechee Gorge Village, Quechee. Small, group fly fishing, canoeing, bird watching, kayaking, and hiking trips (or any combination thereof). Rentals available.

(1) Simon Pearce Glass (295-2711), The Mill, Main St., Quechee.

(1) Wilderness Trails (295-7620), Quechee Inn at Marshland Farm, Clubhouse Rd., Quechee. Bike and canoe rental, guided trips on Connecticut and White rivers, fly fishing school, hiking maps, mountain and hybrid bike rentals and trails; winter activities.

(2) Taftsville Country Store (800-854-0013 or 457-1135), Rte. 4, Taftsville. One of--if not the--biggest selections of Vermont cheeses, and an excellent assortment of moderately priced wines; fresh baked breads and pastries.

(3) Kedron Valley Stables (457-1480), Rte.106, S. Woodstock. Trail rides; 1-4 day inn-to-inn trail trips.

(3) Pleasant Street Books (457-4050), 48 Pleasant St., Woodstock. More than 10,000 antiquarian books. Daily June-Oct.; Thurs.-Sun. Nov.-May.

(3) Shiretown Books (457-2996), 9 Central St., Woodstock. Village bookshop carries New England and Vermont books; "thoughtfully chosen fiction and non-fiction for all ages."

(3) Sugarbush Farm, Inc. (800-281-1757), Hillside Rd., Woodstock. Working farm has a sugar house tour, nature trails, farm animals, and store with cheeses and maple products made on the premises.

(3) The Cyclery Plus (457-3377), Rte. 4, W. Woodstock. Bike rentals.

(4) Bridgewater Mill (672-3332), Rte. 4, Bridgewater. Charles Shackleton Furniture/Miranda Thomas Pottery (800-245-9901) are among the specialty shops, gourmet foods, arts and crafts dealers, bookstore, and antiques shop in this historic woolen mill.

(4) (R) Long Trail Brewing Company (672-5011), Rte. 4W, Bridgewater Corners. Tours, tastings, pub fare.

(5) The Workshop Store (672-5175), The Mill, Bridgewater. Handmade pottery, Charles Shackleton furniture, wooden accessories.

(6)(L) Hawk Inn and Mountain Resort (672-3811), Rte. 100 S, Plymouth. Guided scenic trail rides.

(7) Mountain Orchids (228-8506), Rte. 100, Tyson. By appointment only.

(8) Bill's Country Store (773-9313), Rte. 4, Killington. Vermont products such as maple syrup, cheeses, cob smoked ham, and homemade jams, Rat Trap store cheese, general merchandise, and gifts.

(8) Blue Ridge Outfitters (747-4878), 20 Chittenden Rd., So. Chittenden. Guided fly fishing and instruction; canoe and kayak rentals and tours; guided upland bird and waterfowl trips.

(8) Killington Music Festival (773-4003), P.O. Box 386, Killington. For more than 20 years internationally-acclaimed musicians, teaching faculty, and students join together to perform "Music in the Mountains" on Sundays in summer at the Ram's Head Lodge on Killington Rd. www.killingtonmusicfest.com

(8) Killington Mountain Bike Center (422-6200), Rte. 100, Killington. Mountain bike and hiking boot rentals.

(9) Green Mountain National Golf Course (422-4653), Barrows-Towne Rd., Killington.

(10) Riverside Farm Stables (746-8544), Rte. 100, Pittsfield. Trail rides.

(11) Vermont River Adventures (234-6361, pager: 877-243-8002), Rte. 107, Gaysville. White River Campground (234-9115) also rents inner tubes.

(13) Barnard General Store (234-9688), Barnard.

Drive 6

Lake Champlain, Middlebury, and Lincoln Gap

137 miles

Follow the shoreline of Lake Champlain south from Burlington (see Drive 10 for Burlington tour and information), stopping at several places along the way to learn the role of this "Sixth Great Lake" in American history. Meander east through prime dairy country to the college town of Middlebury, then climb through Lincoln Gap before descending into Mad River Valley ski country. Head back to Burlington via the tortuous Appalachian Gap, skirting -- or maybe conquering on foot -- a prominent mountain peak with a history of colorful animal names.

(1) Begin in Burlington and head south on Rte. 7 (Shelburne Road), navigating your way through one of the (thankfully) few parts of Vermont that truly deserves the label "urban sprawl." It's also the home of the state's worst rush-hour traffic. Suburban Rte. 7 does offer a choice of inexpensive chain and independent motels and restaurants, but other than that it will appeal to you only if your idea of a Vermont souvenir is a dining room set or a new car.

Turn right onto Bay Road in **Shelburne**, just over the town line from South Burlington (there's a big antiques center on the corner) and follow along the south shore

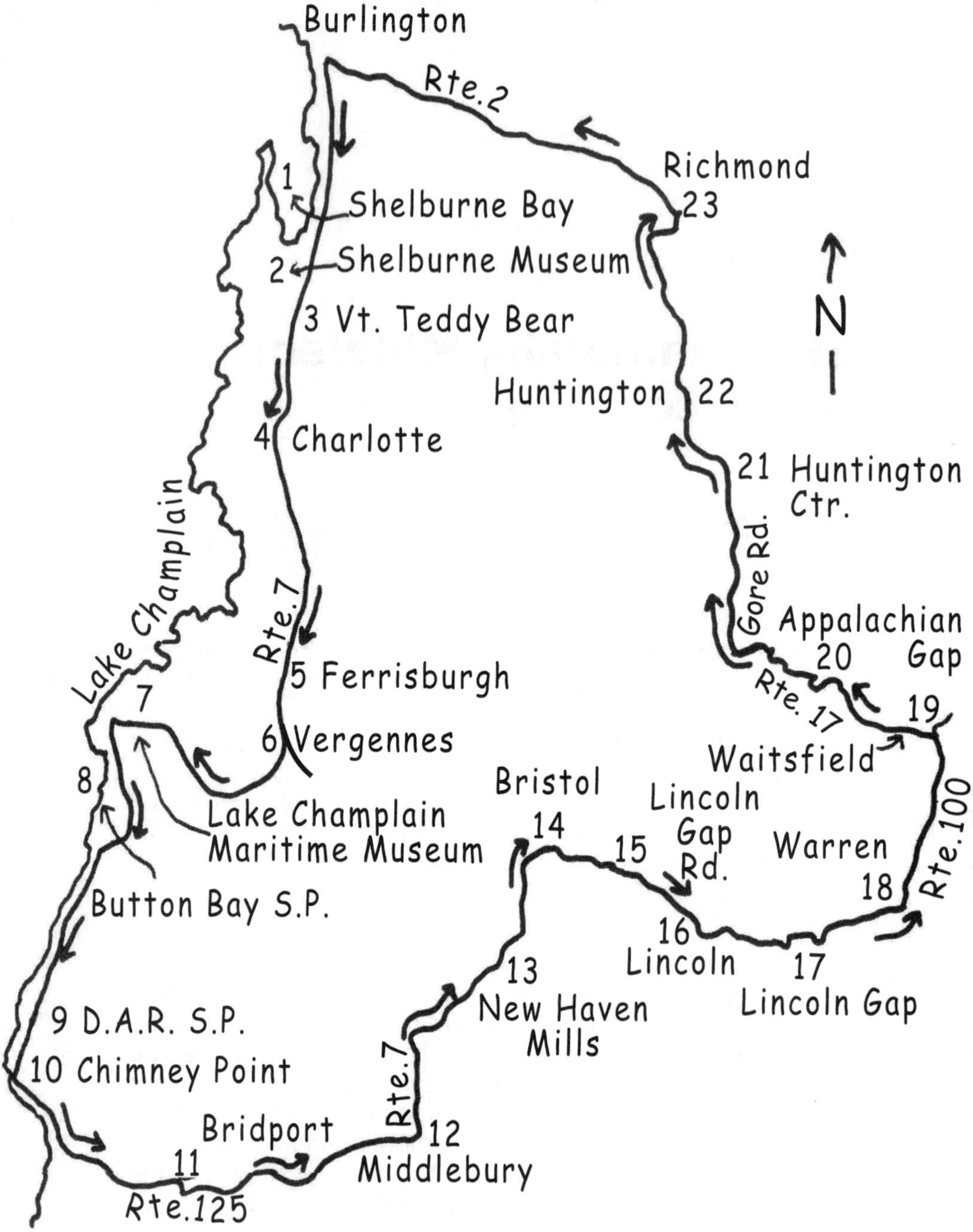
Burlington
Rte.2
Richmond
23
1
Shelburne Bay
2
Shelburne Museum
3 Vt. Teddy Bear
N
Huntington
22
4 Charlotte
21 Huntington Ctr.
Lake Champlain
Gore Rd.
Rte.7
Appalachian Gap
20
5 Ferrisburgh
7
Rte. 17
19
6 Vergennes
Waitsfield
8
Bristol
Lincoln Gap Rd.
Lake Champlain Maritime Museum
14
15
Warren
Rte.100
18
Button Bay S.P.
16
Lincoln
17
Lincoln Gap
13
New Haven Mills
9 D.A.R. S.P.
10 Chimney Point
Rte.7
Bridport
12
Middlebury
11
Rte.125

of Lake Champlain's Shelburne Bay. It was here, during the War of 1812, that the "poor forlorn looking [American] squadron" under the command of Thomas Macdonough wintered in 1812-13 before moving south to Vergennes.

Just ahead is **Shelburne Farms**, the 1880s retreat of railroad magnifico William Seward Webb and his wife, Lila Vanderbilt Webb. The 1,400-acre estate overlooking Lake Champlain was landscaped by Frederick Law Olmsted, and was originally nearly three times as large as it is today. Webb's descendants now maintain the property as a model farm, agricultural education center, and cheese making operation -- its cheddar has won awards -- complete with bucolic footpaths and a barnyard where children can meet farm animals. The Webbs' 1889 110-room summer "cottage" is now the elegant **Inn at Shelburne Farms**, but perhaps the property's greatest architectural attractions are its monumental barns. The restored Farm Barn, built in an Arcadian version of Richardson Romanesque, is, at more than 400 feet in length, actually large enough to house a polo match, were anyone inclined to stage one. In addition to the regular program of tours, Shelburne Farms' grounds are open for a variety of seasonal special events, including Vermont Mozart Festival and Vermont Symphony concerts (see Drive 9 for information).

(2) Back on Rte. 7, continue south through the tidy **Shelburne Village** Historic District to one of the Vermont's premier attractions, the **Shelburne Museum**. The forty-five-acre complex contains thirty-seven buildings, most of them representative late-eighteenth and early-nineteenth-century structures moved here from sites around New England.

The museum's collection of fine and folk art, and of Americana ranging from quilts to farm tools to hand-carved decoys to toys to horse-drawn carriages -- some 80,000 objects in all -- had its origins in the vast trove bequeathed by its founder, the late Electra Havemeyer Webb, a sugar heiress who married J. Watson Webb of the Shelburne Farms Webbs.

Highlights include a Gilded Age private railroad car (a princely indulgence that makes a corporate jet look like a flimsy and inconsequential toy); shops at which artisans demonstrate old-time trades; and everyone's favorite, the SS *Ticonderoga*, last of the side-wheeler steamships to ply Lake Champlain. (It was moved to its high-and-dry location nearly fifty years ago, on railroad tracks specially constructed for the task, and has just been given a keel-to-wheelhouse restoration. A "Fabulous '50s" exhibit features a fully-furnished (right down to the canned goods in the cupboards) post-WW II Shelburne ranch house.

Plan to spend *at least* a half-day at the museum.

Next door to the museum, on Bostwick Road, is the **National Museum of the Morgan Horse**, which celebrates the life and times of Justin Morgan, the schoolteacher who first introduced the doughty breed to Vermont, and of course the horses themselves. (The original Morgan Horse was also called Justin Morgan -- more on both of them when we get to Weybridge, down near Middlebury.)

As you travel south toward Charlotte, you'll notice the open and rolling rural landscape. Several years ago Dr. Stephen Rockefeller, a professor emeritus of religion at Middlebury College, decided that he wanted to do something to preserve the view that he had enjoyed so often when driving along Route 7. He joined with the Conservation Fund to form The Demeter Fund (named for the Greek goddess of grain, fertility and agriculture) to purchase and conserve 850 acres. Today the Charlotte Park and Wildlife Refuge encompasses Mr. Rockefeller's panoramas as well as trails, wetlands, forestlands, and more than 500 acres of preserved farmlands. To get to the park, turn right just past the Shelburne Museum onto Bostwick Road, past the Morgan Horse Museum, to the entrance on Greenbush Road.

(3) Continue south on Rte. 7. If you're traveling with kids, they'll love a tour of the **Vermont Teddy Bear Factory**, a short distance ahead on the left. There's a museum of teddy bear history, and a work area where you can make your own bears.

(4) As you continue south into **Charlotte**, you'll understand what Professor Rockefeller was afraid of. The fields of the one-time farming community have sprouted posh homes on the ten-acre lots that have come to symbolize upscale sprawl. But there's relief at the **Vermont Wildflower Farm**, six lumi-

nous acres of wildflowers where pathways punctuated with explanatory plaques thread through fields and glades. The seed shop will get you started on transforming your own back forty.

(5) In **Ferrisburgh**, the highly-regarded **Starry Night Café** is in a cluster of buildings with the **Ferrisburgh Artisans' Guild**. The renovated complex once housed a depot, farm house, and cider mill (the restaurant is in the mill). The Guild provides work and gallery space for some of Vermont's finest artists. The restaurant (which opens the outdoor deck in nice weather), serves up a host of creative appetizers, and entreées such as rare roasted duck breast and lobster-stuffed sole. Reservations are highly recommended.

A bit further south on Rte. 7 is **Rokeby**, home of one of Vermont's favorite authors, Rowland Robinson (1833-1900). Robinson, who is noted for his stories written in upcountry Yankee and French-Canadian dialect, was a Quaker and a passionate abolitionist, and his farmhouse is believed to have been a stop on the Underground Railroad. In his book *A Study of Independence*, he reported that "[the railroad] held its hidden way through Vermont along which many a dark skinned passenger secretly traveled, concealed during the day in quiet stations, at night passing from one to another, helped onward by friendly hands until he reached Canada ..." At Rokeby, Robinson's books and illustrations are exhibited along with memorabilia of the four generations of his family who lived here.

(6) Bear right off Rte. 7 onto Rte. 22A, past **Kennedy Brothers Marketplace**, to **Vergennes**. New England's third oldest city and Vermont's oldest was founded in 1788. The downtown area is a compact district of Victorian homes and public buildings. Main Street slopes down to Otter Creek Falls, where, during the War of 1812, furnaces and forges turned out 170 tons of cannonballs. It was just below the falls, in 1814, that Thomas Macdonough oversaw the building of three ships -- including the 734-ton *Saratoga* -- in the incredibly short span of forty days, enabling him to seize victory over the British at the battle of Plattsburgh and earn his memorial on Vergennes' green.

When Macdonough took command of the Lake Champlain naval squadron in October of 1812, it was a sad assemblage of small, poorly armed vessels manned by untrained crews. Two years later he commanded a sizable fleet manned by a crack fighting force. Still, he knew that it would be folly to meet the British on the open waters of the big lake. So he strategically placed his ships in the harbor at Plattsburgh, on the New York side, and waited for the enemy to come to him. They did, on September 11, 1814. The ensuing battle ranks with Perry's Lake Erie victory, in the same war, as one of the most swiftly decisive engagements ever fought by the United States Navy on fresh water. It decimated His Majesty's fleet, forced the British army to retreat into Canada, and assured that the Great Lakes would remain in American hands

Side Trip

Head east on Rte. 17 seven miles to the 2,858-acre Dead Creek Wildlife Management Area, home to a wealth of bird and animal life including black bear, wild turkey, and several species of duck. The 1,000-acre Waterfowl Area serves as a major stopover for snow geese on their fall migration. The marshy tract is popular with canoeists, birders, and, in season, duck hunters.

(7) Just west of Vergennes, turn right onto Panton Road to Basin Harbor Road and the **Lake Champlain Maritime Museum**. The museum, which serves as a conservation center for artifacts brought up from the lake bottom (a spectacular recent find was one of Benedict Arnold's Revolutionary War gunboats) offers exhibits chronicling the military, mercantile, and recreational history of Lake Champlain. Maps and vintage water craft tell the lake's story, from the era of the Indians and French explorers, down through its role as the birthplace of the American Navy in the eighteenth century and its later importance in the freight and passenger trade ... not to mention Prohibition-era bootlegging. Moored in a cove adjacent to the museum is a modern replica of another Arnold gunboat, the *Philadelphia*. Clamber aboard, and conjure up this far outpost of the days of fighting sail.

(8) Back on Basin Harbor Rd., continue directly to the 700-acre **Basin Harbor Club**, a serenely luxurious old resort on

Lake Champlain which has it has its own airstrip, and still asks gentlemen to wear jackets and ties at dinner. Or turn left onto Button Bay Rd. to **Button Bay State Park**, one of the loveliest public-access areas on Lake Champlain. The name of the park comes from the little button-shaped stones, oddly pierced at their centers, that turn up on the beach here. The stones, which have become rarer in recent years, were formed when sediment collected around the stems of prehistoric vegetation.

At the fork, bear right onto Arnold Bay Rd. and follow along the shore of Lake Champlain past Arnold Bay. Here in October of 1776, the still loyal Benedict Arnold, pursued by the British after the battle of Valcour Island (see Drive 10), ran his flagship *Congress* and four other vessels ashore and burned them -- with colors flying -- rather than let them be captured by the British.

(9)   Continue south along the lakeshore, following Arnold Bay Road as it turns into Lake Road past **Yankee Kingdom Orchard**, and then onto Lake Street, which merges with Rte. 17. Continue south on Rte. 17 to the turnoff for **DAR State Park** and the **John Strong Mansion**. This handsome Georgian mansion, built in the 1790s with bricks fired on site, stands near the site of Strong's original home, burned by the British in 1777. Check out the four "hidey holes": historians are unsure whether they were meant to hide family members during Indian attacks, to protect them from bears (one had entered Strong's first house looking for food), or both.

(10) Just past the park, at the junction of Rtes. 17 and 125 in the shadow of the bridge to New York State, is **Chimney Point State Historic Site**. It is believed that Samuel de Champlain stood here on July 30, 1609, and named the lake after himself. In 1690 a party of French colonists from the vicinity of modern-day Albany, New York, established what became a vital outpost here. The French fled in 1759, shortly before Mohawk raiders torched the settlement. All that remained were blackened chimneys; hence the name.

The site's museum, which traces the area's Native American and French heritage, is housed in a late eighteenth-century tavern and inn which was built on the remains of a prehistoric

Indian campsite and the French settlement. According to legend, Green Mountain Boys Ethan Allen and Seth Warner were surprised by the British in the inn's taproom (the Boys knew every taproom in Vermont) and narrowly escaped capture. However, architectural evidence points to the present structure having been built after the time of the alleged incident.

(11)   Turn left (east) onto Rte. 125 to the tiny village of **Bridport**, where 125 takes a short jog to the south along Rte. 22A before heading east again on its own.   Approximately three miles from the village, watch on the left for the tiny cemetery near the intersection with Snake Mountain Road.   There are several interesting old headstones here, including one for Mr. Benedict, who "was slain by apoplexy without warning and entered into spirit life 6/20/1881."

(12)   Continue on Rte. 125 into **Middlebury**, passing the campus of **Middlebury College** before reaching downtown. Middlebury, an esteemed liberal arts institution with no present-day religious affiliation, was founded in 1800 as a godly alternative to the University of Vermont, then just getting off the ground itself but suspect because of its nominal association with the freethinking Allen brothers.   Its chief benefactor was local squire Gamaliel Painter -- his Federalist mansion still stands downtown -- for whom the oldest campus building, the elegantly simple Painter Hall (1816), is named.

The Middlebury campus building of greatest interest to visitors (aside from those heading for the admissions office) is the college's **Museum of Art**.   Highlights of the collections include sculptures by Auguste Rodin and the nineteenth-century Woodstock, Vermont native, Hiram Powers; as well as ancient Cypriot pottery and works by contemporary painters. Middlebury's downtown, which bustles with the shops and restaurants of a typical New England college community, clusters against the banks of Otter Creek.   At this point, the "creek" is more of a full-fledged river complete with a lovely waterfall -- for a good view, look out the big picture window at the **Vermont State Craft Center at Frog Hollow**. This is the place to see what Green Mountain glassblowers, jewelers, potters, furniture makers, weavers, and other artisans are up to; if you haven't already noticed, the state has attracted more than its share of creative individuals.

For that matter, Middlebury itself is a handsome creation. The town's historic district has almost 300 buildings that were built during the eighteenth- and early-nineteenth centuries, when it was a major wool processing center and site of Vermont's first major marble quarrying operation (1803). An 1829 marble merchant's home houses the **Henry Sheldon Museum of Vermont History** and its superb collection of nineteenth-century Vermont paintings, furniture, decorative arts, household items and farm tools, as well as the contents of an old-time pharmacist's establishment. Another marble-era relic is the Historic Marble Works, off Elm Street just north of downtown. The complex, which is actually built of marble, now houses shops, offices, and restaurants.

Downtown Middlebury's most distinctive structure is the 1809 Congregational Church, on the north side of the Green. With its arched doorways, magnificent Palladian window, and 136-foot, four-tiered spire incorporating an octagonal belfry, the church joins Bennington's First Congregational (see Drive 1) and Strafford's Town House (see Drive 7) as, in our opinion, the most graceful ecclesiastical structures in Vermont. Also worth a look, or a stroll through the lobby, or even a night's stay, is the **Middlebury Inn**, an inviting 1830 brick hostelry facing the Green.

There are two covered bridges in Middlebury: Pulp Mill Bridge, built between 1808 and 1820; and Vermont's highest, the 1824 Halpin Bridge, built to carry wagon loads of marble forty-one feet over the Muddy Branch of the New Haven River. Ask in town for directions to both bridges, which are on the northern outskirts.

(13) Leaving Middlebury, head north on Rte. 7 for just under three miles and turn right onto River Road toward **New Haven Mills**. This once-thriving community on the banks of the New Haven River was devastated by the 1927 flood. But one building -- a Victorian Italianate structure perched high on a hill in town -- was left unscathed and now stands out like a sore thumb in this farm country. It was the gift of native son Curtis Miranda Lampson, who left Vermont in his early

years, made good, and in the 1860s sent $8,000 to his home-town to build a school. Lampson School served the community until World War II. Today, after years of abuse, it's being restored by new owners.

(14) Turn left (north) at the intersection with Rte. 116 (which soon merges with Rte. 17) to reach **Bristol**. The tidy little town with its red brick, vest-pocket downtown today calls itself the "Gateway to the Green Mountains," but it once had a less glamorous nickname. It was known as the "Coffin Community" back when the National Casket Company was one of several wood products enterprises that took advantage of Bristol's proximity to a vast sea of lumber. Several are still in business, though coffins are no longer part of the picture.

If you're traveling through Bristol on a Tuesday between 7:30 A.M. and 1 P.M. don't be surprised if you get behind a refuse wagon pulled by horses: Patrick and Cathy Palmer haul the town's trash with their team of Percherons.

As you continue east out of Bristol on Rte. 116/17, watch for the Lord's Prayer Rock. A Buffalo physician named Joseph Greene, who grew up near Bristol, recalled teamsters swearing mightily as they cracked their whips to coax overworked horses up the muddy hill. In 1891, Dr. Greene had the rock inscribed as a counter to the teamsters' profanity.

(15) A short distance from town, at the Squirrel's Nest Restaurant, bear right onto **Lincoln Gap** Road, which twists and turns alongside the New Haven River as it descends through the New Haven River Gorge in a series of rapids, cascades, and waterfalls. There are two wonderful swimming holes along the road: Bristol Falls, on the right immediately after the turn-off (one of the best pools is at the upper waterfall, approximately .4 mile up the road); and, a short distance up the road, also on the right, Circle Current.

Side Trip

Bristol is the gateway to Bristol Cliffs Wilderness, one of central Vermont's most intriguing natural areas. At Bristol Cliffs, a 3,740-acre tract of the Green Mountain National Forest maintained as a roadless area off-limits to logging and mechanized travel, vertical crags rise from the rugged shoulder of South Mountain to tower 1,500 feet above the Champlain valley. One protrusion, Devil's Pulpit, is a bulging mass of quartzite that may have been used for Indian arrowheads. Although the peripheral parts of the present-day wilderness were once logged, the deep interior of the parcel is covered by what is believed to be one of Vermont's only old-growth virgin forests. Both Lower Notch Road, which extends south from River Street in downtown Bristol, and Lincoln Gap Road off Rte. 116/17 east of town offer access to Bristol Cliffs trailheads. Hikers should note, however, that in keeping with the tract's wilderness status, trails peter out and the use of compasses and topographical maps is recommended.

(16) **Lincoln**, settled by Quakers more than 200 years ago, retains the look and feel of a frontier logging town. In fact, the **Old Hotel B&B** was built in 1820 to house lumberjacks. One note of sophistication is the

brick Burnham Library, which was refurbished after sustaining extensive damage in the 1997 winter floods.

(17) The road through **Lincoln Gap** (closed in winter) is the highest automobile route in the state, cresting at an altitude of 2,424 feet. It snakes through a steep, narrow pass surrounded by mountains, including Mt. Ellen, Vermont's third highest (4,135 feet). The Long Trail crosses the highway near the top, where there are sweeping panoramas of the Green Mountain Range, the Champlain Valley, and the Adirondacks. A moderately difficult 1.25 mile trail at the top passes through the Bread Loaf Wilderness, a 21,480-acre primitive tract which is the Green Mountain National Forest's largest wilderness (see Drive 6), and offers expansive views that include Warren to the east, Mount Abraham to the north, Bristol and the Bristol Cliffs to the west, and Mount Grant to the south.

Side Trip

The moderately difficult but nevertheless popular Battell Trail (4.6 mi.) climbs to the Battell Shelter, which sleeps eight. From the shelter, which is maintained by the Green Mountain Club and the U.S. Forest Service, a steep 0.8 mile trail leads to the open summit of Mount Abraham (there's a connection here with the Long Trail) and fabulous views of the White Mountains, Bristol Cliffs, Lake Champlain, and the Adirondacks. Be sure to watch where you walk on the summit: it shelters a variety of rare, arctic-alpine plants. To reach the Battell Trail, head north out of Lincoln village on Quaker Street, then turn right on Elder Hill Road. Bear right at the fork and follow signs for trail parking.

(18) The road through Lincoln Gap descends to Rte. 100, the main street of the Mad River valley. The surrounding region is home to two of Vermont's major ski areas -- Sugarbush and Mad River Glen. At the intersection with Rte. 100, turn left (north) for a short distance, then take the second right, Covered Bridge Road, for **Warren** village. The road crosses the Mad River through the 1879-1880 Warren Covered Bridge. Most of the town's Greek Revival homes were built much earlier, when Warren was a thriving mill village.

Today it exists primarily as a service town for the ski areas, and is home to the elegant **Pitcher Inn**, one of only two Relais & Châteaux properties in Vermont (the other is The Inn at Sawmill Farm in West Dover--see Drive #1). Enjoy a home-baked pastry or lunch on the deck overlooking the waterfall at the historic **Warren Store**, across from the inn.

Side Trip

(19)   Return to Rte. 100 and continue north, past one of the access roads to Sugarbush, to the junction with Rte. 17. To visit **Waitsfield**, the main service area for the ski resorts, continue north on Rte. 100 for about a mile. The 1833 Village Bridge, most likely the state's second oldest covered bridge, and one of the few

If you're thinking more about swimming than skiing in the Mad River Valley, detour south on Rte. 100 for a few miles to Warren Falls, one of the state's most popular swimming holes. Park in the lot on the right by the sign that reads, "43rd Infantry Division Memorial Highway."

with an attached walkway, is on Bridge Street. Graton Associates, the company that restored the bridge in 1973, was committed to using only wood, rather than add the steel I-beam supports found in many rehabbed covered bridges. Look for their craftsmanship in the roof bracing, which incorporates "ship knees" -- right-angle timbers cut from the junctures of branches and trunks on large trees.

(20)   Backtrack to Rte. 17 and continue west, past access roads for Sugarbush and Mad River Glen -- the former a modern, two-mountain mega-resort, and the latter a proud, cooperative-owned throwback boasting Vermont's only no-snowboard policy and the last single chairlift in operation in the U.S. The road now ascends through a tortuous series of switchbacks into unorganized Buels Gore (2000 population: 12) and crests the **Appalachian Gap** at 2,365 feet in the shadow of Baby Stark Mountain. Just as abruptly, Rte. 17 begins its descent into the Champlain valley, with outstanding westward views at the summit and along the way.

Several small and remote pieces of land in Vermont , have the word "Gore" in their names. What's a gore? No, it's not a place where an especially bloody battle was fought. The word's closest related use is in tailoring, in which a gore is a triangular piece of material inserted between two larger pieces to alter or expand a garment's shape. Similarly, a gore on the map is a triangular or nearly triangular parcel of land that was left over when two more uniformly-shaped townships were surveyed.

(21) At the bottom of the gap, turn right onto Gore Road, which soon changes names and becomes Main Road, and head north toward Hanksville and Huntington Center. In Huntington Center, turn off at the sign for **Camel's Hump State Park** and 4,083-ft. Camel's Hump, one of the Vermont's most popular hikers' destinations. The summit offers a look at examples of subalpine vegetation, along with views that range over hundreds of square miles and take in the highest peaks of three states: Vermont's Mt. Mansfield (north); New York's Mt. Marcy (west, across Lake Champlain); and New Hampshire's Mt. Washington (east, among the other summits of the Presidential Range). There are several trails, of varying degrees of difficulty, that meet the Long Trail at the summit of Camel's Hump. The best source of information is the Green Mountain Club, in Waterbury (see Drive 11) and its *Guide Book of the Long Trail* .

(22) Back on Main Road, head north through **Huntington**, once a logging and dairying communiy but now a bedroom town for people who work in the Burlington area. Just ahead, look for the **Green Mountain Audubon**

Samuel de Champlain called Camel's Hump le lion couchant -- the couching lion -- because he felt its ridge line resembled just that when seen from the east or west. On Ira Allen's 1798 map, it was called "Camel's Rump," but Vermont gazetteer compiler Zadock Thompson, no doubt sensing the Victorian era just around the corner, changed the name to Camel's Hump -- in any event, a more pronounced feature of the beast.

Nature Center and the adjacent **Birds of Vermont Museum**. Visitors to the 230-acre nature center can wander a network of trails through woodlands, meadows, and apple orchards, and alongside beaver ponds.

(23) Continue on to **Richmond**, home of the **Old Round Churc**h. The sixteen-sided structure with its octagonal belfry, completed in 1813, was a joint undertaking of five sects, who held services here until they each eventually broke away. The building served as the town hall for several years. The interior still has the original pews, pulpit, and gallery. Richmond itself has suffered two calamities: a fire destroyed the entire business section in 1908, and nineteen years later, in the Great Flood of 1927, much of the village was inundated when the Winooski River roared over its banks. Today, the thriving center, home to several businesses and restaurants, including The **Daily Bread Restaurant and Bakery** -- a local institution for almost 25 years -- is frequently praised as an example of how even a small community can have a well-planned, working downtown, despite all the trends to the contrary.

Turn left on Rte. 2 to return to Burlington via Williston (the latter part of this route is heavily commercialized), or hop onto I-89 northbound.

Information

Addison County Chamber of Commerce (800-733-8376 or 388-7951), 2 Court St., Middlebury 05753. www.midvermont.com

Green Mountain National Forest (767-4261), U.S.D.A. Forest Service, RD #1, Box 108, Rochester 05767. www.fs.fed.us/r9/gmfl

Lake Champlain Regional Chamber of Commerce (863-3489), 60 Main St., Suite 100, Burlington 05401. www.vermont.org/chamber

Sugarbush Chamber of Commerce (800-828-4748 or 496-3409), Rte. 100, P.O. Box 173, Waitsfield 05673 www.madrivervalley.com

Lodging

(1)(R) Inn at Shelburne Farms (985-8498),1611 Harbor Rd., Shelburne Farms, Shelburne 05482. The Webbs' 45-room, lakefront, Queen Anne-style mansion has 24 rooms (17 with private bath) of varying size and amenities, and 2 cottages. The formal Marble Room prepares contemporary regional dishes, with entreés such as sauteed Maine salmon and grilled Coleman naturally raised beef tenderloin. Sunday brunch is a real treat, and includes admission to the grounds.Guests have use of the tennis courts, boats, and beach. Mid-May-mid-Oct. (no heat or air conditioning). www.shelburnefarms.org $$-$$$

(11) Lemon Fair B & B (758-9238), Crown Point Rd., Bridport. 4 comfortable guest rooms (2 with private bath) in 1796 home. Entire house can be rented. $

(8)(R) Basin Harbor Club (800-622-4000 or 475-2311), Basin Harbor Rd., Basin Harbor. 38 rooms in the main inn and two lodges; and 77 1-3 bedroom cottages (some with fireplaces, decks, and porches). The dining room ($$-$$$) serves classic American fare such as pan roasted breast of duck or Dijon garlic marinated grilled shrimp, and offers a Sunday jazz brunch. Jackets are required in the restaurant and common rooms after 6 PM. 18-hole golf course, tennis, swimming pool, water sports, children's programs. Pets welcome in cottages ($). Mid-May-mid-Oct. www.BasinHarbor.com $$$

(12) The Inn on the Green (888-244-7512 or 388-7512), 71 South Pleasant St., Middlebury 05753. Gracefully restored 1803 National Historic Register Landmark Federalist on the Green has 11 elegant rooms and suites. www.innonthegreen.com $$-$$$

(12) Middlebury Inn (800-842-4666 or 388-4961), 14 Courthouse Sq., Middlebury 05753. All 55 rooms in the inn, as well as those in the contemporary motel and Victorian-era Porter House Mansion are furnished with period pieces and have TVs, phones, and hair dryers. The inn's front rooms can be a bit noisy if window is open. The restaurant ($$) serves traditional Yankee fare at breakfast, lunch and dinner, and complimentary afternoon tea with home baked treats for guests. Sun. bruch. www.middleburyinn.com $$-$$$

(12) Swift House Inn (388-9925), cor. Stewart Lane & Rte. 7, Middlebury. 21 luxurious guest rooms in 3 buildings on an elegant 1815 estate just two blocks from the center of town. Some fireplaces and double whirlpool tubs. www.swifthouseinn.com $$-$$$

(14) Firefly Ranch (453-2223), P.O.Box 152, Bull Run Rd., (Lincoln) Bristol 05443. Horse lovers (and others) will enjoy this country B & B, which offers equestrian packages with meals, and trail rides. Small pets welcome. www.fireflyranch.com $$

(16) The Old Hotel B&B (453-2567)233 E. River Rd., Box 560, Lincoln. The recently renovated historic inn offers six second-floor guest rooms with shared bath. www.oldhotel.net $-$$

(18)(R) Pitcher Inn (888-867-4824 or 496-6350), Warren 05674. Each of the 9 luxurious rooms and 2 2-bedroom suites--all with jacuzzis and many with steam showers and fireplaces--was designed by a different architect. The elegant restaurant ($$$) serves contemporary American dishes such as lobster and corn chowder, and sesame crusted ahi tuna. The wine list is spectacular. D, Sun. brunch. www.pitcherinn.com $$$

(19) Inn at Mad River Barn (800-631-0466 or 496-3310), Waitsfield 05673. 15 guest rooms with TVs and some steambaths in a decidedly laid back, down-home

environment. Dinner is served in winter.
ww.madriverbarn.com $-$$

(19) Inn at the Round Barn Farm (496-2276), 1661 E.
Warren Rd., Waitsfield 05673. The round barn houses
a pool and greenhouse; some of the 12 luxurious,
antiques-filled guest rooms and suite in the farmhouse
have fireplaces and steam showers or jacuzzis.
Children 15 and over welcome. X-c ski trails.
www.roundbarninn.com $$-$$$

(19)(R) Millbrook Inn and Restaurant (800-477-2809
or 496-2405), Rte. 17, Waitsfield. Seven guestrooms
with hand-stenciling, antique bedsteads and
handmade quilts; the 2-bedroom Octagon House ($$$)
sleeps 4-5. Dinner ($-$$) specialties include lasagna
with homemade spinach noodles, and Indian dishes.
Pets by arrangement. www.millbrookinn.com $$-$$$

(19) The Wait Farm Motor Inn (800-887-2828 or 496-
2033), 4805 Main St., Waitsfield 05673. Spacious
and tidy in-town motel with standard units and
efficiencies. $

(23) Richmond Victorian Inn (888-242-3362 or 434-
4410), 191 E. Main St., Rte. 2, Richmond 05477.
Beautifully restored 1880's Queen Anne home has 6
antique-furnished guest rooms. Children 12 and older.
www.richmondvictorianinn.com $$

Restaurants

(1) Buono Appetito Italian Restaurant (985-2232),
Rte. 7 (next to the Econo Lodge), Shelburne. Great
pizza and regional specialties. D. $

(2) Cafe Shelburne (985-3939), Rte. 7, Shelburne.
One of the most popular upscale restaurants in the
area has been serving delicious French bistro cuisine
for 30 years. D; closed Sun. and Mon. $$-$$$

(5) **The Starry Night Cafe** (877-6316), 5467 Rte. 7, Ferrisburgh Artisans' Guild, Ferrisburgh. D. $$

(6) **Christophe's on the Green** (877-3413), 5 Green St., Vergennes. Excellent upscale chef-owned French restaurant located in a former downtown hotel. A 3-course prix fixe dinner, is available for $41. D, Tues.-Sat.; Dec. and Feb.-April, D Thurs-Sat.; closed Nov and Jan. $$-$$$

(6)(L) **Roland's Place** (453-6309), Rte. 7, New Haven Junction. In a beautifully restored 1796 house, French chef Roland prepares hearty entrees using fresh local products. " Early bird" specials are a great deal. L May-Oct., D and Sun. brunch. year-round. $$

(6) **Eat Good Food** (877-2772), Main St., Vergennes. Super sandwiches, salads and soups to eat in or take out; great place to stock up on picnic supplies. $

(12) **De Pasquale's Delicatessen** (388-3385), Marbleworks Complex, Middlebury. Italian subs, fresh fried fish, salads, Italian meats, cheeses and wine -- all for take-out. $

(12) **Dog Team** (388-7651), Dog Team Rd., just off Rte. 7N, Middlebury. Good, solid New England fare, including prime rib, a relish "wheel," and sticky buns. D Tues.-Sun; open Sun. at noon. $$

(12) **Fire & Ice** (800-367-7166 or 388-7166), 26 Seymour St., Middlebury. Prime rib, steaks, fish and a great salad and bread bar. Special "kids' room" to entertain the small ones while parents dine. L Tues.-Sat., D nightly; open Sun. at 1 PM for dinner. $$

(12) **Rosie's Restaurant** (388-7052), Rte. 7S, Middlebury. Hearty family-style meals, homemade pies and soups. B, L, D. $

(14)(L) **Mary's at Baldwin Creek** (453-2432), Rtes. 116/17, Bristol. A highly creative chef, and a 1790s farmhouse dining room with a fieldstone fireplace and pewter oil lamps keep the crowds coming. Among the house specialties--cream of garlic soup and braised pork shank. There are four second-floor guest rooms ($$-$$$) and a two-room suite. D Wed.- Sun., L in summer, Sun. brunch. $$

(18) The Common Man Restaurant (583-2800), 3209 German Flats Rd., Warren. Romantic restaurant in a 19th-century barn, serving imaginative European dishes for over 25 years. D; closed Mon. $$

(19) American Flatbread (496-8856), Lareau Farm, Rte. 100, Waitsfield. The pizzas, baked in a wood-fired clay oven, have crisp crusts and only the freshest toppings. Specials include oven-roasted chicken. Fri. and Sat. 5:30-9:30 PM. $

(23) Blue Seal Restaurant (434-5949), Bridge St., Richmond. The creative and eclectic menu in this renovated 1854 feed store may include spicy shrimp and crabmeat Quesadilla, and house smoked pork loin with grilled tropical fruits, cous cous, and honey orange glaze. D, Tues.-Sat. $$

(23) Daily Bread Bakery & Cafe (434-3148), 27 Bridge St., Richmond. Bountiful breakfasts, creative sandwiches, and a dinner menu featuring seasonal fresh, local ingredients, with entrees such as lamb steak, pan-seared salmon, and vegetarian caviar on blinis. B, L, D Tues.-Sat. $-$$

Attractions

(1) Shelburne Farms (985-8686), Harbor Rd., Shelburne. Mid-May-mid-Oct. $. Farm store, Visitor Center and walking trails open year-round (no walking trail fee Nov.-Apr.).

(2) National Museum of the Morgan Horse (985-8665), 122 Bostwick Rd., Shelburne. Exhibits, gift shop, Morgan horse demonstrations. Closed Sun., closed Sat. off-season. Donation.

(2) **Charlotte Park and Wildlife Refuge, Greenbush Rd., Charlotte.** Open dawn to dusk.

(2) **Shelburne Museum (985-3346), Rte. 7, Shelburne.** Late-May-mid- Oct. daily. Mid-Oct.- late May, guided tour of selected buildings at 1, weather permitting, exc. holidays. Museum store open all year. $

(3) **Vermont Teddy Bear Company (800-829-2327), 6655 Shelburne Rd., Rte. 7, Shelburne.** Tour, museum, and factory store. Adult tour $2.

(4) **Lake Champlain Ferry (864-9804), Charlotte.**

(4) **Mt. Philo State Park (425-2390), 5425 Mt. Philo Road, Charlotte.** Camping. Mid-May-mid-Oct. $

(4) **Vermont Wildflower Farm (985-9455), Rte. 7, Charlotte.** Early May-late Oct., daily. $ (no admission to seed and gift shops).

(5) **Rokeby Museum (877-3406), Rte. 7, Ferrisburgh.** Mid-May-mid-Oct., Thurs.-Sun. Guided tours at 11, 12:30 and 2. $

(6) **Bixby Memorial Library (877-2211), Vergennes.** Closed Sat. and Sun.

(7) **Dead Creek Wildlife Management Area (759-2398).**

(7) **Lake Champlain Maritime Museum (475-2022),4472 Basin Harbor Rd., Vergennes.** May-mid-Oct. $

(8) **Button Bay State Park (475-2377), Vergennes.** Camping, swimming pool, boat rentals, picnic tables, playground, hiking trail, nature center. Late May-Columbus Day. $

(9) **D.A.R. State Park and John Strong Mansion (759-2354 or 483-2314), Rte. 17, West Addison.** Campground, picnic area, and shale swimming beach. Late May-Columbus Day. $

(10) Chimney Point State Historic Site (759-2412), Rtes. 17 & 125 (Lake Champlain Bridge), West Addison. Memorial Day-Columbus Day, Wed.-Sun. $

(12) Middlebury College Museum of Art (443-5007), Center for the Arts, Middlebury. Closed Mon.

(12) Henry Sheldon Museum of Vermont History (388-2117), 1 Park St., Middlebury. Closed Sun. $

(12) UVM Morgan Horse Farm (388-2011), off Rt. 23, Middlebury. May-Oct. $

(12) Vermont Folklife Center (388-4964), 3 Court Square, Middlebury. Exhibits and information on the traditional arts and folkways of Vermont, as well as area information. Gallery closed Sun. and Mon.

(18) Sugarbush Resort (583-2381), Warren. Super Quad chairlift rides late June- mid-Oct.

(21) Camels Hump State Park, Huntington: Vermont Department of Forests, Parks and Recreation (241-3655), 103 South Main St., Waterbury. $

(22) Birds of Vermont Museum (434-2167), 900 Sherman Hollow Rd., Huntington. Lifelike carvings of more than 150 species of birds, wild bird viewing area, carving demonstrations, 43 acres of nature trails, and gift shop. May-Oct. (trails open year-round). $

(22) Green Mountain Audubon Nature Center (434-3068), Sherman Hollow Rd., Huntington. Visitor Center closed some Sat. and every Sun.; trails open daily.

Activities and Shopping

(1) Harrington's of Vermont (985-2000), Rte. 7, across from Shelburne Museum, Shelburne. Gourmet goodies, cob-smoked bacon and ham, and the "World's Best Ham Sandwich."

(5) Dakin Farm (800-993-2546),Rte. 7, Ferrisburgh. Cob-smoked ham, cheddar cheese, maple syrup, and other specialty foods -- and plenty of free samples. (Also next to Barnes & Noble Books on Dorset St., South Burlington).

(5) Ferrisburgh Artisans' Guild (877-3668), 5467 Rte. 7A, Ferrisburgh.

(6) Kennedy Brothers Marketplace (877-2975), Rte. 22A, Vergennes. Almost 200 crafts and antiques booths, Ben & Jerry's Scoop Shop, deli, Vermont foods and syrup. Play area.

(9) Yankee Kingdom Orchard (759-2387), Lake St., West Addison. Apple orchard, greenhouses and country store with fresh baked goods. Pick apples, strawberries, and pumpkins. Petting zoo, play area.

(12) Bike and Ski Touring Center (388-6666), 74 Main St., Middlebury. Bike rental. Call ahead on Sun.

(12) Danforth Pewter (88-0098), 52 Seymour St., Marble Works, Middlebury. Pewter buttons, jewelry, oil lamps, and tableware.

(12) Maple Landmark Woodcraft (800-421-4223 or 388-0627), 1297 Exchange St., Middlebury. The new home of the high-quality Montgomery Schoolhouse wooden toys; locally-made giftware and ornaments.

(12) Otter Creek Brewing (800-473-0727), 85 Exchange St., Middlebury. Guided 1/2 hr. tours Mon.- Sat. at 1, 3 & 5 PM; samples, gift shop. Closed Sun.

(12) Vermont Bookshop (388-2061), 38 Main St., Middlebury. Full-service book shop; hardcover, paperbacks, and tapes; one of the region's finest collections of current and out-of-print Vermont authors, including the works of Robert Frost.

(12) Vermont Soapworks (388-4302), 616 Exchange St., Middlebury. Soapmaker/ factory outlet/seconds.

(12) Vermont State Craft Center at Frog Hollow (388-3177), downtown Middlebury. The state-subsidized shop overlooking Otter Creek falls sells the works of more than 200 local artists. Mon.-Sat. 9:30-5; Sun. afternoon spring-fall.

(12) Woody Jackson's Holy Cow Store (388-6737), 44 Main St., Middlebury. The man who put Vermont's Holsteins on the map sells them in every form but live in his store.

(14) Art on Main (453-4032), 25C Main St, Bristol. Vermont arts and crafts exhibited and sold.

(14) Firefly Ranch (453-2223), Bristol. Horse rentals, with a 2-hour minimum; no beginners (see 'Lodging' above).

(14) Robert Compton Pottery (453-3778), Rte. 116N, Bristol. Japanese wood fired kiln, raku, pit fired and stonewear pottery, and unique clay fountains and aquariums. Compton's wife, Christine, sells her handwoven textiles. May-Oct.; closed Wed.

(14) Rocky Dale Gardens (453-2782), 62 Rocky Dale Rd., Bristol. 3 acres of display gardens showcase perennials, dwarf conifers, and unusual trees and shrubs. Closed Tues.

(16) Lincoln General Store (453-2981), 17 East River Rd., Lincoln Center, Lincoln. Vermont products and general provisions.

(18) Warren Store (496-3864), Warren Village. Bakery, sandwiches, picnic goodies. Upstairs, jewelry and gifts.

(18) Warren Village Pottery and Gifts (496-4162), Main St., Warren. Functional and decorated handcrafted pottery made on the premises.

(19) Green Mountain Cultural Center (496-7722), Joslyn Road Barn, Waitsfield. Concert and exhibit

space hosts summer concerts and a foliage-season art exhibit.

(19) Luminosity Stained Glass (496-2231), Old Church, Rte. 100, Waitsfield. Barry Friedman creates jewelry, Tiffany lampshades, art glass. Off season, closed Tues.

(19) Vermont Icelandic Horse Farm (496-7141), The Commons Rd., Waitsfield. Year-round trail rides and inn-to-inn treks on pony-sized, smooth-gaited horses described as "the most comfortable riding horses in the world." Also, skijorring.

(19) Waitsfield Pottery (800-496-7155), 4366 Main St., Rte. 100, Historic Waitsfield Village. Hand-thrown, functional pieces.

Not on Drive

Chipman Point Marina (948-2288), Rte. 73, Orwell. Houseboat, sailboat and pontoon boat rentals.

Drive 7

Montpelier, Barre, and Orange County

96 miles

Tour Vermont's town-sized state capital, then drift south and east via a floating bridge and the homes of two famous Vermonters -- one a would-be congressman who learned that life can imitate art, and the other very much the real thing. Head back north through one of the state's least-traveled corners, finishing the drive with a look at the gargantuan quarries of a city that yields nothing to that "Granite State" next door.

(1) **Montpelier**, the smallest state capital (in population) in the nation, hugs the north bank of the Winooski River. If you were to spend your time on and about State Street, downtown's main drag, you could easily be forgiven for concluding that Montpelier consisted of a State House with a village attached. There's more to it than that, but the **Vermont State House** is a good place to start. Built in 1836 of Barre granite, Vermont's capitol is, on the outside, a demure Greek Revival expression of agrarian democracy -- right down to the statue of Ceres, the Roman goddess of agriculture, atop its golden dome. Inside, things get a bit more ornate, as a fire resulted in an 1859 Victorian remodeling (a meticulous recent restoration has preserved that style). A tour, guided or

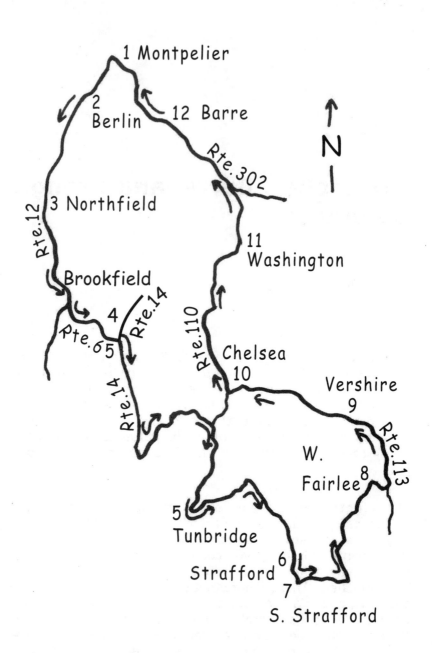

self-guided, takes in the House and more intimate Senate chambers, the lobbies where legislators conduct business with constituents (they don't have private offices), and the Cedar Creek Room, dominated by a splendid painting depicting Vermont troops in one of their major Civil War engagements. If you're visiting between January and mid-April, while the legislature is in session, you're welcome to sit in.

The brick Victorian edifice with the mansard roof that stands next to the State House is the Pavilion Building. If it looks like an old-time hotel, there's a good reason: it was a hotel in its last incarnation. The original structure, which was a virtual dormitory for out-of-town legislators, was torn down in the 1970s, and replaced with a near-replica.

Today's Pavilion Building contains state offices rather than hotel rooms, and is the home of the **Vermont Historical Society** and its museum. The Society's collections include paintings, furniture, photographs, farmers' and tradespeoples' tools, toys, costumes, and ephemera. Temporary exhibitions are built around various Vermont themes. *Note: as of this writing, the Society's premises are undergoing renovations, and operations have been moved to the Spaulding Graded School in Barre (see #12 below). Call the society for a progress report.*

Head east down State Street to where it meets Main Street and try to imagine what this busy intersection looked like one awful spring day in 1992, when it was waist-deep in water. The Winooski River rose over its banks and inundated the entire business district. One institution that fortunately stood on high enough ground to escape damage is the **T.W. Wood Gallery and Arts Center**, four blocks east on the Vermont College Campus. Founded by Montpelier-born artist Thomas Waterman Wood (1823-1903), a well-known portrait and genre painter who contributed his art collection to the city in 1895, the gallery's holdings run heavily to nineteenth-century landscapes and portraits, but also include paintings done by WPA artists such as Joseph Stella and Reginald Marsh. A contemporary gallery highlights Vermont artists of today.

Another Montpelier campus offers not so much a fountain of knowledge as a menu. The **New England Culinary Institute**, a nationally-renowned institution for training chefs, showcases its students and instructors' skills at a trio of fine restaurants in Vermont's capital: the Chef's Table, Main Street Grill & Bar and La Brioche Bakery & Cafe.

Before you head out of town, head up Main St. for 2 1/2 mi. to **Morse Farm Sugar Works**, one of the state's oldest maple sugar farms.   The 200+-year-old establishment has a folk art maple museum, free maple tours and tastings, a video theatre, store, and Vermont crafts emporium.

(2) Drive south out of Montpelier on   Rte. 12, crossing the bridge over the Winooski River and heading uphill and beneath the high overpass of I-89. At this point you enter the town of **Berlin** (accent on the first syllable, unlike the German city). Along its entire route through Berlin,   Rte. 12 follows the Dog River, a tributary of the Winooski system, whose waters eventually empty into the Connecticut River. The Dog River flows through a narrow, constricted valley where such farms as there were are gradually giving over to Montpelier's suburbs.

The last settlement in the town of Berlin is **Riverton**, a bump in the road distinguished today by little more than a miniature golf course.   But for a brief period in 1941 this hamlet was the home of Hungarian composer Bela Bartok (1881-1945), who lived in a borrowed farmhouse nearby.

(3) Just past Riverton, cross into the town of **Northfield**. The town's northernmost settlement, at the intersection of   Rte. 12 with Cox Brook Road, is Northfield Falls, where there are four covered bridges, all within a mile of each other, crossing the Dog River and Cox Brook. The town of Northfield boasts six covered bridges in all (including a tiny, private structure), which puts it in a tie with Montgomery (see Drive 11) for the most covered bridges in a Vermont town.

Continue south on   Rte. 12 into Northfield (by "Northfield", we're referring to the main settlement within the town of Northfield. Others are Northfield Falls, which we just passed through, Northfield Center, which is south of the central settlement of Northfield, and the charmingly-named South Northfield, which, in a rare outburst of Vermont geographical logic, is south of Northfield Center). Northfield clusters around a little red brick downtown crossroads, dominated by a four-story business block typical of Vermont towns of this size. With nearly a dozen businesses -- including a print shop which is also the office of the Northfield News -- it's a fully-functioning town center of the type many Vermonters have been trying to preserve against the threat of big-box stores and suburban sprawl.

Northfield got a boost in the mid-1800s because it was the hometown of Vermont Governor Charles Paine, who saw to it that the Vermont Central Railroad ran through his town rather than Montpelier, which would have made a lot more sense. Northfield's liveliness also owes a good deal to the presence of **Norwich University**, the nation's oldest private military college. The university, which occupies a campus just south of the town's center, offers a four-year program leading to a commission in the U.S. Army, as well as civilian academic degrees. Norwich owes its name to the fact that it was first located in the Vermont town of Norwich, in the Connecticut River Valley (See Drive 8). It moved here in 1867. By that time, the school had trained approximately 300 officers who served in the Civil War. Artifacts and documents chronicling the University's history are on exhibit at a museum on campus.

As you continue this drive, there will be few places to stop for lunch. You might want to stop in town at DeFelice's Cafe for one of their fine specialty sandwiches to go. Or, just out of town, the Red Kettle Family Restaurant, a popular local eatery, serves standards including burgers, liver and onions, a Thursday night all-you-can-eat buffet, and their popular breakfasts--with specials such as stuffed French toast with cream cheese and blueberries--all day.

(4) Just south of the university, at Northfield Center, bear left at the junction of Rtes. 12 and 12A to stay on Rte. 12. Following little Sunny Brook, Rte. 12 cuts across a corner of the town of Roxbury and, at Baker Pond (there's a state boat access on the shore) intersects with Rte. 65 in **Brookfield**. Turn left onto Rte. 65 just opposite Baker Pond. This is a dirt road that climbs quite steeply; it can be daunting in winter, but is plowed and kept open throughout the year.

On the right, just after the road levels out, is the entrance to **Allis State Park**, named after Wallace Allis, who willed his farm to the state. The park, built by the CCC in 1933 and 1934, takes in the summit of Bear Mountain, where visitors can climb a fire tower for spectacular views.

Rte. 12 continues through lovely high country of mixed meadow and forest; just after the park entrance there are beautiful views of the Connecticut Valley to the east.

From late spring until first snowfall, continue along Rte. 65 as it descends and passes under I-89 to head into Brookfield village via its famous Floating Bridge. (During the winter, when the bridge isn't plowed, follow detour signs into Brookfield.) Getting into Brookfield might have been a little less circuitous and a lot less picturesque if the townspeople had accepted the state highway planners' offer of an interchange back when I-89 was being built in the 1960s. But Brookfield opted against the exit and entrance ramps, just has it has always preferred to keep its lone downtown street unpaved.

But who needs an interstate highway exchange when you've got a floating bridge? There's been one here, spanning Sunset Lake, since 1820. (The latest structure, number seven, floats on pontoons rather than the original barrels). Driving across the bridge is a strange sensation -- you can actually feel it wallow slightly beneath you. Even though the bridge is closed in the winter, Sunset Lake is still worth a visit in late January when it's the site of the Brookfield Ice Harvest Festival. The event is a throwback to the days when Vermont's lakes and ponds yielded a supply of ice that lasted through the summer when packed in ice houses between insulating layers of sawdust or straw.

Tiny Brookfield's other claim to fame is its Free Public Library. Founded in 1791 -- the same year Vermont joined the Union -- "to promote useful knowledge and piety," it's the oldest library in continued existence in the state, and one of the oldest in the country. It is on a steep uphill drive off Northfield Street, Brookfield's main thoroughfare.

Brookfield, by the way, is the home of Edward Koren, the *New Yorker* cartoonist noted for his caricatures of leftover sixties types given to saccharine political correctness. Koren serves on the Brookfield's volunteer fire department, and his work turns up from time to time in local Vermont publications.

Continue southeast on Rte. 65, which follows Sunset Brook and passes the handsome First Congregational Church of Brookfield, with its pair of elegant Doric columns. Rte. 65, paved now, drops down through a deep valley to East Brookfield, where it ends at the intersection with Rte. 14. Turn right here, following Rte. 14 south as it parallels and occasionally crosses the Second Branch of the White River.

Continue through the tiny hamlet of North Randolph; roughly two mi. south, at East Randolph (where Rte. 66 comes in from the west), look for a little country store on the left. Just past the store, a left turn takes you onto Chelsea Road, which climbs into lovely countryside on and around Osgood Hill before descending to meet Rte. 110, between Chelsea and Tunbridge.

(5) Turn right onto Rte. 110. Keep an eye to your left -- there are three covered bridges between here and Tunbridge village. One of them, the Flint Bridge at Bicknell Hill, leads to a memorial stone for Justin Morgan's horse, Figure, sire of a line of Vermont horses that would become renown for their strength and gentle spirit (see Drive 6). The actual Justin Morgan Horse Burial Ground is up the road apiece, on private property, and off limits to visitors. (Mr. Morgan is buried in Randolph). To visit the marker, after crossing the bridge turn right onto Harolyn Hill Rd. and continue for a few miles. The marker is on the right.

Back on Rte. 110, continue into **Tunbridge** along the First Branch of the White River. The **Tunbridge Village Store** occupies the building where the parents of Joseph Smith, founder of the Mormon religion, reputedly first met. It's also the place to buy souvenirs of Tunbridge's own Fred Tuttle, hero of the 1996 movie, "Man With a Plan," which tells the story of an old Vermont farmer (Tuttle as himself) who decides to run for Congress. Life imitated art in 1998, when Tuttle was put up as a candidate in the Vermont Republican senatorial primary against a fellow perceived to be a carpetbagger from Massachusetts. Tuttle, who was expected merely to embarrass the serious Republican, actually won the primary. This put him in the position of being the official Republican candidate facing incumbent Democratic Senator Pat Leahy, whom Tuttle announced he had no desire to beat.   Nor did he.

The Tunbridge World's Fair has been held each September since 1867. The grandiosely-named event is a throwback to the harvest fairs of old, with activities ranging from livestock displays to horse pulls to fiddlers' contests. Well into this century, the fair had the reputation of being a colossal community bender known as the "Drunkards' Reunion" in a Vermont still known as a teetotalers' preserve. We don't know whether it's true that they used to throw sober people off the grounds at 3:00 P.M., but today the World's Fair, held in a field just south of town, is a family event, with imbibing confined to a beer tent.

To continue the drive, backtrack at the store and bear right just before you get to the bridge. This will put you on Strafford Road, otherwise known as the Justin Smith Morrill Highway. (After you cross the line into Strafford, it's known as the Tunbridge Road, because that's the way it is in Vermont: a road that connects two towns is nearly always named after the town it's going to until it gets there, after which it takes the name of the town it just came from, unless of course you were headed in the other direction, in which case ... you get the idea.)

(6)   Continue through woods and meadow into **Strafford** village, your first sight of which will be the magnificent 1799 Town House, on your right as you come into town. This beautifully-kept Georgian gem, with its towering steeple, was built both for town meetings and interdenominational church services. Beyond the town hall, the pretty little village extends for all of about two blocks. But the structure which puts Strafford on the map stands just ahead and to the left. This is the **Justin Morrill Homestead**, a seventeen-room pink Carpenter Gothic house, dripping with gingerbread along its gables. It was built between 1848 and 1851 by Justin Smith Morrill, a Strafford-born storekeeper who ran for Congress on an Abolitionist platform and served as a Vermont representative and senator for forty-five years.

Morrill's greatest legacy as a legislator was his sponsorship of the 1862 Morrill Acts, which established America's system of land grant colleges and universities. The Acts provided for federal land to be granted to each state; states were to use proceeds from the sale of the land to endow colleges that would be accessible to "farmers, mechanics, and all those who must win their bread by labor" -- not a bad legacy for a man who dropped out of school at the age of fifteen. The house includes family furnishings and memorabilia of Morrill's long political career.

(7) Continue south out of Strafford on Tunbridge Road; in about two mi. you'll come to **South Strafford** at the intersection of Rte. 132. Note the lovely stained glass on the Unitarian-Universalist Church as you come into town. Bear left at the church and head through the village.

(8) Follow Rte. 132 east out of South Strafford for roughly 2 1/2 mi., then make a left onto Miller Pond Road. The road, which turns to gravel after the first couple of miles but is open all year, offers spectacular foliage viewing in the fall. Miller Pond, ahead on the left, has a boat launch and fishing for brook and rainbow trout. Its wooded shores are undeveloped. Just past the pond, at the bottom of the hill, turn right at a T intersection in a hamlet called Beanville.

Within a mile, turn left onto Rte. 113 at **West Fairlee**, once a copper-mining town (see Vershire, below) and head north along the Ompompanoosuc River. We aren't sure why the little cluster of houses up ahead on the Vershire town line is called "Brimstone Corner;" it looks placid and not at all sulfurous or damned. But then, a right turn at the fork a couple of miles ahead will take you to Goose Green, where there aren't any geese, and there isn't a green.

(9) Don't take that right, though. To continue this drive, bear left at the fork and follow Rte. 113 through **Vershire**, which looks every bit the way its name sounds: it even has an acclaimed riding academy, and an upcountry branch of a Massachusetts prep school. But back when it was called Ely, this town was anything but bucolic. Dur-

ing the decades immediately following the Civil War, Ely's mines turned out well over half of America's copper.

In 1883, Ely was the scene of one of Vermont's few major labor confrontations. The trouble began when some 300 miners, who were owed $25,000 in back wages, armed themselves and began to destroy company property. When the miners issued an ultimatum -- give us our pay or we'll blow up Ely and West Fairlee (did they keep their explosives at Brimstone Corner?), the governor called in the National Guard, who arrested their leaders at gunpoint. The "Ely War" ended with the miners being paid $4,000 of the $25,000 they were owed -- that was all the mine operators possessed -- and the permanent closing of the mines.

(10) Leaving Vershire village, follow Rte. 113 as it descends along Judgment Ridge into the valley of the First Branch of the White River. Here Rte. 113 ends, at a T intersection with Rte. 110 in the Orange County shire town (or county seat, as it's called in some states) of **Chelsea**.

The early citizens of Chelsea seem to have taken literally the biblical admonition to "render to Caesar what is Caesar's, and render to God what is God's." Plenty of Vermont towns have steeple-shadowed greens, but in Chelsea, Caesar and God each have their own. The former lies at the foot of the 1847 Greek Revival Orange County Courthouse, which wears a little gilded dome atop its square, two-tiered tower. The latter green, one block away, is faced by the 1812 United Church of Chelsea, a bit less overtly Greek-inspired, but with a more handsome, hexagonal tower. Chelsea's other architectural highlights include a little Richardson Romanesque library with fat pepperpot towers at each end, and a matched set of 1818 Georgian brick structures at the intersection of routes 110 and 113, each housing a store. And even if you aren't staying or dining at the **Shire Inn**, take a look at the lovely Georgian fanlight above the door.

(11) Turn right at the T intersection in Chelsea where Rte. 113 ends, and follow Rte. 110 north. For much of the distance between Chelsea and **Washington**, ten miles to

the north, the road follows the First Branch of the White River. The river valley (the flow is in the opposite direction from the route you are driving) is narrow, and leaves little room for agriculture; like many rural Vermont communities riven by the steeply-cut courses of swift streams, Chelsea once had an economy supported in part by small, water-powered industries. One of these now-vanished operations is recalled by the name of a byway that branches off from   Rte. 110 just north of town: Bobbin Mill Road.

Washington itself is a tiny crossroads village, hardly prepossessing enough to suggest its one-time status as a shire town named Kingsland. But the county of which it was the seat -- Gloucester County -- existed only on paper, as the wishful conjuring of the New York grantees who believed they had claim to the lands between Lake Champlain and the Connecticut River. We've seen elsewhere what Vermonters thought of New York land claims; in 1780, after the "Yorker" threat had been dismissed, the legislature of the then-independent Republic of Vermont renamed the town Washington, and issued new grants within its boundaries. It has been settled since 1785.

(12)   After clipping a small corner of the town of Orange, Rte. 110 enters **Barre**, where it ends at   Rte. 302 in a part of town called East Barre (which is quite a ways south of South Barre).   At East Barre, turn right for the junction with 302, where a left will take you to the city center. (Just after making this last turn, look for a funky old roadside eatery called the Dugout (right), opposite which is one of Vermont's newest covered bridges, a 1962 span that leads across Jail Brook to private property. But to visit the site that has made Barre internationally famous, turn left at East Barre and follow signs for **Rock of Ages**, the world's largest granite quarry.

Barre lies atop a bed of granite that measures roughly four by six miles near the surface and runs ten miles deep. Since the early 1800s, this 335-million-year-old vein has been quarried for the durable, dense-grained gray stone that is always in demand for construction and monuments. A tour of the quarries offer a look at how workers separate 25-ton blocks of granite from sheer 475-foot walls, using low-velocity explosives and 4,200° F jet torches. (These same forbidding cliffs were used for Arnold Schwarzenegger's "Mr. Freeze" ice-cave scenes in the 1997 film "Batman and Robin.") At the company's Craftsman Center, an elevated walkway overlooks a vast workroom where statuary and architectural details are carved, and where memorial stones are cut and polished. It's the one factory tour where even .if they were giving out free samples, we'd all rather wait.

Side Trip

For a look at just how versatile a material granite is in the right hands, drive north for one mile out of downtown Barre on Rte. 14. The city's Hope Cemetery has long been a showplace for monument art, much of it done by Barre's celebrated granite carvers for each other. Don't miss the granite easy chair, the granite soccer ball, the relief carving in which a young Italian soldier's wife appears in a puff of his cigarette's smoke, and the gripping life-sized representation of Elia Corti, a young labor leader shot at a socialist rally in 1903. It was carved by his brother, Guglielmo. Like the Cortis, many of Barre's granite workers were Italians,

Continuing west, Rte. 302 leads directly into downtown Barre. As you come into town, watch on the right for a large brick building called the **Spaulding Graded School**. It's the newest acquisition and temporary home of the Vermont Historical Society, and now houses the society's public library collection. The school was built in 1891 when Barre's granite industry flourished, and gives visitors an idea of what a state-of-the-art school looked like more than 100 years ago.

Take a walk down North Main Street to see the city's three most distinctive pieces of civic sculpture -- all of them carved, of course, from granite. The 1899 Robert Burns Memorial, on the grounds of the Spaulding Graded School, celebrates the poet beloved of Barre's first great wave of immigrant stonecutters, the Scots. The memorial consists of a statue of Burns standing on a plinth ornamented with carved scenes from his poetry. The second sculpture, "Youth Victorious," stands in City Park opposite City Hall; it's a muscular young man holding a sword, done in that blunt, supposedly inspiring style that the Stalinists used to call "Socialist Realism."

The city's most poignantly relevant work of sculpture stands at the intersection of North Main Street and Maple Avenue. This is a larger-than-life statue of a typical Italian stone cutter of the early twentieth century, heroically mustachioed and outfitted with a cap, a leather apron, and a stout hammer. It says more about what got Barre off the ground than any number of naked youths with broadswords.

Across from the statue, on Granite Street, is the National Historic Landmark **Old Labor Hall**, home to the Socialist Labor Party in the 1900s. The two-story red brick building with the Barre granite arm and hammer medallion on its facade served as a meeting place for the Italian immigrants and granite workers who built it until it closed in 1936. In 1995 the Barre Historical Society bought the building and is in the process of renovating it. In 2002 the building, one of only 14 National Histroric Landmarks in Vermont, received a National Trust Historic Preservation Award.

Granite memorials aside, downtown Barre is well worth a stroll. It's a fine example of a fully-functioning small urban downtown, that *rara avis* in this era of big-box suburban discount stores. Jewelers, clothiers, hardware stores, pharmacies and florists -- even, wonder of wonders, three or four independent bookshops: Barre is indeed a working period piece. What makes the little city an even livelier place is the presence of the **Barre Opera House**, a turn-of-the century venue for concerts and plays rescued from oblivion and restored by private contributions during the 1980s. (It's located right upstairs from City Hall.)

Return to Montpelier via Rte. 302 and Rte. 2, both commercial strips; or pick up I-89 at Barre for points north and south. As you head towards Montpelier, watch on the left for a large building in the process of being renovated: it's the future home of the Granite Museum, which will trace the history of that industry.

Information

Central Vermont Chamber of Commerce (877-887-3678 or 229-5711), Box 336, 33 Stewart Rd., Barre 05641. www.central-vt.com

Northfield Business & Professional Association (485-4999), P.O. Box 432, 15 Depot Sq., Northfield 05663.

Randolph Chamber of Commerce (877-772-6365 or 728-9027), 31 VT Rte. 66, P.O, Box 9, Randolph 05060. www.randolphvt.com

Vermont Chamber of Commerce (223-3443), Box 37, Montpelier 05601. www.vtchamber.com

Lodging

(1) Betsy's B & B (229-0466), 74 E. State St., Montpelier 05602. 12 nicely furnished rooms and suites with TVs and phones (some with kitchens) occupy 2 adjacent Victorian homes in the Historic District. Exercise bike and weight machine. www.betsysbnb.com $-$$

(1) Capitol Plaza Hotel & Conference Center (800-274-5252 or 223-5252), 100 State St., Montpelier 05602. Tastefully-furnished rooms and suites in Colonial-themed, full-service downtown hotel; restaurant and shops. www.capitolplaza.com $$

(1) Comfort Inn at Maplewood (229-2222), 213 Paine Turnpike North, Berlin (exit 7 off I-89). Well-appointed chain motel close to the highway has 89 rooms and 18 2 1/2 room suites with kitchens. www.comfortinnsuites.com $-$$$

(1) The Inn at Montpelier (223-2727), 147 Main St., Montpelier 05602. Both the main inn and annex, in the Historic District, are early-1800s Federal buildings, and offer a variety of accommodations, including fireplaces. www.innatmontpelier.com $$-$$$

(1) Montpelier Guest Home (229-0878), 138 North St., Montpelier 05602. 1890s Victorian with 3 antiques-filled guest rooms (shared bath) with handmade quilts and antiques just a few minutes from town. Spacious yard with gardens. Specially-priced family rooms sleep 4. www.guesthome.com $

(3) The Northfield Inn (485-8558), 27 Highland Ave., Northfield. 12 spacious, antiques-filled guest rooms and family suites (9 with private bath) in a restored, 1902 Victorian mansion on a hill overlooking the village. Brass or carved wood beds with European feather bedding. www.thenorthfieldinn.com $$-$$$

(4) Birch Meadow Luxury Log Cabins and B & B (276-3156), 597 Birch Meadow Dr., Brookfield 05036. 200-acre hilltop retreat has 3 year-round housekeeping cabins that sleep 6, and 1 suite with a private entrance in the home (breakfast served in room). www.bbhost.com/birchmeadow $$

(4) Green Trails Inn (800-243-3412 or 276-3412), By the Floating Bridge, Brookfield 05036. 12 guest rooms (8 with private bath) in 2 historic buildings on 17-acre estate. Fishing, swimming, canoeing, biking, hiking and x-c skiing. Children over 10. Across from Ariel's Restaurant (see below). www.greentrailsinn.com $$

(6) Marge's B&B at Round Robin Farm (763-7025), Fay Brook Rd., Strafford 05972. This sixth-generation dairy farm, which houses its Holsteins in a classic, 1917 round barn, has four guest rooms in the original farmhouse. Guests can tour the sugar house and farm, watch the milking, or hike or xc ski around 350 acres. www.vermontfarms.org/central.htm#22 $

(10) Shire Inn (800-441-6908 or 685-3031), Main St., P.O. Box 37, Chelsea 05038. 1832 In-town, Federal-era home on 22 acres abutting the river has elegantly-furnished, antiques-filled rooms (4 with fireplaces). Children under 7, and pets, welcome in the 2-bedroom cottage. An elegant six-course, candlelight dinner is available to guests only. www.shireinn.com $$- $$$

(12)(R) Autumn Harvest Inn and Restaurant (433-1355), 118 Clark Rd., Rte. 64, Williamstown 05679. 18 clean, comfortable guest rooms and 2 suites in a farmhouse on a 100-year-old dairy farm with spectacular views. Dinner (Wed.-Sun., $$), served on the verandah in nice weather, might begin with crabcakes with Dijon sauce, and include an entreé of pasta Alfredo or prime rib. Pond, sleigh rides, horseback riding packages. Pets welcome. www.autumnharvestinn.com $-$$$

(12) The Hollow Inn and Motel (800-998-9444 or 479-9313), 278 South Main St., Barre 05641. 15 inn rooms and 26 motel rooms in a complex just a mile out of town; outdoor heated pool and jacuzzi; fitness center with whirlpool, sauna and exercise equipment. Some rooms with fridge and microwave. www.hollowinn.com $-$$

Restaurants

(1) The New England Culinary Institute of Montpelier has three downtown restaurants: the Chef's Table (229-9202), 118 Main St., serving innovative and classic American fare; the Main Street Grill & Bar (223-3188), 110 Main Street, an American-style bistro with upscale and creative dishes; and La Brioche Bakery & Cafe (229-0443), 89 Main St., with pastries, breads, and sandwiches. $-$$$

(1) Sarducci's (223-0229), 3 Main St., Montpelier. Italian cuisine featuring wood-fired pizza and imaginative pasta dishes, and fabulous homemade bread. Patio overlooking river. L Mon.-Sat., D. $-$$

(3) DeFelice's Café (485-4700), Main St., Northfield. Subs, sandwiches, salads, seasonal soups. Mon.- Fri., 8:30-4; Sat. in foliage. $

(3) Red Kettle Family Restaurant, Rte. 12, Northfield. B, L Sun.-Wed.; B. L, D Thurs.-Sat. $

(4) Ariel's Restaurant and Pond Village Pub (276-3939), Brookfield. Highly-acclaimed, lakefront dining specializing in "Cuisine of the sun" -- dishes from the world's warmer climes. Full dinner menu served Fri. and Sat., pub menu Wed., Thurs. and Sun. evening. $-$$

(12) A Single Pebble (476-9700), 135 Barre-Montpelier Rd., Barre. The place for authentic Chinese cuisine: traditional clay pot and wok specialties. D; closed Sun., Mon, and month of Aug. Reservations suggested. $

(12) Green Mountain Diner (476-6292), 240 North Main St., Barre. Good, down home cooking; great daily specials. B, L; D Mon.-Sat.; B & L Sun. $

Attractions

(1) Capital Walking Tour (229-4842), 134 State St. (in front of Tourist information Center), Montpelier. Guided 1 1/4-hour walking tour (flat terrain) of city's architectural and historical heritage. Sat., 10:30 a.m. spring-fall. Donation.

(1) T.W. Wood Gallery & Arts Center (828-8743), Vermont College, College Hall, Montpelier. Daily noon-4; closed Mon. $ (free on Sun.)

(1) Vermont Historical Society Museum (828-2291), Pavilion Building, 109 State St., Montpelier. Closed for renovations: call for update (see #12 below).

(1) Vermont State House(828-2228), State St., Montpelier. Tours 10-3:30, Sat. 11-2:30. or by appt.; call for off-season hours.

(3) Norwich University Museum (485-2379 or 485-2999), Northfield.

(4) Allis State Park (276-3175), Rte. 12, Randolph. Camping and hiking trails.

(6) Justin Morrill State Historic Site (765-4484), Strafford. Memorial Day-Columbus Day, Wed.-Sun. $

(12) Old Labor Hall, Granite St., Barre. For information: Barre Historical Society (476-0567).

(12) Rock of Ages (476-3119), 773 Main Street, Graniteville. Visitors center open May-Oct. Mon.-Sat. 8:30-5 and Sun. noon to 5; guided tour ($) June-mid-Oct. Mon.-Fri. 9:15-3; manufacturing facility Mon.-Fri. 8-3:30.

(12) Spaulding Graded School, Vermont Historical Society (828-2290), North Main St., Barre.

Activities and Shopping

(1) The Artisans' Hand (229-9492), 89 State St., Montpelier. Cooperative gallery displays and sells works of more than 100 local artists. Open Mon.-Sat.

(1) Bear Pond Books (229-0774), 77 Main St., Montpelier. 40,000+ titles.

(1) Lost Nation Theater (229-0492), Old City Hall, Main St., Montpelier. Comedies, drama, musicals and, in foliage season, Shakespeare, performed by resident professional company. June-Oct. $

(1) Morse Farm Sugar Works (223-2740), Main St. Ext., Montpelier.

(1) Rivendell Books (223-3928), 100 Main St., Montpelier. New and used books (with an emphasis on the latter).

(5) Tunbridge Village Store (889-5588), Tunbridge.

(12) Barre Opera House (476-8188), City Hall, Barre. Concerts and plays in restored, 1899 opera house.

Drive 8

The Upper Connecticut Valley from Windsor to Waterford

80 miles

Follow the great river highway of early Vermont settlement, beginning at the place where an independent republic forged its tools of self-government. Tour a little city where cowcatchers once meant a lot more than cows, and drive north along the river (with, perhaps, a stop for a balloon ride) through a string of little towns where steamboats used to call. Find out why "Caledonia" is an appropriate name for the county at the northern end of this route, and end the day at a gracious country inn.

(1) Begin your drive in **Windsor**. "The Birthplace of Vermont" earned its sobriquet in July of 1777, when delegates from the New Hampshire Grants who had determined to create an independent Republic of Vermont gathered at Elijah West's tavern to draft a constitution. Using as a model Benjamin Franklin's constitution for Pennsylvania, they wrote the first constitution in America that banned slavery, gave voting privileges to all males, and mandated a public school system. The story is told in the tavern, renamed the **Old Constitution House** and moved to its present location.

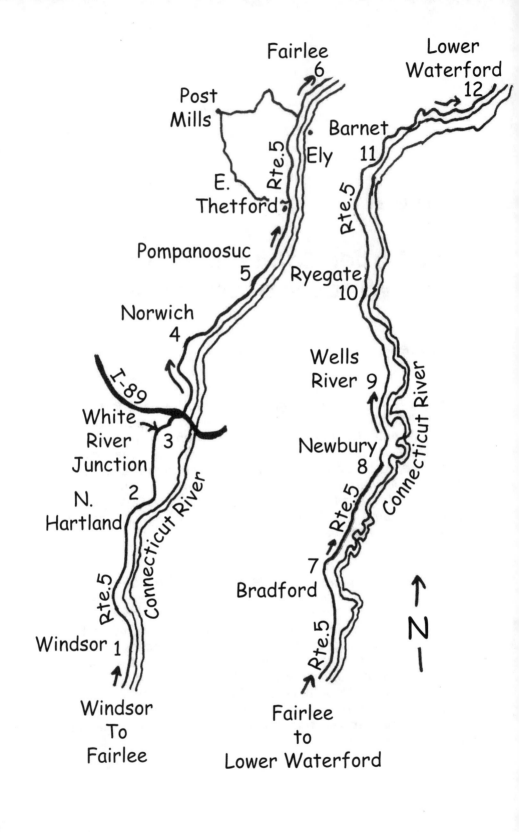

Fairlee
6

Lower
Waterford
12

Post
Mills

Barnet
11

Rte.5

Ely

E.
Thetford

Rte.5

Pompanoosuc
5

Ryegate
10

Norwich
4

Wells
River 9

I-89

White
River
Junction 3

Connecticut River

Newbury
8

N.
Hartland 2

Rte.5

Connecticut River

Rte.5

7

Bradford

Rte.5

Windsor 1

N

Windsor
To
Fairlee

Fairlee
to
Lower Waterford

Today, it's hard to imagine that in 1820 this quiet little town was the largest in Vermont, and just thirty years later, a thriving industrial center. The town was fertile soil for tinkerers, too: it was the home of more inventions, and inventors, than any other community in the state. Interchangeable parts were first produced for everyday use at the 1846 Robbins and Lawrence Armory, now the National Historic Landmark **American Precision Museum**.

While delegates from Vermont towns were busy hammering together the new republic's constitution at Windsor on July 8, 1777, reports of British General John Burgoyne's incursion into the Lake Champlain valley caused such consternation that the assembly very nearly broke up. They decided to stick with their task, though, when a sudden thunderstorm made a virtual island of their meeting place, Elijah West's tavern. So it was that the representatives gathered at the "Birthplace of Vermont"

At one time Windsor had a less flattering nickname. From 1809 until it closed in 1975, "Prison Town" was home to the Vermont State Prison. The last person to be executed by the State of Vermont went to the electric chair here in 1952.

Be sure to visit the **Vermont State Craft Center at Windsor House**, which exhibits and sells the works of nearly 200 juried artists and craftspeople. The graceful, white Old South Church on Main Street, built in 1798, is believed to have been designed by Asher Benjamin, a

Side Trip

In Windsor, turn east onto Bridge Street and cross over the Connecticut River into New Hampshire on the 460-foot-long, 1866 Cornish-Windsor Bridge, the longest covered bridge in the country and the longest two-span covered bridge in the world. Head north a short distance on Rte. 12A to Saint-Gaudens National Historic Site, the home, studio, and formal gardens of the famed sculptor.

well-known Connecticut Valley architect who lived in Windsor for several years. If you're a diner aficionado, plan a stop at the newly-restored **Windsor Diner**, a 1950 classic from the workshops of the Worcester Lunch Car Company

(2) Head north on Rte. 5; turn into the Windsor Industrial Park to visit the **Harpoon Brewery & Beer Garden**, and   one of the factory showrooms of **Simon Pearce Glass** (the other is in Quechee; see Drive 5).

In Hartland, 4/10 of a mile past the overpass of I-91, covered bridge fans will want to detour onto Martinsville Road to the 1881 Martinsville Bridge, a Town lattice bridge (see Drive 11 for more on this design) spanning Lull's Brook. Hartland's first settler, Timothy Lull, gave the brook his name when he arrived with his family in a canoe in 1763, after paddling upstream on the Connecticut River from Dummerston. According to local lore, Tim christened the brook with a bottle of liquor he had brought along (saving some, we hope, for himself). In *Covered Bridges of Vermont*, Ed Barna advises that the bridge has become a hangout for local kids, and it would be wise to visit only during the day.

There's yet another covered bridge a few miles farther north off   Rte. 5 in **North Hartland**. Turn right (east) onto Mill Road to the Willard Bridge, also a Town lattice construction; the Ottauquechee Woolen Company's mill stood near the bridge until it was destroyed in the Great Flood of 1927.

The **North Hartland Lake** recreation area, created when a flood control dam was built by the U.S. Army Corps of Engineers on the Ottauquechee River, is a good place to swim, or fish for brown and brook trout.

(3) **White River Junction** is a once-important railroad town, where the tracks took their cue from the junction of the White and Connecticut rivers -- and where the theme is carried on by the meeting of Interstate routes 91 and 89. The railroad reached White River Junction in 1847; fifty years later, fully ten percent of all rail traffic between the U.S. and Canada passed through the town. Aside from Amtrak's *Ver-*

monter, which stops on its daily north- and southbound runs between Washington, D.C. and St. Albans, downtown's only reminder of the glory days of the high iron is the Boston and Maine's Number 494, a late-nineteenth-century 4-4-0 steam locomotive parked permanently near the station with its tender and a caboose. (The designation "4-4-0," by the way, refers to the wheel arrangement of a steam loco -- in this case, four pilot wheels, four drivers, and no trailing wheels.)

White River Junction's downtown area is a National Register Historic District: pick up a walking tour brochure at the Chamber of Commerce. Highlights include the 1926 Hotel Coolidge (named for the president's father, John Coolidge), a rare example of a surviving "railroad hotel" just across from the station. It's the successor to a line of hotels, originally named the "Junction House," that stood on this site beginning just two years after the trains first arrived. Lillian Gish stayed at the Coolidge's immediate predecessor when she was filming D.W. Griffith's 1920 silent *Way Down East* on the ice floes of the White River. Take a look at the murals in the hotel cafe (a barn dance) and in the Vermont room (Vermont history) -- they were done in return for lodging by a Dartmouth student in 1949.

The **Briggs Opera House** is another downtown landmark. It's the venue for fall and spring productions by Northern Stage, a professional regional theater company, and for occasional visiting performers. Vermont's only African restaurant, **Taste of Africa's Karibu Tulé**, occupies a corner of the opera house.

Side Trip

Just 1.9 mi. from the Junction, turn right off Rte. 5 onto Depot Street and follow signs to Wilder Dam. If you're here between the last week of May and the first week of July, you're in luck: it's the time of year that salmon and shad pass through on their upstream spawning run. Fish ladders at the U.S. Generating Company dam help them over the otherwise impossible hurdle. Keep your eyes peeled for bald eagles, who know a good fishing spot when they see one.

(4) Continue north on   Rte. 5. Bakers will want to make a pit stop at the **King Arthur Flour Baker's Store**, a 200-plus-year-old Vermont-based company that has grown to national proportions. The company's retail store is packed to the rafters with every conceivable necessity for the home baker, and -- to see how it all should taste -- the bakery sells everything from breads to biscotti. Manicured **Norwich** is often held up as an example of what the perfect Vermont village is supposed to look like; truth be told, however, much of its polish derives from its status as a bedroom community for **Dartmouth College**, located just across the river in Hanover, New Hampshire. Regardless of who's paying the bills, the town is still a visual treasure, filled with magnificent late eighteenth- and early nineteenth-century homes. On your stroll along lovely Main Street, stop in at Jasper Murdock's Alehouse in the 1794 **Norwich Inn** for a pint of their home brew.

Norwich's **Montshire Museum of Science**, off   Rte. 5 along the shores of the Connecticut River, is a manageably-sized yet fascinating trove of informative hands-on exhibits for kids of all ages. In 2002 the museum opened the Leonard M. Riser Learning Center, which added 40% of exhibit space, and a Science Park with two acres of exhibits in a park-like setting. Be sure to save time to walk at least one of the nature trails that thread through the museum's 100 riverside acres.

Side Trip

It might be too late for you to go to Dartmouth, but at least you can go take a look at it. The nation's ninth-oldest college (it was chartered by King George III in 1769) occupies a movie-set campus in Hanover, N.H., a short hop from Norwich via a Connecticut River bridge. The handsomest buildings are along "Dartmouth Row" on College Street opposite the Green; at their center is Dartmouth Hall, a 1904 replica of the graceful Georgian original built on this site in 1791. Other campus attractions include Baker Library, with its Hough Room of rare books and its cycle of allegorical murals on the social history of the Western Hemisphere painted in the early 1930s by Mexican artist Jose Clemente Orozco, then a member of the Dartmouth art faculty. The Hood Museum houses Dartmouth's fine arts collections.

Head north on Rte. 5 through Pompanoosuc, where the Ompompanoosuc River meets with the Connecticut, and **East Thetford**, home to another successful company that began as a cottage industry. The handmade furniture business that Dwight Sargeant started in his home several years back is now known as **Pompanoosuc Mills**, and ships its sturdy, clean-lined hardwood wares around the world.

(5) Continue through **Ely**, the one-time railroad station for the Ely Copper Mines (see Drive 7). Turn left (west) onto Rte. 244 to visit densely-wooded Lake Fairlee, accessible primarily to those who have waterfront summer cottages.

(6) **Fairlee**, nestled in the lee of a 600-foot rock barrier called the Palisades, is often thought of as the homely stepsister to stately Orford, just across the river in New Hampshire. Fairlee is the service town for Lake Morey, named for the inventor Samuel Morey who experimented with a steamboat fourteen years before Robert Fulton launched his *Clermont*. Many a fine day Mr. Morey could be seen chugging up and down the Connecticut River or across the lake in his contraption. Later, bitter at Fulton's fame, the inventor supposedly cried,

"curse his stomach, he stole my patent," and to have sunken his craft in Lake Morey. The remains have yet to be found.

(7) **Bradford**, the next town of any size along the Vermont side of the Connecticut, got some publicity a couple of years back from an unexpected quarter: *Travel and Leisure* magazine listed its downtown thoroughfare as one of the top ten Main Streets in America, commenting that this string of utilitarian blocks is "so ordinary it's extraordinary." Bradford was home to some not-so-ordinary citizens, though. James Wilson was a local farmer and self-taught engraver, who in the early 1800s created America's first geographical globes. Admiral Charles Clark, born in Bradford in 1843, commanded the battleship *Oregon* during its rush around Cape Horn to victory at Santiago Bay, Cuba in the Spanish-American War. (Landlocked Vermont, by the way, had the unlikely distinction of supplying two naval heroes in that conflict. Admiral George Dewey, who sank the Spanish fleet at Manila Bay, was a Montpelier boy.)

Not content to rest on its Main Street laurels, Bradford also hosts one of the state's finest wild game suppers every year on the Saturday before Thanksgiving, serving up almost 3,000 pounds of delicacies including wild boar, bear, and venison to some 1,000 customers. To receive a brochure write: Game Supper Committee, Bradford, VT 05033; or call Barbara at 222-4670.

(8) At **Newbury**, the Connecticut River goes through a tortuous series of loops called "oxbows," one of which makes a near-circle of four miles, only to reach a spot scarcely half a mile from where it began. The Abenaki Indians were attracted to the fertile meadowlands and fine fishing grounds created by the oxbows, and had a permanent settlement in present-day Newbury long before Revolutionary War General Jacob Bayley and his party made their way north from Newbury, Massachusetts in the early 1760s to establish the then-furthermost northern outpost on the Vermont side of the Connecticut.

Bayley was also on hand to organize and oversee the construction of the first fourteen miles of the Bayley-Hazen Military Road, from Newbury to Peacham. He promised his 110 men the equivalent of $10 a month plus food, and a half-pint of rum a day; they finished the job in just forty-five days. Unfortunately, the Continental Congress was unable to pay the bill that Bayley presented. We hope the men did get their rum; they had built the first real road in Vermont.

As you head north out of Newbury on Rte. 5, watch for the Ox-Bow Cemetery, where the citizens of Newbury have been interring the departed since 1761. It's the final resting place of Old Joe, the Indian guide who befriended early settlers (see Drive 12).

(9) **Wells River** is a curious place: it's a small Vermont community that feels like it would be more comfortable alongside its more workaday mill town sisters across the river in New Hampshire. Altogether it's an unlovely collection of stolid, red brick buildings and ho-hum store fronts. But it has a sort of utilitarian dignity, and maybe *Travel and Leisure* should take a look at it. We could well imagine Jimmy Stewart walking down Main Street on his way back to the bank after lunch.

Wells River had its glory days during the nineteenth century, when steam-

Newbury is a classic Vermont village of post-Colonial homes and graceful churches, with the 1794 Congregational Church a particular standout. One distinctive local structure, however, has not survived. The 1805 Bedell Bridge between Newbury and Haverhill, N.H. had been battered mercilessly by storms over the years, and was rebuilt no fewer than four times. In the late 1970s, local citizens contributed to finance a thorough restoration of the 396-foot span, which was rededicated and opened to foot traffic only in July, 1979. The banners had barely been taken down when, on September 15, 1979, violent winds tore the bridge to splinters. It was raining heavily, and a party of campers had just taken refuge inside the structure; all eight campers were rescued, although one seriously injured individual had to be cut out of the wreckage with a chainsaw. It could have been much worse: a wedding was to have taken place on the bridge the following day. All that remains of the Bedell Bridge are its piers, visible at the end of a dirt road off Rte. 5.

boats chugged upstream to dock at this northernmost navigable point on the Connecticut River. Later, it was a thriving railroad junction. Wells River's present-day link to the transportation industry is the **P & H Truck Stop**, the only 24-hour diner in northeastern Vermont and a mecca for hungry teamsters barreling up and down I-91.

(10) In 1773 a party of would-be emigrants in Glasgow, Scotland banded together to form the Scotch-American Company of Farmers. They wanted to purchase land in North America, and the Reverend John Witherspoon, president of the institution which evolved into Princeton University, sold them 23,000 acres in the town of **Ryegate**. In a short time the Scots, under the leadership of James Whitelaw, had settled into their new home and set about dairying, raising oats, and making maple sugar. Whitelaw would later be recognized as one of early New England's finest surveyors and mapmakers.

Ryegate, and nearby Barnet to the north, were the only two towns in the state to be settled by people who came directly from across the sea, rather than from the older American colonies to the south and east. The Scots gave the old Latin name of their homeland, Caledonia, to the county that begins at Ryegate.

(11) Continue north on Rte. 5 through McIndoe Falls to **Barnet**. Two Buddhist retreats have established themselves here -- the Karme-Choling Buddhist Meditation Center, a Tibetan Buddhist

Side Trip

Early Scottish settlers built their first church -- the United Presbyterian Church -- in Barnet Center in 1791. The church's cemetery is a testament to the people who first settled the surrounding hills: Wallaces, Buchanans, Lairds, MacNabs, McPhees, and one Thomas Clark, a native of Scotland who defied all the odds of his era and died in Barnet April 5, 1827, at the age of 88. Also among those interred here are David Goodwillie and his son, Thomas, who together served eighty years as the church's pastors. To reach Barnet Center, head west out of Barnet on West Barnet Road, and take a right after roughly two miles.

facility founded by Trungpa Rinpoche; and Milarepa Center, another Tibetan Buddhist retreat more closely affiliated with the Dalai Lama. **Samedhi Cushions**, an outgrowth of the Karme-Choling Center, sells brightly-colored, Barnet-made meditation cushions, along with Tibetan products, at a shop in the village.

(12) In East Barnet, turn right off   Rte. 5 and follow signs for **Lower Waterford**. You can easily see why this gem-like town perched high on a hill overlooking the Connecticut River got its nickname, the "White Village." The 1798 Congregational Church has a rather unusual double-decked cupola. The major attraction here, other that the sheer loveliness of the town, is the highly regarded **Rabbit Hill Inn**.

Information

Upper Valley Bi-State Regional Chamber of Commerce (888-663-6656 or 295-6200), P.O. Box 697, White River Junction 05001. www.uppervalleyvt-nh.com

Windsor-Mt. Ascutney Chamber of Commerce (674-5910), P.O. Box 341, Windsor 05089. www.windsorvt.com

Canoeing on the Connecticut River **is a free, 47-page guide published by PG & E (603-653-9232), 46 Cetera Parkway, Lebanon, NH 03766. Attn: Ken Alton.**

Lodging

(1) The Inn at Weathersfield (263-9217), Rte. 106 (near Perkinsville), Box 165, Weathersfield 05151. 1792 inn on 21 acres offers 12 guest rooms and suites with canopy beds and some fireplaces, whirlpool tubs and private decks. Fine restaurant and afternoon tea. www.weathersfieldinn.com $$-$$$

(1)(R) Juniper Hill Inn (800-359-2541 or 674-5273), Juniper Hill Rd., Windsor 05089. Elegant and

secluded National Historic Register hilltop mansion across from 400-acre Paradise Park has 16 guest rooms (11 with fireplaces), a pool, gardens, and grand common rooms. A four-course candlelight dinner, served Tues.-Sat., might include baked brie in puff pastry with almonds and apricots, a house salad, herb-crusted rack of lamb, and the house special "creme" in puff pastry topped with seasonal fruit. www.juniperhillinn.com $$-$$$

(4)(R) The Norwich Inn (649-1143), Main St., Box 908, Norwich 05055. Charming 1797 inn (originally a stage stop) has 16 guest rooms in the inn, 4 efficiency suites in the Vestry, and 7 units in the motel: all have traditional country furnishings and Victorian antiques, along with phones and TVs. The dining room ($$-$$$) smokes its own meats and poultry, and serves dishes such as grilled twin beef tournedos and Maine crab cakes. It's open for B,L, and D Mon.-Sat., and Sun. brunch. A pub menu is available in Jasper Murdock's Alehouse, which handcrafts its own brews. www.norwichinn.com $-$$

(4)(R) Hanover Inn (800-443-7024 or 603-643-4300), Box 151, The Green, Hanover, NH 03755. Just across the river from Norwich, the 4-story Georgian brick inn owned by Dartmouth College has 92 rooms and a formal restaurant ($$$) which serves regional American fare. A wine bar offers a lighter menu. www.hanoverinn.com $$$

(6)(R) Lake Morey Inn Resort (800-423-1211 or 333-4311), Clubhouse Rd., Fairlee 05045. Newly-renovated 600-acre resort has 137 guest units, a championship golf course, indoor and outdoor swimming pools, a spring-fed lake, tennis, boating, and kids' programs; winter x-c and snowmobile trails.
 www.lakemoreyinn.com $$-$$$

(6) Silver Maple Lodge & Cottages (800-666-1946 or 333-4326), 520 Rte. 5 South, Fairlee 05045. Rambling, 1855 farmhouse has 8 pleasant guest rooms (6 with private bath), and 7 cottage units

(some with kitchens and fireplaces). Biking, hot air balloon and canoe packages. Pets allowed in cottages. Continental bkfst. www.silvermaplelodge.com $-$$

(8) Peach Brook Inn B & B (866-3389), Doe Hill (just off Rte. 5), South Newbury 05051. Colonial home overlooking the Connecticut River and valley offers 3 rooms with shared or private baths. Children 10 and older. $

(9) Nootka Lodge (800-626-9105 or 603-747-2418), jct. Rte. 302 and Rte. 10, Woodsville, NH 03785 (just across the river from Wells River). 27 spacious units: the second-floor rooms have cathedral ceilings and balconies. Pool, barbecue pit, jacuzzi, game and exercise rooms. Special rooms for pets. $-$$

(11)(R) Rabbit Hill Inn (800-762-8669 or 748-5168), Rte. 18, Lower Waterford 05848. "An Inn for Romantics," the award-winning hostelry has been accommodating overnight guests since 1795. Each of the 19 rooms and suites have canopy beds and antiques: some have fireplaces and 2-person hydromassage tubs, and private porches. The intimate, candlelit dining room (just 15 tables) serves a 5-course dinner ($$$) featuring regional New American cuisine, with dishes such as sauteed hazelut encrusted foie gras, roasted bacon-wrapped pheasant breast, and kumquat creme bruleé. Pub. Closed first 3 weeks April and 1st two weeks in Nov. Children 13+. www.RabbitHillInn.com $$$

Restaurants

(1) Windsor Diner (674-5555), 135 Main St., Windsor. Homemade clam chowder and pies, daily specials, and diner favorites including fried liver and onions. B, L, D Fri. & Sat. B & L Sun.- Thurs. $

(3) Taste of Africa's Karibu Tulé (295-4250), Briggs Opera House, White River Junction. Authentic cuisine from countries throughout Africa. D Wed. - Sun. $$

(4) La Poule a Dents at Carpenter Street (649-2922), Corner of Main and Carpenter Sts., Norwich. Elegant and delicious French cuisine and an excellent wine list served in a historic 1820s home. Fixed price menu available. Reservations essential. D. $$$

(7) Colatina Exit (222-9008), Main St., Bradford. A genuine Italian trattoria -- with candles and red checkered tablecloths no less -- in the heart of Vermont. Owner/chef Carol Perry has been serving up moderately priced dishes for 30+ years; the menu includes 7 kinds of pasta with 12 different sauces and hand thrown, hearth baked pizzas. D. $-$$

(9) P & H Truck Stop (429-2141), Rte. 302, just off exit 17 of I-91, 3 mi. west of downtown Wells River. Hearty diner fare. B, L, D. $

(9) Warner's Gallery Restaurant (429-2120), Rte. 302, east of downtown Wells River. The "home of the sticky buns" serve up great prime rib, fish, and poultry and offers a 50-item salad bar in a large, family-friendly establishment. D and Sun. brunch; closed Mon. $-$$

Attractions

(1) American Precision Museum (674-5781), 196 Main St., Windsor. Late May-Nov. 1. $

(1) Mt. Ascutney State Park (674-2060), Rte. 44A, Brownsville. Late May-mid-Oct. $

(1) Old Constitution House (672-3773), Windsor. Late May-Mid Oct., Wed.-Sun. 11-5. $

(1) Saint-Gaudens National Historic Site (603-675-2175), Rte. 12A, Cornish, N.H. Sun. afternoon concerts July & Aug. at 2 PM. Late May-Oct. Grounds open dawn-dusk. $

(1) North Hartland Lake (295-2855), 112 Clay Hill Rd., North Hartland. Swimming, boating, picnicking, hiking trails. $

(3) Wilder Dam (291-8112), Wilder Dam Rd., Wilder. Memorial Day weekend-Labor Day, Thurs.-Mon.

(4) Dartmouth College (603-646-2808), Hanover, N.H.: Baker Memorial Library, 1 Elm St.; Hood Museum of Art, Wheelock St., closed Mon.

(4) Montshire Museum of Science (649-2200), Montshire Rd., Norwich. $

Activities and Shopping

Wilderness Trails (295-7620), Inn at Marsh Farms, Quechee. Canoe and fly fishing trips on the Connecticut River.

Vermont Waterways (800-492-8271 or 472-8271). Inn-to-inn guided tours on the upper Connecticut River.

***

(1) Ascutney Mountain Resort (484-3511), Brownsville. Mountain bike rentals.

(1) Morningside Flight Park (603-542-4416), 357 Morningside Lane, N. Charlestown, NH. Hang gliding; introductory courses.

(1) North Star Canoe Rental (603-542-5802),   Rte. 12A, Cornish, N.H. Daily and overnight trips on the Connecticut River (camping and inn accommodations arranged); shuttle. May-Oct., closed Mon./Tues.

(2) Harpoon Brewery (888-427-7666 or 674-5491), 336 Ruth Carney Drive, Windsor. Brewery/gift shop open Tues.-Sat. 10-6; free tours daily at 11 and 3. Indoor/outdoor beer garden, serving sandwiches, open Tues.-Sun. 11-6.

(2) Simon Pearce Glass (800-774-5277 or 674-6280), Windsor Industrial Park, Windsor.

(1) Vermont State Crafts Center at Windsor House (674-6729), 54 Main St., Windsor.

(3) Briggs Opera House (296-7000).

(4) Dan and Whit's General Store, Main St., Norwich. Classic general store with everything from widgets to wine and the place to find out what's happening.

(4) King Arthur Flour Baker's Store (800-827-6836 or 649-3361), Rte. 5S, Norwich. Store, bakery, education center.

(4) The Norwich Bookstore (649-1114), Main St., Norwich. First-rate bookstore in a house next to the post office: call for special events.

(4) Norwich Farmers' Market, Rte. 5S, Norwich. Saturdays, 9 a.m.-1 p.m. May-Oct. Fresh produce, crafts, music.

(4) Opera North (603-643-1946): Headquartered in Norwich, this semiprofessional opera group performs throughout the area. Call for schedule.

(4) Ledyard Canoe Club (603-643-6709), on the river by Dartmouth College, Hanover, N.H. Canoes, kayaks and sea kayaks for rent hourly or daily.

(4) Stave Puzzles (295-5200), Olcott Commercial Park, off Rte. 5, Norwich. High-quality, hand-crafted wooden jigsaw puzzle factory; store open Mon.-Fri.

(5)(L) Post Mills Airport (333-9254), Robinson Hill Rd., Post Mills.

(6) Pompanoosuc Mills (785-4851), Rte. 5, East Thetford. Home base for the region-wide manufacturer of fine quality wooden furniture.

(6) **Fairlee Drive-In Theater (333-9192),   Rte. 5, Fairlee.**

(6) **Fairlee Marine (333-9745),   Rte. 5S, Fairlee. Pontoon, rowboat (with small motors), and canoe rental; fishing supplies.**

(6) **Chapman's (333-9709),   Rte. 5, Fairlee. Old-time former pharmacy with a modern twist: hand-tied flies, more than 400 bottles of wine, rare and used books, and jewelry.**

(11) **Samadhi Cushions (800-331-7751 or 633-4440), Church St., Barnet.   Closed weekends.**

Drive 9

Burlington

2 - 3 miles on foot, with a maximum 5 miles of driving to outer points

When is a Vermont drive not a drive? When it's a walk through the "Queen City," a metropolis by local standards but the smallest largest city any state has. With five colleges, Burlington is right up to date (or perhaps a little farther, depending on which bands are playing at the clubs). But its history goes all the way back to Ethan Allen, and the merchants who made Lake Champlain a major avenue of trade. Walk (and eat) your way through the Church Street Marketplace, join the waterfront promenade, and take a free course in American architecture simply by strolling through the campus of the University of Vermont.

(1) Begin your Burlington walk where the heart of downtown begins, at the intersection of Church and Main streets. If you're facing up Church Street, the brick Georgian Revival building on your left is City Hall, an uninspired 1926 example of the great architectural firm McKim, Mead, and White's declining years. (The park just behind City Hall is the site of a popular Saturday farmers' market from late spring through fall.) That big marquee just over your left shoulder belongs to the **Flynn Center for the Performing Arts**, sole survivor of Burlington's grand prewar movie houses. This 1930 Art Deco structure survived not as a competitor of the suburban megaplexes, but because it was splendidly restored in the 1980s to serve as the city's premier performing arts venue. Each year, the Flynn's directors put

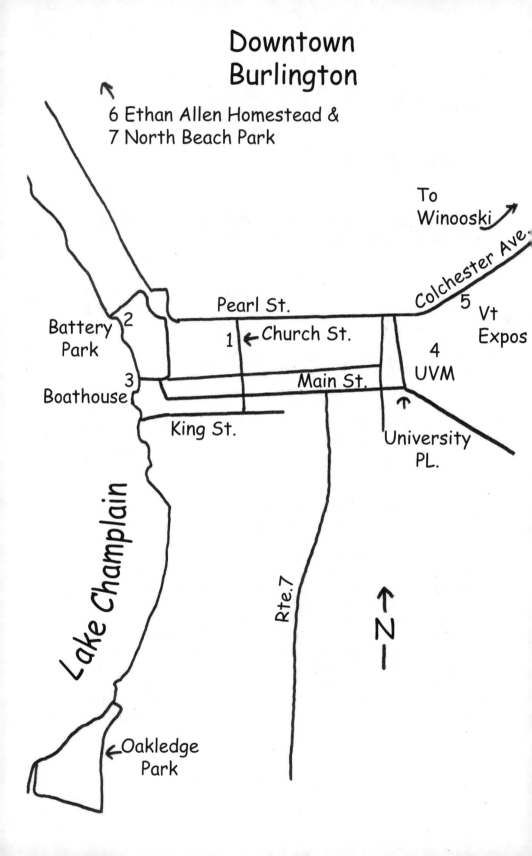

together an exciting and truly eclectic calendar, ranging from touring opera companies to African dance to Japanese drums.

The same decade that saw the restoration of the Flynn also saw the debut of the **Church Street Marketplace**, which on a bright spring or summer day is itself something of a performing arts venue -- and not just because of the street entertainers. Church Street is Burlington's grand promenade, a place where people-watching is rewarded by the immense variety of people to watch. Twenty-five years ago, the four-block stretch between Main and Pearl streets was open to automobile traffic, and lined with shops that met a small city's everyday demands -- it was easy, on a weekday afternoon or evening, to entirely forget that this is a college town. All that changed when the core blocks of Church Street went all-pedestrian, and the hardware stores, stationers, and 5 & 10s gave way to boutiques, sidewalk cafes, street sculpture and musicians, along with an entrance to an indoor mall, Burlington Square. Next door to City Hall, an old fire station became the **Firehouse Center for the Visual Arts**, emphasizing works by Vermont artists in various media. (Their artisan counterparts are represented up the street, at the **Vermont State Craft Center**.)

To mix in a little of the flavor of pre-Marketplace downtown, while enjoying the passegiata and deciding where to stop for a microbrew or a glass of Zinfandel, cast your glance up beyond (and, in your mind's eye, through) the modern-day shop fronts. At Church and College streets, two stately old banks have been reborn as the pub-restaurants **Sweetwater's**, on the right, and **Ri-Ra**, on the left (the name of the latter is Irish, as is the imported interior, the potables, and the bill of fare). That *chanson* by Edith Piaf is coming from Leunig's Bistro, Burlington's answer to Paris' Left Bank. One block up and also on the left, you'll have to look to the upper stories to piece together the architectural unity of the 1878 Howard Opera House, divided into individual shops and restaurants below but in its day a regular Flynn Theater of a place. It was built in 1878 by John Howard (you'll see his bewhiskered bust set into the facade of the Old Mill, on the UVM campus) at a cost of $100,000, and was once a prime stopover for traveling operatic and theatrical troupes.

Two other stolid, confident piles of late nineteenth-century brickwork flank the north end of the marketplace, at Pearl Street. On the left is the 1897 Masonic Temple, capped with an enormous pyramidal slate roof that seems an embodiment of what to do with the mystic compass and square, while opposite stands the turreted, cast-iron-balustraded one-time premises of Abernethy Clarkson Wright, which survived into the 1970s as the sort of department store where you expect to see floorwalkers wearing boutonnieres. Today, both the Masonic Temple and Abernethy's are anchored by chain retailers that sell apparel for casual Friday, *sans* boutonniere.

But the finest architectural monument of downtown Burlington still serves its original purpose. This is the 1816 First Unitarian Church, which stands at the head of Church Street, on Pearl. The red brick church and its great white steeple are late Georgian at its most chaste and sublime; it was designed by Peter Banner, who was responsible for the understandably more elegant and urbane Park Street Church in Boston, and it is said that Charles Bulfinch himself had a hand in the plans. The first bell to hang in the steeple was cast in the Massachusetts foundry of Paul Revere, while the old man was still alive; it has since been replaced with one crafted to duplicate the original's tone.

(2) Turn left onto Pearl Street, which, on its way down to the lakefront, passes two examples of ecclesiastical architecture that couldn't differ more from Peter Banner's commission for those long-ago Unitarians. Within a span of less than a year at the beginning of the 1970s, fires claimed the cathedral churches of Burlington's Roman Catholic and Episcopal dioceses. Both denominations immediately rebuilt. The Catholics put up the odd, greenish Cathedral of the Immaculate Conception (between St. Paul and Pine streets, on the left), which looks like a church that has been half-buried in a lawn; while the Episcopalians went in for a bold concrete statement (also left, a long block farther down, near Battery Street) in their St. Paul's Cathedral, which is as devoid of exterior ornament as an airport control tower. Both cathedrals, though (particularly the Episcopalian) have pleasant, serene interiors.

Pearl Street ends at Battery Street, across from which stands **Battery Park** on a bluff overlooking Lake Champlain. The park got its name from an artillery battery set up here to repel the British during the War of 1812. Wander over to the escarpment by the playground, opposite the police station, for Burlington's finest panorama of the lake at its broadest point, with the Adirondack Mountains in the background. A century ago, novelist William Dean Howells said that the sunsets here were the loveliest in the world. Some Burlingtonians would say that the description also fits the French fries served up at **Beansie's Bus**, the yellow school bus/restaurant that's parked here daily in season.

(3) Leaving Battery Park, head south (the opposite direction from which you walked up Church Street) and follow Battery Street past the Radisson Hotel Burlington to College Street. Turn right on College Street, and Burlington's newly revitalized waterfront lies directly ahead.

Like many other cities whose livelihood once depended on their harbors, Burlington long took a strictly utilitarian approach to its waterfront. While some evidence of those days is still easy to find (to the north, for example, stands the Burlington Electric Department's power plant), this city has done a remarkable job, over the past fifteen years, of making its doorstep on Lake Champlain into an accessible and inviting recreational asset. At the end of the pier off the foot of College Street stands the Community Boathouse;just alongside, the cruise vessel *Spirit of Ethan Allen III* departs for excursions around the lake. Another option for a lake voyage, with or without your car, is the ferry to Port Kent, New York. The trip takes an hour each way. Boats leave from the **Lake Champlain Transportation Company**'s dock at the foot of King Street, two blocks south of the Boathouse. A lakeside promenade extends for several hundred yards north from the Boathouse, although it's possible to walk, bike, or rollerblade much farther in either direction on the Burlington Recreation Path. The 10 mi., mostly flat **Cycle the City** path, which connects the waterfront, Ethan Allen Homestead, the Intervale, the University and the Hill Section, begins at Union Station. (Maps of the paths are available at downtown bike shops; Main Street's **Ski Rack** --which also rentals rollerblades -- and **North Star Cyclery** are closest).

The northern end of Burlington's recreation path is at the mouth of the Winooski River, about five miles north of downtown. But for the past couple of summers, the path has been extended north onto a bike route in the town of Colchester by means of a little ferry capable of carrying five riders and their bikes at a time. It's probably the most unusual water excursion in Vermont -- it's free, takes less than ten minutes, and leaves from a tackle shop and boat livery that hasn't changed since the Truman administration. Area bike enthusiasts would like to see the ferry eventually superseded by a bicycle bridge, the first link in a route that would bring cyclists up to the Champlain Islands (See Drive 10) and all the way to Montreal.

One block south of the Boathouse (again, that's left, if you're facing the lake), Burlington's Union Station caps the water end of Main Street. No longer a major rail depot -- Amtrak's *Vermonter* terminates in Essex Junction, eight miles from here -- the station is still in use as the terminus for the **Champlain Valley Weekender** summer excursion trains between Burlington and Middlebury. For some reason, it was decided that Union Station would look good topped with a pair of flying monkeys, straight from The Wizard of Oz. They're up on the roof, life-size (what is the life size of a flying monkey?), having done prior service as a come-on for a waterbed outlet on Shelburne Road. No, this wasn't a college prank. This is Burlington. It's official.

Also at the foot of Main Street, right near the station, is the **Leahy Center for Lake Champlain**, newly reopened after a major renovation and expansion. The Center's focus is the history, culture, and ecology of the Lake Champlain region, and it houses more than 2,200 live fish, amphibians, and reptiles in aquarium and terrarium exhibits. There are plenty of interactive, hands-on activities for children.

Before heading uphill to the UVM campus, take a look at two of Burlington's most distinctive houses, both in the waterfront vicinity. That big colonnaded temple of a place one block up on College Street is Burlington's finest example of pure Greek Revival. Built in 1845 by lawyer and railroad president Timothy Follett, it was designed by Ammi B. Young, best known for the U.S. Custom House in Boston and the Vermont State House in Montpelier. After many decades of neglect as the home of a succession of institutions and clubs, the Follett House was purchased by a local developer and restored for office use in the 1980s.

Tucked away in a more obscure location at 35 King Street, a block up from the ferry landing, is the Gideon King House, a foursquare Georgian brick residence now used as offices. Dating from about 1798, this is one of the oldest structures in Burlington. For twenty-eight years, until his death in 1826, it was the home of Gideon King, Jr., known in his day as the "Admiral of the Lake." Engaged in enterprises ranging from freight forwarding to importing horses from Canada, King more than anyone put Burlington on the map as a shipping hub. It was in this house on June 22, 1798, in fact, that a map was put on Burlington. The downtown grid of streets that still exists -- including the outlines of City Hall Park -- were agreed upon here after being presented by William Coit, one of King's fellow movers and shakers.

(4) It's a ten-block uphill climb to the next stop on this walk, the campus of the **University of Vermont**, and cheating by hopping into your car (or by taking one of the free trolley-style shuttle buses that run up and down College Street) is perfectly acceptable. Tackling the climb on foot will reward architecture buffs, though, because the slope between downtown and the campus is lined with houses that grow ever more handsome the higher you climb. Many were in fact middle-class homes, built in an era in which even modest Burlington burghers expressed themselves extravagantly in brick and wood.

Head towards UVM either on Main or College streets. Both are commercial for the first few blocks, but give way to residential (increasingly, this means "student" hereabouts) neighborhoods once you get east of Union Street. Two grand old houses in particular stand out along Main Street. The first is the General William Wells House on the southeast corner of South Willard Street. With its mansard roof and central, similarly mansarded tower, this red brick stalwart typifies the French Second Empire style (called, in American terms, "General Grant") popular in the 1870s. Built by Gen. Wells in 1877 for $15,000, it was later the home of Dr. H. Nelson Jackson, who married the general's daughter, Bertha. Dr. Jackson was the first person to cross the United States in an automobile, in 1903. The Winton he drove on the epic trip is now in the Smithsonian. His home is now a fraternity house.

One block up from the Wells House, at Main and Summit streets, is Grassmount, a brick Georgian mansion built in 1804 by Thaddeus Tuttle and still surrounded by spacious lawns. Now housing department offices for UVM, Grassmount is the last surviving Burlington home to suggest the still-rural character of the hilltop estates that flourished when the city was new.

Also new in 1800 was the University of Vermont, founded in 1791 by Ira Allen, brother of Green Mountain Boy Ethan. Ira, who is commemorated by a statue facing Prospect Street on the UVM Green, was a real estate promoter who, although he eventually died broke, was instrumental in bringing settlers to Burlington and environs under the aegis of his Onion River Land Company. Ira Allen got the University off to a start with a grant of fifty acres. Instruction began in 1800, a year after axemen started clearing the Green. (This manicured open space nowadays receives the attention of a different sort of arboreal professionals -- its few surviving elms have been inoculated and nursed against the ravages of Dutch Elm disease, which destroyed the vase-shaped trees that once made leafy tunnels of Burlington's residential streets.)

Before taking a walk around the campus, we should stop to explain the meaning of the initials "UVM." Why not "UV"? The answer is simply that the early nineteenth-century scholars who came up with the abbreviation were thinking, as scholars did then, in Latin: "UVM" stands for Universitas Viridis Montis, the University of the Green Mountains.

UVM's most distinctive buildings face the Green on University Place. Follow one of the pathways across the grass to begin at the north (left) end of the row, at the corner of University Place and Colchester Avenue. The newest building in the row is the 1927 Ira Allen Chapel, a Georgian Revival effort by McKim, Mead, and White that is considerably more successful than downtown Burlington's City Hall. The red brick non-denominational chapel's most impressive feature is its 170-foot campanile, which houses a mellifluous sixty-four bell carillon. Alongside the north wall of the chapel is the grave of Vermont-born philosopher and educational reformer John Dewey (1859-1952), UVM 1879.

Directly behind the Ira Allen Chapel, facing Colchester Avenue but with its entrance at the rear, is the **Robert Hull Fleming Museum**, which houses UVM's art collection. On display among the museum's European and American works are canvases by painters of the Hudson River School (including two Bierstadts); and by Sargent, Homer, Corot, and Fragonard. Ethnographic collections include an Egyptian mummy in its painted wooden sarcophagus. Special exhibits often highlight the work of Vermont artists.

The finest structure on the UVM campus -- and in Burlington -- stands just to the right of the Chapel as you walk south. This is the 1886 Billings Student Center (formerly Billings Library), whose blunt Romanesque massing, heroically arched entryway, and masterful use of rough-cut sandstone mark it as the work of Henry Hobson Richardson. The baronial interior, warm with the glow of honey-colored Georgia pine, long ago outlived its usefulness as library space, and now serves as a student lounge and activities headquarters. Step inside for a look at the great rotunda, the balconied main hall, and especially the exquisitely carved mantel and standing clock opposite the entrance. All of the carvings were done by Albert H. Whittekind, a German-born artisan who came to Burlington expressly to work on the library and remained for the rest of his life, nearly another sixty years. Whittekind carved exterior ornaments for many fine turn-of-the-century homes. If you're strolling around the residential blocks near the university, look for examples at 61 Summit Street, 376 and 384 College Street, 301 South Willard Street, and 282 Pearl Street.

Moving southward along the row, the next building is the 1896 Williams Science Hall, which boasts intricate terra-cotta detailing. Popular Victorian architect Frank Furness is said to have designed Williams to be the first completely fireproof building in the United States. It's a relief to know this, since Williams is the home of the irreplaceable brainchild of two UVM profes-

Henry Hobson Richardson (1838-1886) was one of America's half-dozen greatest architects, and the only one whose name is used to define the dominant style of his era: Richardson Romanesque. It's no small feather in Burlington's cap that the architect called UVM's Billings Library "the best thing I've done" near the premature end of a career that included Boston's Trinity Church, much of the New York State Capitol, and dozens of other public buildings and magnificent private homes. Richardson was chosen for the Burlington commission by the library's donor, railroad baron Frederick Billings (see Drive 5), who had promised a fine home for the 12,000-volume collection of his late friend, the scholar, diplomat, and environmentalist George Perkins Marsh, which he was presenting to the university. Billings wrote UVM President Matthew Henry Buckham, "For such a building really the proper thing to do is to employ Richardson." Billings backed the uncompromising Richardson with his purse -- having initially pledged $85,000 for the library's construction, he eventually sprung for $150,000.

sors: WHAMKA is an acronym for Williams Hall Art Museum of Kitsch Art. It's on the first floor, just to the right of the entrance.

The Old Mill, just to the south, is the oldest building on campus. Its cornerstone was laid in 1825 by the Marquis de Lafayette, who was progressing through an American tour to mark the fiftieth anniversary of the Revolution he had fought in as a young man. (Among the festivities surrounding Lafayette's visit to Burlington was a sumptuous banquet at Grassmount, the Georgian mansion we visited earlier.) For a number of years after its oldest section was constructed, the Old Mill (presumably not yet known by that name) contained the entire university, including lecture rooms, dormitories, the library and the chapel. It was extensively restored in 1996-1997, and the long-disused fourth floor has been partly dedicated to an informal museum of artifacts uncovered during the renovations -- including nineteenth-century student quarters where one must have had to study extra hard to keep warm.

The last two structures on University Place are the Royall Tyler Theater, named after the Vermont jurist whose 1787 comedy "The Contrast" is generally held to be the first American play; and Morrill Hall, a ponderous yellow-brick 1907 building with one of Vermont's few tile roofs. It houses the offices of UVM's Agricultural College, and was named to honor Justin Smith Morrill, the Vermont senator who wrote the 1862 legislation launching America's land-grant colleges (see Drive 7).

(5) Ethan Allen -- living and dead -- and a clutch of fine city parks are the focus of side trips that expand this Burlington city walk with several short drives.

At the corner of University Place (by Ira Allen Chapel), Pearl Street becomes Colchester Avenue. Head east, away from downtown and the lake, and watch on the right for the entrance to Greenwood Cemetery. (It's just past the right-hand turnoff for Centennial Field, where the Single-A minor-league **Vermont Expos** baseball team plays.) Somewhere in the vicinity of the tall column topped by his statue -- no one is sure of the exact location -- lie the mortal remains of Ethan Allen. At least the old Green Mountain Boy's burial site is easier to pin down than that of his brother Ira, who is buried in an unmarked grave in a Quaker cemetery in Philadelphia. A couple of years back, someone floated the idea of using DNA testing to identify Ira's bones, and bringing them back to Burlington. But when the project's backers realized that they would have to dig up every pauper in the field to run the tests, it was decided to leave UVM's benefactor wherever it is that he is.

For a vivid reminder of the living Ethan Allen, take Pearl Street back downtown to Battery Park, then head north (right, by the police station) on Battery Street to North Avenue. Stay on North Avenue for just under two   miles to Rte. 127 North, following signs for the **Ethan Allen Homestead**. Allen moved to this plain but cozy farmhouse in 1787, and died here two years later after taking ill during a trip across the frozen lake from South Hero. The homestead has been restored to show how Allen and his family -- and many another pioneer Vermonter -- lived in the days when northern New England was as much a wild frontier as the later American west. An on-site museum places Allen into the historical context of the American Revolution and early federal period. The homestead's spacious grounds, with trails, picnic areas, and access to the Winooski River banks, offer expansive views of the northern Green Mountains.

(6) Leaving the Ethan Allen Homestead, backtrack on North Avenue for roughly a half mile to **North Beach Park** (as you head back toward Burlington, turn right onto Institute Road). Along with a swimming beach, picnic sites, and access to the Burlington Recreation Path, this is the only Burlington park -- for that matter, the only place anywhere in town -- to offer camping, making this a great place to camp for anyone attracted by the idea of hopping out of their tent, onto a bike, and straight into downtown Burlington. The Recreation Path also leads to Leddy Park, on the lake north of North Beach, and south beyond downtown all the way to Oakledge Park, where a scenic swimming beach anchors the southern end of the gentle arc of Burlington Bay.

Information

Lake Champlain Regional Chamber of Commerce (877-686-5253 or 863-3489), 60 Main St., Suite 100, Burlington 05401. Closed weekends. www.vermont.org

Note: in this chapter we've given a small sampling of lodging, dining, and shopping options; for a full listing, be sure to contact the chamber.

Lodging

Note: there are many moderately-priced chain and independent motels south of Burlington on Rte. 7, and to the east along Rte. 2.

(1/3) 78 Main Street Sunset House B&B (864-3790), Burlington 05401. Restored, downtown Historic Queen Anne-style, c. 1854 boarding house has 4 air-conditioned guest rooms with shared baths.

www.sunsethousebb.com $$
(1/3) Willard Street Inn (800-577-8712 or 651-8710),
349 So. Willard St., Burlington 05401. Historic, 1880s
brick mansion with lake views has 14 elegant rooms
with private baths. Breakfast is served in the solari-
um. www.wilardstreetinn.com $$-$$$

(1/3) Burlington Redstone B & B (862-0508), 497 S.
Willard St., Rte. 7, Burlington 05401. 1906 National
Historic Register home has 2 guest rooms with shared
bath (with a soaking tub) and a suite with its own
bath. Lake views, lovely gardens. Children over 13.
www.burlingtonredstone.com $$

(1/3) Lang House (877-919-9799 or 652-2500), 360
Main St., Burlington 05401. Restored 1881 Eastlake
Victorian has 9 well-appointed rooms with period fur-
nishings and antiques. www.langhouse.com $$$

(3)(R) Radisson Hotel Burlington (800-333-3333 or
658-6500), 60 Battery St., Burlington 05401. Many
of the 255 rooms in Burlington's only waterfront ho-
tel overlook Lake Champlain and the Adirondacks.
Indoor pool, jacuzzi, health facility. $5 parking.
www.radisson.com $$-$$$

Not on Walk

Anchorage Inn (800-336-1869 or 863-7000), 108
Dorset St., South Burlington 05403. Pleasant 2-story
motel with indoor heated pool, hot tub and sauna just
across from University Mall and next door to Barnes &
Noble. Continental breakfast.
www.vtanchorageinn.com $-$$

(R) The Inn at Essex (800-727-4295 or 878-11000),
70 Essex Way, Essex 05452. 120 rooms (30 with fireplaces) in a colonial-style hotel/inn near Essex Outlet Fair. Outdoor pool. Restaurants operated by New
England Culinary Institute. Continental breakfast.
www.innatessex.com $$$

Sheraton-Burlington Hotel & Conference Center (800-325-3525 or 865-6600), 870 Williston Rd., Burlington 05401. 309 rooms, indoor pool, fitness center, and jacuzzis; popular Sun. brunch; English pub. www.sheraton.com $$-$$$

Restaurants

(1) Bove's (864-6651), 68 Pearl St., Burlington. This unpretentious family-run eatery has been serving up good, plain Neapolitan fare for more than 60 years. The meatball sandwich ($1.60) is a bargain. L, D. Closed Sun. and Mon. $

(1) Five Spice Cafe (864-4045), 175 Church St., Burlington. Vietnamese, Indonesian, Thai, Burmese and Chinese. L, D, and Sunday dim sum brunch. $-$$

(1) Leunig's Bistro (863-3759), 115 Church Street, Burlington. Outdoor seating; call for schedule of live music and/or cabaret. L, D; open until midnight. $-$$

(1) Mirabelle's (658-3074), 198 Main St., Burlington. Informal café serves sandwiches on fresh-baked baguettes, omelettes and homemade soups and chowders. Closed Sun. $

(1) Nectar's (658-4771), 188 Main St., Burlington. Legendary for its french fries with gravy and as the place the band Phish was launched. Solid, diner-type fare and evening entertainment. $

(1) Paradise Burritos Mexican Café (660-3603), 88 Church St., Burlington. One of Church Street's best meal deals: great tacos, man-sized burritos, and a seat outside to people-watch while you eat. L, D. $

(1) Parima Thai Restaurant (864-7917), 185 Pearl St., Burlington. Fine ethnic fare in an upscale environment of dark wood, stained glass and plants. L, D. $

(1) Penny Cluse Café (651-8834), 169 Cherry St., Burlington. Popular with college kids, who know where to find a good deal. Healthy and hearty fare, including homemade soups, vegetarian specials, and huge breakfasts. B,L. $

(1) Ri-Ra (860-9401), 123 Church St., Burlington. Traditional Irish and American fare in a restored pub shipped from Ireland. Live entertainment. B Sat. and Sun., L, D, and late night menu. $-$$

(1) A Single Pebble (865-5200), 133 Bank St. The place for authentic Chinese cuisine: traditional clay pot and wok specialties. D Tues.-Sun. $

(1) Sweetwaters (864-9800), cor. of College and Church sts., Burlington. Creative sandwiches, local micro brews, hamburgers, buffalo burgers and more. patio and porch seating. L, D, Sun. brunch. $$

(1) Trattoria Delia (864-5253), 152 St. Paul St., Burlington. Award-winning, authentic Italian trattoria specialties include handmade pastas and hardwood-grilled entrees. D. $$-$$$

(2) Beansie's Bus, Battery Park. L spring-fall. $

Not on Walk

Al's French Frys (862-9203), 1251 Williston Rd. (Rte. 2), Burlington. Folks may disagree about who makes the area's best French fries, but nobody can dispute that this +50-year-old "diner" is the queen of the Queen City's fast food eateries. L, D. $

Pauline's Café and Restaurant (862-1081), 1834 Shelburne Rd., So. Burlington. For more than 15 years, serving "wild and cultivated edibles from the Lake Champlain Region" in a casual downstairs café ($$) or a more formal upstairs dining room ($$-$$$). The early-bird special (5 PM-6 PM; $) is a deal. L, D, Sun. brunch. $$

Peking Duck House (655-7474), 79 West Canal St., Winooski. Well-prepared dishes served in an airy brick-and-beam upscale atmosphere in one of the area's finest Chinese restaurants. L, D. $

The Sirloin Saloon (985-2200), Shelburne Rd. (Rte. 7), Shelburne. Steaks, seafood, and a great salad bar. $$

Attractions

(1) Burlington Farmers' Market, City Hall Park, Burlington. Seasonal Saturdays from 10 am- 2 pm.

(1) Firehouse Center for the Visual Arts (865-7166), Church St., Burlington. Wed., Thurs., Sat. and Sun. noon-6.

(1) Flynn Theatre for the Performing Arts (863-5966 for tickets; 863-8778 for tours and information), 153 Main St., Burlington. $

(3) Leahy Center for Lake Champlain (864-1848), 1 College St., Burlington. Mid-June-Labor Day, 11-5; rest of the year, weekend and school vacation afternoons. $

(3) Lake Champlain Historic Underwater Preserves (475-2022). Scuba divers can visit 1800s-era historic shipwrecks (4 in greater Burlington Harbor) maintained by the Vermont Division for Historic Preservation. Equipment rental at Waterfront Diving (865-2771), 214 Battery St., which also provides maps and information.

(4) Robert Hull Fleming Museum (656-0750), 61 Colchester Ave., Burlington. Closed Mon. $

(4) University of Vermont (656-3131 for general info.; 656-3370 for tour schedule), 85 South Prospect St., Burlington. Maps available at information office in Waterman Building, library, and bookstore.

(5) Ethan Allen Homestead (865-4556), off Rte. 127, Burlington. Mid-May-mid-Oct. daily. $

(6) North Beach Park (865-7247).

Activities and Shopping

(1) Bennington Potters North (863-2221), 127 College St., Burlington. Pottery, home furnishings and accessories; seconds department.

(1) Lake Champlain Chocolates (864-1807), 750 Pine St., Burlington. Watch chocolates being made and sample the wares; factory seconds. Retail store at 63 Church St.

(1) Vermont Mozart Festival (800-639-9097 or 862-7352), 110 Main St., Burlington. Mid-July - early-Aug. Concert series features world-class classical, jazz and other musical events at outdoor venues throughout Northern and Western Vermont, as well as in Burlington's concert halls. $

(1) Vermont State Craft Center/Frog Hollow on the Marketplace (863-6458), 85 Church St., Burlington. Vermont crafts.

(1/3) Ski Rack (658-3313), 81 Main St., Burlington.

(3) Lake Champlain Cruises (864-6830), King Street Dock, Burlington. Narrated daily excursions; Sun. brunch and dinner cruises. Adm.

(3) Lake Champlain Ferries (864-9804), King Street Dock, Burlington. Seasonal ferries from Burlington to Port Kent, NY and Charlotte to Essex, NY; year-round from Grand Isle to Plattsburgh, NY. $

(3) Burlington Community Boathouse (865-3377), foot of College St., Burlington. Sailboat rentals, fishing charters, captained day sails. Late May-Oct.

(3) Lake Champlain Weekender (800-707-3530 or 388-0193), Union Station, cor. of Main and Battery sts., Burlington. One-way or round-trip. Bicyclists welcome. July-early Sept.

(3) North Star Cyclery (863-3832), 100 Main St., Burlington.

(3) PaddleWays (660-8606), 89 Caroline St., Burlington. Sea kayaking trips: 3 hour, full day trips; overnight inn-to-inn voyages; Champlain Island family excursions. $

(3) Spirit of Ethan Allen III, Lake Champlain Shoreline Cruises (862-8300), Burlington Community Boathouse, College St. Scenic lunch, sunset dinner, and Sun. brunch cruises aboard the 500-passenger Spirit. May-mid-Oct.

(3) True North Kayak Tours (860-1910), Burlington Community Boathouse, Burlington. Guided wilderness trips (lodging arranged): day trips; no experience required.

(3) Whistling Man Schooner (862-7245), Burlington Community Boathouse, Burlington. Two-hr. cruises at noon, 3, and 6 pm; 3-day B&B theme cruises in July; historical cruises of the lake with lectures by the Lake Champlain Maritime Museum.

(3) Winds of Ireland (863-5090), Burlington Community Boathouse, Burlington. Sailboat cruises , charters (28 ft.-41 ft.) and bareboat charters.

(4) Vermont Expos (655-4200), Centennial Field, Colchester Avenue, Burlington. $

Not on Walk

Burton Snowboards Factory Outlet Store (660-3200), 80 Industrial Parkway, Burlington. Vermont's own -- the originator of the snowboard craze -- sells seconds and demos as well as first quality boards and gear at their factory outlet.

Gardener's Supply Company (The Intervale) (660-3505), 128 Intervale Rd., Burlington. The home of America's largest mail-order gardening catalogue has a two-story greenhouse, display gardens, walking trails, and bike paths.

Magic Hat Brewery (652-2515), 5 Bartlett Bay Rd., South Burlington. Guided tours Wed.-Sat., self-guided tours daily; gift shop and free samples.

Pizza Putt (862-7888), 1205 Airport Parkway, South Burlington. Imaginative indoor miniature golf course, pitching machines, arcade, and small kids' playground make this a good destination for a rainy day. And the pizza is pretty good, too. $

Drive 10

The Champlain Islands and St. Albans

80 miles

This is a trip to the Champlain Islands, the archipelago that forms Grand Isle County off Vermont's "West Coast." It's a heroic trip, you might say, since the two main islands are called South Hero and North Hero, after those celebrated titans of Vermont's frontier days, Ethan and Ira Allen. Leaving the islands and their scenic string of state parks, visit a National Wildlife Refuge on the way to St. Albans, the stately "Rail City" and an unlikely player in a Civil War drama.

South Hero and North Hero, along with Isle La Motte and the Alburg peninsula, come as somewhat of a surprise for those who think of Vermont as a mountain state. There are no mountains out here -- but there are few places as perfect for viewing them. Look across the vast northwestern arm of Lake Champlain called the "Inland Sea," and take in the peaks from Camel's Hump to Jay; turn in the other direction, and there are the northern Adirondacks. In between, surrounded by all that water, is gently rolling orchard and dairy country, slowly suburbanizing towards the southern end of South Hero Island but still largely bucolic and serene, with a handsome scattering of state parks offering plenty of shoreline access.

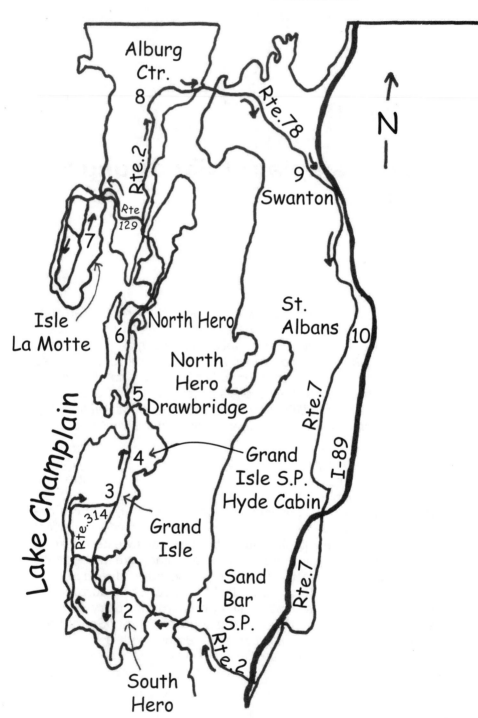

Canada

Alburg
Ctr.

8

Rte.78

Rte.2

Rte
129

N

9
Swanton

7

Isle
La Motte

6   North Hero

North
Hero
Drawbridge

St.
Albans

10

5

4

Grand
Isle S.P.
Hyde Cabin

Rte.7

3

I-89

Rte.314

Grand
Isle

Sand
Bar
S.P.

1

Rte.7

2

Lake Champlain

South
Hero

Rte.2

Begin the drive at Exit 17 (Champlain Islands exit) off I-89, turning west on Rte. 2. At the finish, you'll be back on the mainland at St. Albans, where you can hop back onto I-89 to return to Burlington and points south, or head north towards the Canadian border.

(1) The first major attraction of this drive isn't really on the Champlain Islands, but on their mainland threshold. **Sand Bar State Park**, on the right side of Rte. 2 just before you reach the causeway, offers one of Vermont's best swimming beaches. There's a smooth, sandy shore, a drop-off so gentle that sometimes it seems as if you could wade over to the islands, and gorgeous vistas of the lake and Adirondack mountains beyond.   With changing rooms, picnic tables and grills, a snack bar, and a windsurfer, paddle boat and canoe rental, Sand Bar is the perfect setup for a summer day. It's so perfect, in fact, that it can get quite crowded on weekends. Get there early to grab a beachside table -- or opt for a weekday evening on one of the longest summer days.

Just beyond the entrance to the state park, Rte. 2 swings out onto the causeway that links the mainland with South Hero Island. The panorama south (to the left of the causeway) towards the broadest part of Lake Champlain and the high peaks of the Adirondacks is spectacular, and became even more so just a couple of years ago. Electric power to the islands used to be transported via overhead wires, strung from poles set into rockpiles located at intervals in the shallow waters to the left of the causeway. When ice jams damaged the poles and cut power, it became apparent that running an underwater cable would not only eliminate the likelihood of future service interruptions, but would drastically improve the view.

(2) The unassuming center of **South Hero** lies four miles ahead at the intersection of Rte. 2 and South Street, marked on the left by an imposing early nineteenth-century stone structure,once an inn and now a bank branch. Turn left onto South Street, passing (on your right) a Congregational Church and cemetery, and keep an eye out (also on the right) for a curious little stone castle, about   four feet high, in a yard alongside a private home. The castle, which is one of several

on South Hero Island, was the handiwork of an early twentieth-century custodian for some of the island's summer homes.

Rich soil and the moderating effect of Lake Champlain on island temperatures make South Hero prime apple-growing country. In early autumn, you can pick your own apples at **Allenholm Farm** and **Hackett's Orchards**, both located along the right side of South Street. The two orchards are the centerpieces of South Hero's Applefest, held each year on a weekend in early October. Although the festival has in recent years gotten a little too heavy on the yard sales, it's still worth a visit if you can get there during the cider-pressing competition, or for the cricket match, featuring expert Jamaican cricketers. Their team is drawn from the hardworking migrant apple pickers who head north from their home island late every summer to help bring in South Hero's apple crop. They play the local Burlington cricket club, and invariably win.

About a mile past the orchards, take a right onto West Shore Rd. (If you continue to the end of South St. you'll reach a quiet residential neighborhood at the southern tip of South Hero Island. If all goes on schedule, beginning in spring 2004 you'll be able to go even farther on foot or by bicycle. Local Motion, which now operates the Winooski River Bike Ferry (see #3, 'Winooski River Bike Ferry', Drive 9) is planning to operate another ferry between here and Colchester. When that happens it will be possible to bike up to the islands from Burlington, via that city's bike path and the Colchester Causeway. Eventually, the planners hope, the causeway will be part of a bicycle route to Montreal.)

On West Shore Rd., just past Crescent Bay Farm, is another stone castle (the last we'll point out, so keep your eyes peeled), and **Snow Farm Vineyard and Winery**, an enterprise which has succeeded here because of the mild island temperatures that also benefit the apple orchards. If you're passing through on a Thursday in summer, pack a picnic and enjoy a concert on the lawn from 6 to 8 p.m. Beyond the winery, West Shore Rd. wanders north past some of South Hero's -- and Vermont's -- choicest real estate, where the views are sold by the foot and come with the opportunity to get very nervous when springtime lake levels react to a winter of heavy snows.

(3) At the **Grand Isle** town line, West Shore Rd. merges with Rte. 314 (as of this writing, there's no sign for Rte. 314). A right turn here will take you back to Rte. 2, on the island's east side. If you continue directly ahead (north), though, you'll soon reach the **Grand Isle - Plattsburgh Ferry** at Gordon Landing. This is the only one of the Lake Champlain ferries to follow an all-year schedule, and makes for a pleasant excuse to take a 20-minute lake cruise (each way) while surrounding yourself with mountain scenery: Adirondacks to the west, Green Mountains to the east.

Almost directly across from the dock, turn right onto Bell Hill Rd. to visit the **Ed Weed Fish Culture Station**, where a self-guided tour of the state-run facility shows how trout and salmon are raised to release size. You can even help raise them; alongside one of the raceways are vending machines that sell fish food.

The hatchery also has tanks with full-grown live specimens of native Vermont fish species, and information on perhaps the greatest threat currently faced by the Lake Champlain ecosystem -- the zebra mussel, a fingernail-sized freshwater mollusk released into the Great Lakes and St. Lawrence River system by foreign tankers disposing of their ballast water. The mussels have begun to encrust the lake bottom and everything on it, including a number of historic shipwrecks, and have even threatened the viability of the Ed Weed hatchery by clogging intake pipes. The hatchery was saved after installation of expensive measures for filtering out the mussels and their spawn, but only after several Vermont politicians argued that the less than ten-year-old facility might have to be closed.

To learn more about zebra mussels and the lake's ecology in general, visit the **Champlain Basin Program**. The Program's headquarters, in an 1824 stone house just past the entrance to the ferry, has information about the lake and its denizens.

(4) Continue north on Rte. 314, which soon veers to the right and leaves West Shore Rd. Within a mile it intersects with Rte. 2: turn left here. Continue north (the official designation of Rte. 2 is E-W, but you're heading north), past the right-turn entrance to **Grand Isle State Park** to the **Hyde Log Cabin**, on the right-hand side of the road.

Revolutionary War veteran Jedediah Hyde, Jr. built his 20' x 25' home out of locally-felled cedar in 1783. Often cited as the oldest surviving log cabin in the country, the doughty little structure contains furnishings and exhibits documenting everyday life on what was once New England's wild frontier.

Side Trip

At the northern tip of Grand Isle, turn right at the blinking yellow light across from a variety store onto East Shore Drive North and continue 7/10 mile, past the town beach, to the Grand Isle Lake House overlooking Pearl Bay. Built in 1903 as the Island Villa Hotel, the building was purchased in 1956 by The Sisters of Mercy for a girls' camp. The camp closed in 1993, and in 1997 the buildings and grounds were donated to the Preservation Trust of Vermont, which is restoring the property as a meeting and events facility. (There are 13 overnight guest rooms on the second floor.) Visitors are invited to tour the building as long as there is no function in progress and a caretaker is on the premises. If you're not planning to visit the Hyde Log Cabin (see above), after leaving the Lake House turn right and follow East Shore Drive as it loops around the "Inland Sea", past one of Vermont's few remaining round barns, and rejoins Rte. 2.

(5) The drawbridge that connects the two islands of South Hero and **North Hero** marks the spot where the British fleet anchored in October, 1776, prior to encountering four gunboats Benedict Arnold -- then still on the American side --dangled in front of them as bait to lure them toward Valcour Island, near the New York shore of Lake Champlain, where the American fleet was waiting in ambush.

After a night of furious battle, Arnold and a small contingent of ships once again lured the enemy away from the major part of the American fleet, allowing it to escape to Ticonderoga and thus delay the English advance for another year. When the British were about to overtake Arnold's retreating force, he ran his boats aground and burned them on the Vermont shore, rather than allow them to be captured (see

Drive #6). By surviving the battle, of course, Arnold lived to turn sides and become a synonym for treachery and treason.

Immediately after crossing the bridge onto North Hero Island, turn left for the entrance to **Knight Point State Park**. A day-use facility (no camping), Knight Point has a sandy beach, a boat rental, a picnic area with cooking grills, and foot trails that meander through meadow and forest comprising a designated State Natural Area. The park is located at the site of the original ferry crossing between North and South Hero islands. Operated by the Knight family for over a century, the ferries finally stopped running with the opening of the first bridge between the islands in 1892. The building that now serves as park headquarters is a vivid reminder of the old ferryboat days: the brick section dates to 1845, while the wooden addition is a reconstruction of Knight Tavern, a 1790 inn at which travelers would stop for a dram while waiting for the ferry.

Approximately a mile beyond the Knight Point entrance is the summer home of the **Royal Lipizzan Stallions**, where descendants of the noble white horses bred in Austria since the sixteenth century perform intricate dressage maneuvers for six weeks each summer. They're owned by Colonel Ottomar Herrmann, a former Austrian army officer, who traces his family's involvement in the training of Lipizzans to 1618, when one of his ancestors was presented with several of the animals by Hapsburg Emperor Ferdinand II. Although the Lipizzans only perform Thursday through Sunday from mid- July through August, guests are welcome to visit the horse barn free when the horses are not performing. Call the Lake Champlain Islands Chamber of Commerce for ticket information.

(6) The town of **North Hero**, on the eastern shore of North Hero Island, is the shire town of Grand Isle County and the islands' prettiest settlement. Don't be misled by the term "town" -- the main street is also the only street. Wooded points of land create a natural harbor, grandiosely and completely misleadingly called "City Bay," that cradles a small cluster of homes, businesses, and municipal buildings, most notably the stately Grand Isle County Courthouse, built in 1824 of marble quarried on nearby Isle La Motte. There are comfortable accommodations and a good restaurant at

the **North Hero House,** and canoes and kayaks for rent at **Hero's Welcome**, one of those omnium-gatherum Vermont emporia where you can buy bait and a decent Merlot. City Bay is a delightful place to paddle around -- you might even want to make your way around Hibbard Point to tiny Hen Island.

Follow Rte. 2 north beyond the narrow neck of land called the Carrying Place (the name harks back to Indian portages). (Bear right at the fork to visit **North Hero State Park**.) Continue across the drawbridge that spans Alburg Passage, a narrow channel of Lake Champlain that separates North Hero Island from the Alburg peninsula, which extends southward from the Canadian border and is at no point connected to the U.S. mainland.

(7) Turn left onto Rte. 129. Continue for approximately two miles, then bear left and follow Rte. 129 across La Motte Passage to reach the most remote and bucolic corner of the Lake Champlain archipelago, two-by-five-mile **Isle La Motte**. Just past the bridge, look left for a bit of history: a monument here commemorates the spot where two Green Mountain Boys, Seth Warner and Remember Baker, camped with

Side Trip

The 625-acre Alburg Dunes State Park, near the southern tip of the Alburg peninsula, is a little bit of Cape Cod in a Lake Champlain setting, with sand dunes created by centuries of erosion of glacially-deposited material, and the relentless action of the wind. The dunes comprise a barrier between the lakefront and an interior cedar swamp; within these shifting hillocks of sand are stands of rare Champlain beach grass and beach pea. Although the fragile dunes themselves are fenced off, the day-use-only park has a fine sandy swimming beach as well as bicycle and pedestrian paths. To reach the park, turn left at the State Park sign onto Rte. 129. Turn left again onto Rte. 129 Extension/Sand Beach Rd., and then onto Coon Point Rd. to the park entrance.

General Montgomery in 1775 on their way to attack Montreal. Follow signs (right) to **St. Anne's Shrine**, at the island's northwestern tip. The French, under the Sieur de la Motte and accompanied by a contingent of Jesuits, put ashore here in 1665 and built a fort as a defense against hostile Mohawk Indians, thus creating Vermont's first (if not permanent) European settlement. The priests celebrated the state's first Roman Catholic Mass here on July 26, 1666. (La Motte with his soldiers and Jesuits weren't the first whites to land here, however: on July 2 and 3, 1609, Samuel de Champlain and his party beached their canoes, hunted, and camped on this yet-unnamed island "three leagues long" in Champlain's eponymous lake.)

The St. Anne Shrine itself, maintained by the Edmundite fathers and brothers, features an outdoor pavilion and small indoor chapel where daily masses are celebrated, along with outdoor stations of the cross, a cafeteria, and a swimming beach with boat dock. Among the shrine's statuary are a 15-foot representation of Our Lady of Lourdes, exquisitely gilded through the bequest of an anonymous donor; and a statue of Champlain sculpted in the Vermont Pavilion of the 1967 World Exposition in Montreal by Vermont artist D.W. Webb. Candlelight processions are held here in summer; contact the Shrine for dates.

To make a short but interesting circuit of Isle La Motte, head south from the Shrine, keeping the lake on your right. The most enticing views are west across the water to the New York shore, but about two-thirds of the way south along the island, keep an eye out on the left for the stone ruins of the estate of one-time Vermont lieutenant governor Nelson Fisk. It was here, while attending a luncheon of the Vermont Fish and Game Club in September of 1901, that Vice-President Theodore Roosevelt learned that President William McKinley had been shot. Next door is **Fisk Farm**, a pleasant little bed-and-breakfast (open summer and fall) that offers art shows, concerts, and poetry readings in an old carriage barn, and Sunday afternoon tea on a lawn overlooking the lake.

Just past Fisk Farm (left) is the entrance to an abandoned quarry that recalls Isle La Motte's most famous industry, but is now better known as one of the world's most significant geological sites (see sidebar below). The island has long been known for its supply of a limestone that is almost but not quite marble, and in particular for a black variety of this stone available at only a few other sites on the globe. It's been used in the U.S. Capitol, in New York's Radio City Music Hall, and in Vermont's State Capitol.

Finish your Isle La Motte exploration by bearing left at the southern end of the island and heading north on The Main Road, which passes the Isle La Motte Historical Society (just beyond, in a field on the right, is another reef outcrop), and heads through the village with its handsome small library and two churches, all made of local stone. The Main Road soon rejoins Rte. 129.

(8) Retrace your route to return to Rte. 2 and continue north to **Alburg Center** and the junction with Rte. 78.

Turn right onto Rte. 78 and head west over the causeway, past the West Swanton Orchard/ Cider Mill, to the 6,000-acre Missisquoi National Wildlife Refuge, which includes much of the marshy estuary of the Missisquoi River as it empties into Lake

A close examination of the exposed rock surfaces in Isle La Motte's Fisk Quarry, and at several of the island's other exposed outcrops, reveals the fossils of prehistoric sea creatures. These animals, primitive bryozoa and stromatoporoids, once inhabited a warm tropical sea that covered Isle La Motte some 400 million years ago, when Vermont was located where Zimbabwe is now. They form part of what is considered the oldest fossil reef in the world -- a reef so old, in fact, that only the more recent of its petrified specimens can properly be called corals, which evolved long after the reef began to form. The reef crops up in several locations on Isle La Motte; this portion was threatened by a reopening of the old Fisk Quarry which was averted in 1998 when concerned citizens led an effort to buy the quarry from its would-be operators and set it aside under the auspices of a newly-formed Isle La Motte Reef Preservation Trust, which has installed walkways and interpretive signs at the old quarry.

Champlain's Missisquoi Bay. The refuge is a haven for waterfowl, ospreys, and other wildlife, and harbors a huge great blue heron rookery on Shad Island. In all, some 201 avian species have been identified on the 6,345-acre refuge since 1943. The refuge headquarters, located right on Rte. 78, can supply information, maps of foot trails and canoe routes ... and the occasional frog license. That's right. If you're visiting between July 15th and September 30th and have a hankering for frog's legs, you can harvest up to 12 tree leopard frogs a day without a permit along Rte. 78 and Mac's Bend Rd. (a permit costs $35).

(9) **Swanton**, a Missisquoi riverside city whose fortunes have ebbed and flowed over the years, served as a campsite for Native Americans as early as 6,000 B.C., and is thus Vermont's oldest community. The tribe later known as the St. Francis Indians lived in the area before the French arrived about 1700. Many of their descendants, grouped today under the tribal designation Abenaki, still reside here. The Abenaki Tribal Museum and Cultural Center exhibits tribal artifacts such as traditional garb, woven baskets, beadwork, and a birch bark canoe.

In 1835, a lead tube was found alongside the Missisquoi River. Inside was a document which read: "Nov. 29. A.D. 1564 -- This is the solme day I must now die this is the 90th day since we lef the Ship all have Parished and on the Banks of this River I die to farewell my future Posteritye know our end -- John Graye." A theory once held that this odd document was written by the last survivor of one of Martin Frobisher's sixteenth-century voyages, but it is now thought to have been a nineteenth-century hoax. The tube has long since disappeared, (it's rumored to be somewhere at the University of Vermont), but a copy of the document survives at the Highgate Historical Society museum, located on Rte. 78 in the nearby town of Highgate (open from 10 to 2 on the first and third Sunday of each month).

The swans in Swanton Park are descendants of Betty and Sam, who were given to the city by Queen Elizabeth in 1961.

In the cemetery just south of Swanton Park, look for the large monument with an angel bearing a cross. This is the burial place of Lieutenant Stephen F. Brown of the 17th Regiment of Vermont Volunteers, a Swanton native who, as the inscription tells it, arrived on the battlefield at Gettysburg without a sword, and wielded a hatchet during the defense of the Union position during Pickett's charge until he got hold of a Confederate sword. His statue adorns the regiment's memorial at Gettysburg.

They were flown here from Norfolk, England.

(10) Rte. 78 intersects with Rte. 7 in downtown Swanton. Finish your drive by heading south on Rte. 7 to **St. Albans**, settled by emigrants from Vermont's lower Connecticut Valley and formally organized as a town in 1788. Shortly after its incorporation, Ethan Allen's Tory brother, Levi, laid claim to so much of the town's land that he addressed his wife in a letter as "Duchess of St. Albans." When he could not validate his claims, he was forced to leave town.

St. Albans, now a city, is the creature of the Central Vermont Railway (now New England Central), which maintained extensive yards and shops here. The glory days of the iron horse in St. Albans are now commemorated by little more than an Amtrak stop (northern terminus of the *Vermonter* service from Washington, D.C.). But St. Albans remains a handsome old Victorian city, with most if not all of its brick downtown blocks rehabbed, and a stately row of civic buildings arrayed along Taylor Park. The Italianate Franklin County Courthouse and Richardson Romanesque public library are especially noteworthy, and the row also contains the **Franklin County Historical Society Museum**, which includes in its exhibits a fully-equipped turn-of-the-twentieth-century doctor's office and railroad memorabilia.

St. Albans earned its place in more than local history on October 19, 1864, when twenty-two Confederate soldiers staged the St. Albans Raid, the most northerly engagement of the Civil War. Dressed in civilian clothes, they simultaneously held up all of the banks in town and escaped to Canada with

$201,000, killing a man as they fled. They were caught and tried in Canada, but acquitted on the grounds that the raid had been a legitimate act of war. (Just to assuage strained cross-border feelings, though, Canada reimbursed the banks $50,000.) The raid had been meant to throw a scare into the north, but it backfired: Union Army enlistments increased. Each year, the raid is reenacted in Taylor Park.

St. Albans now seeks notoriety in different ways: in 1983, townspeople concocted a 26,000 lb. sundae, which made the Guinness Book of Records. It also cooked up the world's largest pancake, a 20- foot-wide flapjack that had to be flipped with a crane; and, in 1982, built a 48-foot snowman. You won't necessarily see any accomplishments on this heroic scale if you drop in at the annual Maple Festival, held in April, but you can try a plate of sugar on snow, made by pouring heated maple syrup onto snow (or shaved ice) so that it turns to a taffylike consistency. It's traditionally served with donuts and pickles. No fooling.

Information

Lake Champlain Islands Chamber of Commerce (800-262-5226 or 372-5683), 3537 US Rte. 2, P.O. Box 213, North Hero 05474. www.ChamplainIslands.com

St. Albans Chamber of Commerce (524-2444), 2 North Main Street, PO Box 327, St. Albans 05478. www.stalbanschamber.com

Swanton Chamber of Commerce (868-7200), P.O. Box 237, Swanton 05488. www.swantonchamber.com

Lodging

(6) Charlie's Northland Lodge (372-8822), Rte. 2, North Hero. Lakefront housekeeping cottages, rooms with shared bath in the 19th-century house, boat and motor rentals, fishing licenses and supplies. $-$$

(6) Shore Acres Inn and Restaurant (372-8722), Rte. 2, North Hero. 23 lakefront units; 4 in an annex without water views. Tennis courts, private beach. The motel is open early May-late Oct., the annex is open year-round. The lakefront restaurant ($$) serves breakfast and dinner, and lunch July and August. www.shoreacres.com $$-$$$

(6)(R) North Hero House Inn & Restaurant (888-525-3644 or 372-8237), Rte. 2, North Hero 05474. Many of the 24 rooms in the main inn and three annexes overlook the lake; all have private baths, phones, TVs and antiques (some have jacuzzi tubs and fireplaces). Cocktails are served in the fireplaced greenhouse; the colonial dining room ($$-$$$) serves Continental fare such as brandied lobster bisque, lobster shepherd's pie, and Dijon crusted rack of lamb. Lobster buffet Friday nights in season. Beach, sauna, lakeside hot tub and boat rental. www.northherohouse.com $$-$$$

(7) Fisk Farm (928-3364), West Shore Rd. (next to Fisk Quarry Preserve), Isle La Motte 05463. Two lakefront cottages: one built in 1800 with fireplace and full kitchen; the other with a lakefront balcony and light cooking facilities. Two rooms in the main house share a bath and lake views. $$

(7) (R) Ruthcliffe Lodge (800-769-8162 or 928-3200), Old Quarry Rd., Isle La Motte. 7 of the 9 motel units face the lake; the restaurant ($$) serves Italian fish and pasta specialties, as well as classics like rack of lamb in the informal dining room or on the deck. Homemade desserts. D mid-May-Columbus Day; L July and August. www.ruthcliffe.com $

(7) Terry Lodge (928-3264), 54 West Shore Rd., Isle La Motte 05463. Family-friendly accommodations include 7 rooms in the lodge (2 with private bath), and 4 motel units, most with lake view. Also, a housekeeping cottage and apartment. Family-style dinner available to guests (others by reservation). Private swimming beach, dock, and raft. Open May 15-mid-Oct. www.geocities.com/terry-lodge $$

(8) Ransom Bay Inn (800-729-3393), 4 Center Bay Rd., Alburg 05440. 4 pleasant guest rooms in an antiques-filled, 1795 one-time stagecoach stop just off Rte. 2. Dinner ($) by advance reservation. $$

(8) Thomas Mott Homestead B & B (800-348-0843 outside VT; 796-4402 in VT), 63 Blue Rock Rd., Alburg 05440. Four simple but clean guest rooms of varying sizes with private baths in an 1838 Shaker farmhouse overlooking Lake Champlain. Private dock and canoes. Kids 12+. www.thomas-mott-bb.com $$

(9) High Winds B & B (868-2521), Hog Island, Campbell Bay Rd., West Swanton 05488. 2 rooms with private bath in an 1800s farmhouse on a dairy farm overlooking the Missisquoi River. Canoes and boats. April-Nov. $

(10) Comfort Inn and Suites (800-228-5150 or 524-3300), 167 Fairfax Rd., St. Albans 05478. Just off I-89, the chain motel has 63 rooms and suites, an indoor pool and fitness room; continental breakfast. www.vtcomfortinn.com $-$$

Off the Drive

The Tyler Place Family Resort (868-4000), Rte. 7, Highgate Springs 05460. One of the country's oldest family resorts offers a full roster of activities for all, including private beach and boating on Lake Champlain. Late May-mid-Sept. www.tylerplace.com. $$$

Restaurants

(4) Margo's (372-6112), Rte. 2, Grand Isle. Bakery-cafe serves up tasty baked goods and sandwiches. $

(9) Sunset Restaurant, Motel & Cabins (527-7965), Rte. 7. Swanton. Traditional Yankee fare including

roast chicken and pot roast in a setting untouched by time. Daily specials. Limited seating. L, D Tues.-Sat. $

(10) Chow! Bella Cafe & Wine Bar (524-1405), 28 N. Main St., St. Albans. Intimate restaurant housed in an historic building serves fine Continental fare including creative pasta dishes and pizzas, sandwiches, salads, and seafood entrees. L, D Mon.-Sat. $-$$

(10) Jeff's Maine Seafood Market (524-6135), 65 N. Main St., St. Albans. Restaurant/market/deli serves creative seafood specialties, fabulous chowders, and a fair selection of meat entrees. L & D Mon.-Sat. $-$$

(10) Old Foundry Restaurant (524-9665), 3 Federal Street, St. Albans. Prime rib, steak, heaping plates of seafood, and a great salad bar. Victorian outdoor dining area. D Mon.-Sat. $$

Attractions

(1) Sand Bar State Park (393-2825), Rte. 2, South Hero. Late May-Labor Day. $

(3) Champlain Basin Program (800-468-5227), 54 West Shore Rd., Rte. 314, Grand Isle. Open weekdays.

(3) Ed Weed Fish Culture Station (372-3171), Bell Hill Rd., Grand Isle.

(3) Grand Isle-Plattsburgh Ferry (864-9804), Lake Champlain Ferries, Gordon Landing, Grand Isle. Fare.

(4) Grand Isle State Park (372-4300), Rte. 2, Grand Isle. Camping/facilities for campers. Late May-Columbus Day. $

(4) Hyde Log Cabin (372-5440), Rte. 2, Grand Isle. July 4 -Labor Day, Thurs.-Mon., 11 am-5 pm. $

(5) Knight Point State Park (372-8389), North Hero. Swimming, picnicking, boat rental. $

(5) Grand Isle Lake House (372-5024 or 865-2522), East Shore Drive North, Grand Isle.

(5) Royal Lippizan Stallions (372-8400), Rte. 2, North Hero. Mid-July - late Aug., Thurs. and Fri. at 6 P.M., Sat. and Sun. at 2:30 P.M. Children free Fri. night. $

(6) North Hero State Park (372-8727), 3803 Lakeview Drive, North Hero. 400 acres on the lake's northern tip. Campsites, swimming, rowboat and canoe rentals, and nature trails. Late May-Labor Day. $

(7) St. Anne's Shrine (928-3362), West Shore Rd., Isle La Motte. Mid-May-mid-Oct.

(8) Alburg Dunes State Park (796-4170), Alburg. One of the state's newest parks has a sandy beach and some fine examples of rare flora and fauna along the hiking trails. Late-May-Labor Day. $

(8) Missisquoi National Wildlife Refuge (868-4781), Rte. 78, Swanton.

(9) Abenaki Tribal Museum (868-2559), 100 Grand Ave., Swanton. Mon. - Fri. Donations.

(10) Burton Island State Park (524-6353), St. Albans Bay, St. Albans. 250-acre island accessible by shuttle (in season) or private boat from Kill Kare State Park. Camping, public launch, marina, beach, picnic area, and boat rental. Late May-Labor Day. $

(10) Franklin County Historical Society (527-7933), Taylor Park, St. Albans. June-early Oct., Tues.-Sat. 1-4. Donations.

(10) Kamp Kill Kare State Park (534-6021), Point Bliss Rd. (off Rte. 35), St. Albans Bay. Boat rental, small beach, dock, shuttle to Burton Island State Park. Late May-Labor Day. $

(10) Knight Island State Park (343-7236), St. Albans Bay, St. Albans. Primitive campsites and nature trails.

Accessible by boat from Burton Island State Park. For water taxi information: 372-6104). Late May-Labor Day. $

Activities and Shopping

Mountain Lake Expeditions (777-7646), 139 East Shore North, Grand Isle conducts half- and full-day kayak tours, and delivers kayak and bikes to locations throughout the islands.

(2) Allenholm Farm (372-5566), 111 South St, South Hero. July-Dec.

(2) (L) Apple Island Resort (372-3922 or 372-5398), Rte. 2, South Hero. Sailboat, rowboat, canoe, and motor boat rentals.

(2) Hackett's Orchard (372-4848), 86 South St., South Hero. Syrup, pies, cider donuts. July-Dec.

(2) South Wind Market (372-3721), Rte. 2, South Hero. Homemade goodies and soups, sandwiches, and a great wine selection. A few tables. B, L, seasonal D.

(2) Snow Farm Vineyard and Winery (372-9463), 190 West Shore Rd., South Hero. Tasting room and guided tours at 11 a.m. and 2 p.m. May-Oct.; self-guided tours year-round.

(4) Mountain Lake Expeditions (777-7646), Grand Isle. Kayak and bike tours and rentals. Inn-to-inn tours.

(5) Sea Trek Charters (372-5391), Tudhope Sailing Center, Grand Isle. 6-8 hour fishing and sightseeing trips aboard 25-foot Baha cruiser.

(6)(L) Charlie's Northland Lodge (372-8822), Rte. 2, North Hero. Canoe rental; fishing supplies and maps.

(6) Hero's Welcome (800-372-4376 or 372-4161).
Rte. 2, North Hero. Kayak, canoe and bicycle rentals.

(7) Bike Shed Rentals (928-3440), West Shore Rd.,
Isle La Motte. Mountain and tandem bikes, trailers,
helmets and maps. Open daily July/August/ weekends
June, Sept., and Oct.

(8)(L) Henry's Sportsman's Cottages (796-3616), 218
Poor Farm Rd., Alburg. Motor boat rentals.

(9) West Swanton Orchard & Cider Mill (868-7851),
Rte. 78, West Swanton. Working cider mill, pick-your-
own apples, fresh fruits and vegetables. June-Dec.

Drive 11

The Bridges of Lamoille County -- and Beyond

140 miles

This longest of our drives begins in the Winooski River valley, then swings north to the celebrated ski town of Stowe and the lofty, rugged passage through Smugglers' Notch. Between Waterville and Montgomery the drive takes in an even dozen examples of that most characteristic expression of Vermont folk engineering, the covered bridge, and then follows an eighteenth-century military road to the western fringes of the Northeast Kingdom. The route then turns due south by way of timeless Craftsbury Common and the sedate resort of Greensboro, returning to Montpelier via a landscape strewn with lakes.

(1) Begin in Montpelier (see Drive 7 for city tour and information). Head west out of the city on Rte. 2, which follows the course of the Winooski River. The Winooski -- the name means "Onion River" in Abenaki -- is one of three major streams flowing west through northern Vermont to empty into Lake Champlain. The others are the Lamoille and the Missisquoi, both farther north. All three rivers actually predate the Green Mountains. As the mountains rose, the rivers kept to their ancient courses, carving deep, fertile valleys across the range.

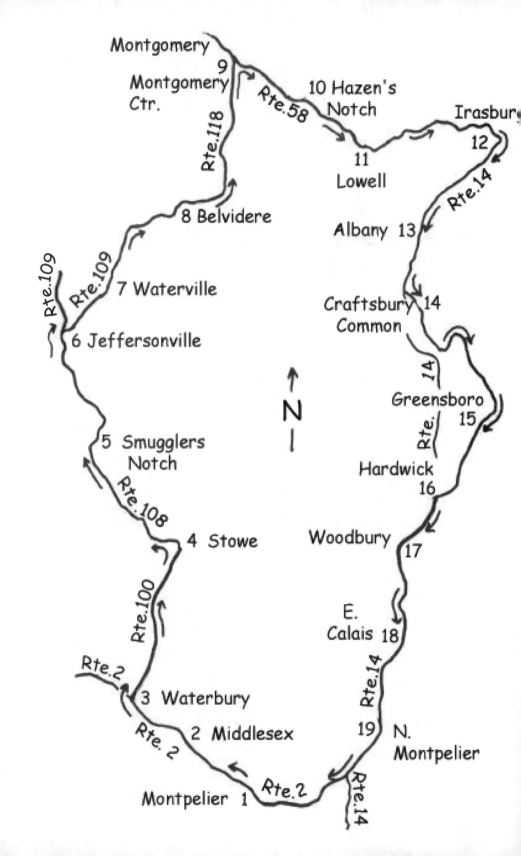

(2) Yes, that's an army tank you see up ahead as you pass through **Middlesex**. It's just one of the many military vehicles on display at **Camp Meade Victory Museum and Lodging**, whose exhibits focus on the events, sights and sounds of the Depression and World War II eras. Rides are given on the vehicles Saturdays from 10 A.M. to 3 P.M. The "canteen" is open daily, and the Sunday morning buffet, from 7 A.M. until noon, sure beats army food. Cabins are available for overnight stays, and you don't have to worry about pulling KP.

Camp Meade was built in the 1930s by the Civilian Conservation Corps (CCC), President Franklin D. Roosevelt's landmark effort to match unemployed urban youth with rural improvement projects. About 200 members of the corps lived here while they installed the rough stone embankments called "rip-rap" along the Winooski in Middlesex to prevent erosion of the riverbank and rich adjacent farmland. The Mad River, which you are not likely to encounter in anything like an angry state except during the weeks of spring snow melt, joins the Winooski here after flowing northeast from its source high in the Green Mountains. Local legend has it that Thomas Mead, the first Middlesex settler (1783), shot three black bears near here in one morning.

(3) Continue west on Rte. 2 to **Waterbury**, Vermont's "Recreation Crossroads," nestled between the Green Mountains and the Worcester Range. For many years the town was home to the sprawling Vermont State Hospital complex, mostly converted into state offices when the trend towards deinstitutionalization coincided with a need for space. Downtown Waterbury, somewhat overshadowed by the red brick campus, occupies a compact cluster of blocks recently enlivened by new pubs and restaurants -- after all, the slopes of Sugarbush and Mad River Glen are just a short hop down Rte. 100. There's also a little old-fashioned train station, which comes to life twice a day when Amtrak's *Vermonter* rumbles in. Just past the center of town, head north on Rte. 100. For the next ten miles, between here and Stowe, you'll be in tourist paradise: pick and choose your stops with care, if you hope to finish this drive before "snow flies," as they say hereabouts. (If it's already flown, you are probably headed for Stowe and aren't stopping anywhere.)

First up is **Ben & Jerry's Ice Cream Factory and Tour**. If you don't want to stop, make sure to cover the kids' eyes before they see the Disneyesque building flanked by a herd of ersatz cows. The wait for the tour -- and/or an ice cream cone -- can be interminable, because common consensus now has it that a trip to Vermont isn't complete without a stop to see the wonderful world built by two jolly sixties souls from Long Island who ... well, you'll hear it all on the tour. Suffice it to say that all this and a couple of other plants, along with hundreds of jobs and the utilization of a significant percentage of Vermont's dairy output, began with a hand-cranked ice cream machine in a barely-converted Burlington gas station less than thirty years ago. Tours (we've listed this below as an attraction, not a retail outlet) last 30 minutes, are given frequently, and, on Sunday, do not include a visit to the production line. The ice cream elves get a day of rest.

Also along this stretch of Rte. 100:
The **Cabot Annex Store**, which houses Green Mountain Chocolates, a Vermont Teddy Bear outlet, a Snow Farm Vineyard Tasting Room (see Drive 10), the Cabot Cheese Annex, Green Mountain Coffee Roasters, and several other retail operations; The **Vermont Clay Studio**, featuring fine ceramics by artists from around the country; and **Ziemke Glass Studio**. **Waterbury State Park** borders Waterbury Reservoir, Vermont's ninth largest body of water, created in the 1930s to control flooding along the Winooski River Valley. The water level has been lowered for dam repairs scheduled to be completed in 2005, but the park, on a 90-acre peninsula, is open to the public -- free of charge -- for picnicking. Up ahead at **Cold Hollow Cider Mill**, you can watch cider being made (and sample the finished product), and then stroll through the store which sells everything from smoked meats to maple syrup. Grand View Winery (see #18 below) has a tasting room here.

Roughly three miles north of Waterbury center, look to the northwest for your first glimpse of Mount Mansfield (4,393 ft.), Vermont's highest mountain. Mount Hunger (3,620 ft.), the highest peak in the Worcester Range, is to the east. **Green Mountain Club** Headquarters, on the left side of Rte. 100 about a mile past the cider mill, has maps, guidebooks, and the latest information on the Long Trail and other footpaths.

(4) Next to skiing, the one thing that probably has brought more visitors to Stowe than anything else is the story of a certain Austrian expatriate family with a talent for singing. To visit the **Trapp Family Lodge**, turn left across from the Burgundy Rose Motel onto Moscow Rd., past Little River Hotglass Studio, and follow the signs. Still owned by descendants of Baron and Baroness Georg and Maria von Trapp, heroes of *The Sound of Music*, the resort is a famous cross-country ski venue and a reminder that if you look in the right place, you can find a place that looks, well, sort of like home. Go for the views from the Tea Room terrace, which go down nicely with a glass of Austrian wine, a plate of wurst, and maybe a slice of Linzer torte *mit kaffe*, even if you aren't staying over or dining at the main lodge.

For decades, **Stowe** has been one of Vermont's premier destination resorts, a place synonymous with skiing in the Green Mountains. In 1914, a Dartmouth College librarian named Nathaniel Goodrich set tongues clucking in this quiet hill farm community by making the earliest recorded descent of Mt. Mansfield on skis. Within twenty years Civilian Conservation Corps (CCC) crews were cutting the mountain's first ski trails, precursors of the "Front Four" and other legendary runs at **Stowe Mountain Resort**, which sprawls across Mt. Mansfield and nearby Spruce Peak. But for all its winter sports fame, Stowe at heart is still a small town -- the cheery, busy village itself runs for only a few blocks, and most of the shopping, dining, and lodging (there are plenty of choices, but we're not talking Aspen or Gstaad here) are strung along the Mountain Rd. (Rte. 108), which leads north out of town to the narrow defile at the crest of Smugglers Notch and the ski resort of the same name on the other side.

For just taking in the scenery, you can't do better than to grab a bicycle, a pair of rollerblades, snowshoes, or just your walking shoes and take to the 5 1/2-mile **Stowe Recreation Path**, which begins right behind the sharp-spired Stowe Community Church and follows roughly the same route as the Mountain Rd. (there are a number of other access points along the way). Mt. Mansfield, always in view, looms sublimely above the valley floor through which the path meanders; from the right angle, you just might be able to make out the reclining human profile that the summit ridge is said to resemble, and which gave its peaks the names "Nose," "Chin," "Forehead," and "Adam's Apple." Among the Stowe Mountain Resort attractions accessible along the Mountain Rd. are the **Stowe Gondola**, a cable-suspended ski lift operating during summer and foliage season as well as in winter (the **Cliff House**, at the upper terminal, serves lunch); and the **Toll Road** for automobiles, which ends just under the Nose and doubles as a gentle ski trail in the winter. On Spruce Peak, opposite Mt. Mansfield, an **Alpine Slide** -- individual rider-controlled sleds on a concrete chute served by a chairlift -- proves that skiers don't have a monopoly on gravity-based thrills. There's also a skate park here.

Stowe is in Lamoille County, which has more covered bridges -- 14 -- than any other county in the state. We'll point out some of the more interesting in this chapter, but if you're an aficionado, be sure to get a copy of the Stowe-Smugglers' Notch Guide, which describes each of them. It's available at the Stowe Chamber of Commerce. or the Lamoille Valley Chamber of Commerce.

(5) Smugglers' Notch Scenic Highway in Smugglers' Notch State Park is one of Vermont's two official designated scenic routes (the other is the Middlebury Gap State Scenic Road; see Drive 6). Take the RV ban seriously: the road to the top is narrow and very steep, with fiddler's-elbow turns that graze gigantic boulders. The 2,162 foot summit is crowded on both sides by towering cliffs and dark, beetling ledges where reintroduced pairs of peregrine falcons nest. The Notch was used by smugglers during the War of 1812 when trade with Canada was forbidden; as an escape route to Canada for slaves during the days of the Underground Railroad; and by bootleggers smuggling liquor from Canada during Prohibition. One caveat: this is one of the state's major attractions, and traffic to the top on a fine summer day can be maddeningly slow. If you want to experience the Notch's grandeur in relative solitude, try to travel in the early morning or evening. Once the first snowfall arrives -- and until the drifts finally melt in early May -- you won't be traveling through the Notch at all. The road is simply too narrow and tortuous to plow.

Several popular hikes begin at the crest of the Notch, including one of our favorites, a short (1.2 mile) but strenuous climb to trout-stocked Sterling Pond, which is the highest significant body of water in the state. Continue past the pond for a short distance to the Sterling Mountain lookoff. Smuggler's Notch Resort, the Lamoille Valley, Jay Peak, and Canada (in exactly that order of distance) are all directly ahead to the north.

(6) Head down the north side of the notch on the flank of 3,640-foot Madonna Mountain, past Smugglers' Notch Resort. As you parallel the Brewster River, watch for the turnoff for Old North Road: here, at the junction, waterfalls plummet into Brewster River Gorge. A bit farther north, at the intersection of Canyon Road, the eighty-five-foot Grist Mill Covered Bridge, built in 1919, spans the river. **Smugglers Notch Canoe Touring**, at the Mannsview Inn next door to **Smugglers Notch Antique Center**, offers guided and self-guided canoe trips down the Lamoille River.

Continue into tiny **Jeffersonville**, a popular artists' retreat for more than fifty years. The **Mary & Alden Bryan Memorial Art Gallery** exhibits the works of more than 250

Side Trip

To view Moss Glen Falls, one of Vermont's highest waterfalls, head north through Stowe Village on Rte. 100 for approximately 3.2 mi. Turn right onto Randolph Rd., and then right onto Moss Glen Falls Rd. to the sign for the falls. Follow a short path to see cascades of water plummet more than 100 feet to a gorge below, creating a cooling, if shallow, swimming hole. (Don't confuse this site with the other Moss Glen Falls, off Rte. 100 in the town of Granville.) Another nice spot for a dip is Bingham Falls -- watch for a sign on the right side of the Mountain Rd., after the turnoff for the Trapp Family Lodge. A waterfall here, in the West Branch of the Waterbury River, cascades through a deep ravine: even if you don't want to swim, the scenery is worth the short (approximately one-third mile) trek down a well-worn dirt path.

regional artists throughout the season. At the intersection with Rte. 15, turn right (east) and continue a short distance to Rte. 108. Turn left onto 108 and cross the old steel truss bridge over the Lamoille River near a small streamside picnic and fishing access area. This bridge, which is scheduled for replacement in the near future (word has it it may be salvaged to carry a bike path across the Missisquoi River north of here) was built in 1931 to replace a wooden covered bridge, which burned when a farmer's cigarette ignited his horse-drawn load of hay. Continue a short distance to the intersection with Rte. 109. Turn right (north) onto Rte. 109 toward Waterville.

In all the world, there's only one Lamoille River. Must be a French word, right? Wrong. According to the most plausible theory, the name came about because of Samuel de Champlain's careless handwriting: on a map detailing his explorations, Champlain supposedly named the river La Mouette -- the Gull. But the father of New France forgot to cross his Ts, and his "e" looked like an "i." So Lamoille it is.

Just a few miles past the turn onto Rte. 109, watch for the large horse farm on the right. It's the home of Vermont HORSE, a retirement home/adoption agency for retired trotting horses.

(7) Continue north, past Miller's Family Farm and its summertime cornfield maze, to **Waterville**. The debate drags on as to whether Chester A. Arthur was born here in 1830. The nearby town of Fairfield also lays claim to the grandly whiskered twenty-first president, and boasts a replica of his boyhood home that is an official State Historic Site. But Watervilleans point to an old tradition that holds Chester was born in their town, and brought by his mother to Fairfield -- where his father was a preacher who had until recently served a Waterville congregation -- when the boy was but a few days old. The boy's birth, Waterville partisans say, was registered in the family's new home town.

Beyond dispute is the fact that Waterville has three covered bridges, all just off Rte. 109 and all spanning the North Branch of the Lamoille River. The Village Bridge (1887 or

1895, depending on your source) carries Church Street over the river; it's on the left just past Dan and Sheila's Country Store in the village center. The 1887 Montgomery Bridge is off to the right 1 1/5 mi. north of the center; and the c. 1877 Jaynes, or "Kissing" Bridge, also on the right, is approximately 1/2 mile past the Montgomery Bridge. Below each bridge is a popular swimming hole.

About four miles north of Waterville center, just after crossing a highway bridge at Belvidere Junction (note the 1851 church, on the right, now a community building), turn left onto a gravel road to reach the 1895 queenpost Mill Bridge, one of two in the town of Belvidere (both, like the Waterville bridges, cross the North Branch of the Lamoille). The foundations of two nineteenth-century mills that gave the bridge its name remain along the riverbank, and there are swift rapids below. Drive through the bridge and bear right onto Back Rd., keeping an eye out on the right for the 1887 Morgan Bridge. Drive through it back onto Rte. 109, turn left and continue north. (If you want to skip the bridges, just continue north on Rte. 109 from Waterville to Belvidere).

You're just a stone's throw from the "World's Best Maple Syrup," made at Waterville's Ledge Maple Farm. Sugarmakers Nelson and Pat Slack were awarded that title at the 1998 Maplerama, an annual Vermont contest. And at the 2001 Vermont Maple Festival in St. Albans, they took top honors (out of more than 190 entries) for their Vermont Grade A Dark Amber. Judges test syrup for density, color, clarity, and -- most important -- taste. The Slacks will be glad to give you a tour of their maple syrup operation if they're home (see "Activities" below).

In **Belvidere Center**, which lies just ahead beyond the cemetery and school, be sure to stop at the general store, one of the most authentic, least "cutesified" mercantile time capsules in New England. Here in downtown Belvidere, it's easy to recall that this stretch of Rte. 109 was the last portion of state highway in Vermont to be paved. That happened in 1981, and not everyone hereabouts was happy about it.

(8) Rte. 109 comes to an end at its intersection with Rte. 118 in Belvidere Corners. If you continue straight here onto 118, a drive of just a few hundred yards will take you past serene little Belvidere Pond, also called Long Pond, which -- along with its totally undeveloped shoreline -- has been acquired by the state and will be preserved as is. The road along the marshy area leading up to the pond is a good place to spot moose browsing for vegetation, especially around dusk -- and also a good place to cut your speed, since the moose is the giant sport utility vehicle of the deer family.

To the east of Rte. 109 as it passes through Waterville and Belvidere is 2,780-foot Laraway Mountain, scene of a tragic plane crash on September 18, 1991. A small cargo jet out of Monckton, New Brunswick plowed into the mountainside when the two-man crew lost track of their altitude and bearings during a storm. Both men were killed. Among the cargo was a shipment of iced lobsters, and the crash is still remembered as the day it rained lobsters in Belvidere.

Our drive calls for a left turn north onto Rte. 118, which passes through another marshy area that is notoriously "moosey," before climbing into higher terrain and approaching the town of Montgomery, through scenic, rolling farm country.

(9) The pretty little village of **Montgomery Center**, a gateway to the **Jay Peak Ski and Summer Resort** to the northeast, was declared a federal disaster area after the Trout River roared over its banks in the July flood of 1997. You'll see no sign of the damage today, other than the shiny new highway bridge that carries Rte. 118 into town. Its predecessor, also made of steel and concrete, was swept away in the flood. Fortunately, none of Montgomery's six wooden covered bridges sustained more than minor damage.

Montgomery and Northfield (see Drive 7) share the honor of each having more covered bridges than any other town in Vermont. Montgomery residents like to point out that they have the edge, because one of Northfield's spans is a tiny, private, pedestrians-only affair; and say that a seventh "Montgomery" bridge, just over the line in Enosburg, should be counted because it was built by the same Montgomery builders who erected all the others in town. All of the Montgomery spans were built between 1863 and 1883 by the Jewett brothers, who favored a design called the "Town lattice" after its originator, Connecticut architect Ithiel Town. You have to look inside a Town lattice bridge to see the genius of its engineering. Beneath the outer sheathing on each side is a frame that resembles a trellis, or a lattice pie crust. Pegged at their intersections and where they meet with the top and bottom horizontal timbers, the lattice frames provide tremendous structural support.

Stop at the Town Clerk's office or at **Kilgore's Store** (opposite each other on the main drag in Montgomery Center) for a map showing the locations of Montgomery's covered bridges -- none are exactly on our route, but all (except one) are within a short drive and several are just a quick turnoff from the main road. Several have nice swimming holes, and the Trout River got its name for a reason. The most picturesque swimming spot is just below Crystal Falls, near the almost spookily remote Creamery Bridge.

From Montgomery Center, backtrack on Rte. 118 over the new bridge that brought you into town, then turn left onto Rte. 58, the Hazen's Notch Road. The road soon changes to dirt (in winter it's open only as far as the cross-country ski places mentioned below) and begins to climb. Be sure to watch to the left for spectacular views of Jay Peak.

Side Trip

Jay Peak Ski and Summer Resort's Gondola is a great ride, popular with mountain bikers in summer as well as with winter's ski crowd. To get to the resort access road, take Rte. 242 east out of Montgomery Center.

On the right is **Hazen's Notch Association and Outdoor Education Center**. The center's owners, Sharon and Rolf Anderson, run ecology, nature, and wilderness summer camps for kids, and also open their thirty miles of trails to the public for hiking (and, in the winter, cross-country skiing and snowshoeing). Just up the road is Hazen's Notch

B & B and Cross-Country Ski and Hiking Center, a small, cozy and secluded lodging place that offers cross-country ski and snowshoe rentals and trails.

> Rte. 58 between Montgomery Center and Lowell is the northernmost portion of the Bayley-Hazen Rd. (see Drive 8), built as part of a planned invasion of Canada during the Revolutionary War. The fact that it doesn't extend all the way to the border -- which is a scant ten mi. from here -- is allegedly due to its planners' realization that if it could be used by Americans to invade Canada, it could be ... you fill in the rest.

(10) Near the height-of-land where a historic marker announces that this is the northernmost point of the Bayley-Hazen Road, the Long Trail crosses Rte. 58 on its way between Haystack and Sugarloaf mountains. At 1,790 feet, this narrow, steep-walled gap is a low point along this particularly grueling section of the trail. Northbound hikers have just descended more than 1,400 feet into the notch, and now have to ascend over 600 feet to get out of it: the Long Trail's designers had a diabolical sense of humor. Surrounding the road-trail intersection is the 197-acre **Hazens Notch Natural Area**. Rare alpine plants grow on the mountain cliffs, which are a popular spot for nesting peregrine falcons. Rock climbing is not permitted.

(11) The road turns to pavement as you approach the quiet hill town of **Lowell**, whose population swelled when French Canadians came south during the early twentieth century to work in the asbestos mines on nearby Belvidere Mountain. The mines operated round the clock six days a week, at one time producing enough raw ore to yield 50,000 tons of asbestos fiber each year. But business tapered off when the extreme respiratory hazards of asbestos fibers were discovered, and the mines were closed by the early 1990s. Lowell today is about as sleepy as a village can get, and passersby wonder when if ever anyone is going to put on a concert in that forlorn little bandstand on the town green, where Rte. 58 meets Rte. 100.

Cross Rte. 100 and continue east on Rte. 58. Between here and Irasburg lie some of the most magnificent vistas in Vermont. Looking to the north (on your left) across open meadowland, you've got a clear line of sight towards Jay Peak. That beaky little protrusion at the summit is the station for the gondola ski lift; if you look carefully enough on a clear day, you can see the cable that carries the cars across the gap between the summit and a lower spur of the mountain.

(12) **Irasburg**, on a plateau above the Black River Valley, was named for Ethan Allen's brother Ira (see Drive 9). It was the birthplace of America's first impressionist painter, Theodore Robinson, who was a great friend of Monet. Today it's home to one of Vermont's finest writers, Howard Frank Mosher (*A Stranger in the Kingdom* and *Where the Rivers Flow North*, both of which have been made into films; *Northern Borders*). Mosher makes poignant and effective use of his Northeast Kingdom locales; he's one of those authors who evokes a spirit of place so strong that neither he nor his characters can be imagined inhabiting any other landscape.

(13) At the broad town green, turn south onto Rte. 14 and follow the Black River through **Albany**, gateway to a collection of hamlets (East Albany, South Albany ...) strung along a nest of dirt roads that is consistently the most confusing in the state. But they also offer some of the most rewarding views -- at places, of Mt. Mansfield to the south -- so if you have a Vermont atlas, a compass, and a lunch, plunge right in. Don't call us if you get lost.

(14) Approximately three miles south of Albany, turn left onto Lackey Rd. and follow signs to **Craftsbury Common**, considered by many seasoned Vermont travelers to be the loveliest village in the state. In 1788, Ebenezer Crafts, Yale graduate and Revolutionary War officer, sold his tavern (the present-day Publick House) in Sturbridge, Massachusetts to pay off war debts, and traveled north, up the Bayley-Hazen Road, to settle here. His son, Samuel, who served as town clerk for thirty-seven years and as governor of Vermont for two terms, founded Craftsbury Academy, which served for many years as the town's public high school. The Reverend Samuel Read Hall (see Drive 14) served as headmaster here.

Craftsbury Common is a perfect exemplar of the old realtor's mantra: location, location, location. The village rambles along a ridge, with views in nearly every direction; unlike valley towns, with their utilitarian tethers to rivers, roads, and rails, this community seems serenely disconnected from the world down below, and likely to float off like a cloud to some part of the Northeast Kingdom that hasn't been discovered yet.

As the home of Sterling College, which specializes in environmental studies, Craftsbury may well be Vermont's smallest college town. It is also a part of Vermont's Hollywood connection: Alfred Hitchcock's 1955 *The Trouble with Harry* -- Shirley MacLaine's first movie, at least in this life -- was filmed here. Rounding out the town's string of unusual associations is the presence of the **Craftsbury Outdoor Center**, a mecca for cross-country skiers, mountain bikers, and scullers. The Center, a year-round resort (see 'Lodging' below) has served as a training facility for Olympic sculling teams, who, like lesser amateurs, enjoy rowing the glassy waters of long, narrow Great Hosmer Pond.

(15)   Less than a mile south of Craftsbury Village, home to two fine country stores, turn left onto East Craftsbury Rd. and continue through East Craftsbury toward Greensboro. After winding for several miles through the woods, you'll reenter civilization at the inviting **Highland Lodge**, with Caspian Lake, elevation 1,404 feet, below on the right. Continue into **Greensboro**, a genteel little resort village located right on the lake. A century ago, Greensboro and its lakeside environs were a getaway favored by families from the Barre-Montpelier area. It later began to attract an academic, literary and professional set, including the late authors John Gunther and Wallace Stegner, and U.S. Supreme Court Chief Justice William Rehnquist. One of the few show-biz types to ever show up here was Greta Garbo, who spent part of a summer with friends. Introduced around Greensboro under an assumed name, the star was finally able to be alone -- although at a local dance, she met a man who told the not-quite-young Garbo that she "must have been a handsome woman in her day."

To take a dip in Caspian Lake without having to plunk down for real estate, turn right just past a shop called **The Miller's**

Thumb (well worth a browse; the Italian pottery is gorgeous) to the town beach. At **Barr Hill Nature Preserve**, a Nature Conservancy property tended by students and staff of Sterling College, two loop trails (one 2/3 mile; the other 1/3 mile) reward hikers with spectacular panoramic views. To get there, turn right at the Town Hall and then left at 6/10 of a mile at the first fork. After passing several dairy farms and a B & B, enter what appears to be a barnyard driveway. Stop, open and close the gate at the George Hill Farm, and watch for the Conservancy sign; proceed another 6/10 of a mile to the parking area.

If you want a tasty souvenir, pick up some of Alice Perron's critically-acclaimed (*New York Times, Yankee, Vermont Life*) tea cakes at Willey's or the **Lakeview Inn**'s gift shop. The Greensboro baker has been baking her mail-order Bien Fait Fruitcakes in her home for five years; the tea cakes are a smaller version of the holiday treat.

The heart of Greensboro is the 200-plus-year-old Willey's Store, a rambling affair that subscribes to the everything-from-salsa-to-balsa school. What they don't have, you don't need. Patrons hate to see any changes: when the owners piped in music, they received phone calls asking at what times the music would not be playing, so shopping trips could be planned accordingly (the system has been removed). On the other end of the scale, Willey's had to remove a wine cooling/soft drink tub from the front of the store when one of the locals began using it to cool his feet on hot days.

(16) Continue straight through town, past the historic Lakeview Inn and down Center Road, which makes a southeasterly beeline through pleasant countryside into **Hardwick**. Entering downtown Hardwick, turn left onto Main Street at the Jeudevine Memorial Library, a Richardson Romanesque gem. The library is brownstone, but in the early 1900s, Hardwick was a granite center nearly on a footing with Barre, its neighbor to the south. Woodbury Mountain to the southwest had one of world's largest granite deposits, and miners flocked to Hardwick from around the country and the world.

But when the men who ran Woodbury Granite Company died, the business died, too, along with the town's prosperity.

Hardwick has since had a tough row to hoe -- a decade ago, a fire leveled downtown's most prominent block -- but its citizens have fought back gamely and the town center is a busy, lively place. There's a small independent bookstore, the **Galaxy Bookshop**, and several restaurants. On a more offbeat note, check out the ancient suspension footbridge that crosses the Lamoille River just off Main Street.

(17) Head south out of Hardwick on Rte. 14. To the west is 2,483-foot Woodbury Mountain, where all that granite came from. The first town along the heavily wooded road is **Woodbury**, which encompasses a total of twenty-eight bodies of water. These include eighty-three-acre Greenwood Lake, popular among anglers seeking brown and rainbow trout, as well as the charmingly named Mud Ponds #1 and #2.

(18) For fresh-picked fruit and homemade treats, stop in at family-owned **Legare Farm Stand** in **East Calais**. If your taste runs more to the grape, turn left off Rte. 14 just past the farm stand onto Max Gray Rd., and continue for two miles to **Grand View Winery**. Owner Phil Tonks makes Vermont country wines, fruit and organic wines and hard cider. Take a tour, visit the learning center and tasting room, and enjoy spectacular views of the Worcester Range, Camel's Hump and Sugarbush.

(19)   At seventy-two acres, North Montpelier Pond in **North Montpelier** is really a small lake. Whatever its classification, it's a good place to fish for largemouth bass, yellow perch, bullhead, and chain pickerel.

At the junction of Rte. 14 and Rte. 2, take Rte. 2 west and follow the Winooski River back to Montpelier. If you've time for one more stop, and room for one more piece of maple candy, stop at **Danforth's Sugarhouse**: they have an excellent video on the sugarmaking process and lots of equipment on display.

Information

Green Mountain Club (244-7037), Rte. 100, Waterbury Center 05766. www.greenmountainclub.org

Hardwick Area Chamber of Commerce (472-5906), P.O. Box 111, Hardwick 05843. Information booth on Rte. 14 open late May-Labor Day weekend. www.hardwickvtarea.com

Jay Peak Area Association (800-882-7460 or 988-2259), P.O.Box 177, Troy 05868. www.jaypeakvermont.org

Lamoille Valley Chamber of Commerce (800-849-9985 or 888-7607), 43 Portland St., P.O. Box 445, Morrisville 05661. www.stowesmugglers.org

Smugglers' Notch Area Chamber of Commerce (644-2239), 1073 Junction Hill, Jeffersonville 05464. www.smugnotch.com

Stowe Area Association (877-603-8693 or 253-7321), P.O. Box 1320, Main St., Stowe 05672. www.gostowe.com

Waterbury Tourism Council (800-684-8210), P.O. Box 468, Waterbury 05676. www.waterbury.org

Lodging

(2) Camp Meade Cottages & Museum & Lodging (223-5537), Rte. 2, Middlesex. www.campmeade.com $-$$

(3) 1836 Cabins (244-8533) Box 128T, off Rte. 100, Waterbury Center 05677. Secluded, modern housekeeping cabins (some with fireplaces) which sleep 2-6, set in the woods on 200 acres in back of the Green Mountain Club. www.1836cabins.com $$

(3) Old Stagecoach Inn (800-262-2206 or 244-5056), 18 N. Main St., Waterbury 05676. Renovated 1826

stagecoach stop has 8 comfortable guestrooms (2 with shared bath), and 3 apartments perfect for kids and pets; library bar. www.oldstagecoach.co $-$$$

(3) Thatcher Brook Inn (800-292-5911 or 244-5911), Rte. 100 N, Waterbury 05676. 22 well-appointed rooms (some fireplaces and jacuzzis) in c. 1899 Victorian inn close to I-89. Candlelight dining. www.thatcherbrook.com $$-$$$

(4) The Burgundy Rose Motor Inn (800-989-7768 or 253-7768), Rte. 100, Stowe 05672. Clean, comfortable 2-floor, 12-unit motel set well off the highway. Efficiencies. Continental breakfast. Pool. $

(4) Green Mountain Inn (800-253-7302 or 253-7301), 18 Main St., Stowe 05672. Historic 1833 inn in the village has 100 rooms and suites, many with canopy beds, fireplaces and jacuzzis. Year-round outdoor pool and health club; two restaurants. www.greenmountaininn.com $$-$$$

(4) The Inn at Turner Mill (800-992-0016 or 253-2062), 56 Turner Mill Lane, Stowe 05672. 10-acre complex close to Mt. Mansfield has 4 rooms and 4 1- or 2-bedroom suites with kitchens. Some fireplaces. Swimming hole, pool, snowshoe rental, xc trails. Breakfast summer & fall $-$$$

(4) Stone Hill Inn (253-6282), 89 Houston Farm Rd., Stowe 05672. One of the area's newest lodgings, set well off the Mountain Rd., offers 9 beautifully-furnished rooms with fireside bedrooms and baths, and two-person jacuzzis. Lovely landscaped grounds. www.stonehillinn.com $$$

(4)(R) Edson Hill Manor (800-621-0284 or 253-7371), 1500 Edson Hill Rd., Stowe 05672. One of Stowe's finest inns/restaurants has 9 rooms -- most with fireplaces -- in the main building, and 4 carriage houses with 3-4 fireplaced units. American cuisine, served in a dining room ($$-$$$) resembling a trellised garden, includes appetizers such as smoked duck French toast, and entrees including seared rare tuna loin and pan broiled duck breast. Stable, trout pond, xc skiing. www.stowevt.com $$-$$$

(4)(R) Topnotch at Stowe Resort & Spa (800-451-8686 or 253-8585), 4000 Mountain Rd., Stowe 05672. A 23,000 sq. ft. spa, year-round tennis, a highly-rated restaurant, and an assortment of accommodations make this plush resort on 120 acres a popular retreat. Year-round tennis. Two restaurants, including Maxwell's, serving appetizers such as seared foie gras, and entrees including pepper crusted loin of venison and Diver sea scallops with Asian vegetables. A 4-course prix fixe menu is offered for $38. www.topnotch-resort.com $$$

(4)(R) Trapp Family Lodge (800-826-7000 or 253-8511), Luce Hill Rd., Stowe 05672. 116 rooms at this 2,800-acre resort offer a variety of lodging options. The main dining room ($$-$$$) serves European-style cuisine, with entrees such as wiener schnitzel and mustard-glazed salmon, and offers 3 & 5 course prix fixe options. Extensive trail network, tennis courts, indoor pool, and sports center. Children's programs. www.trappfamily.com $$-$$$

(6) Mannsview Inn (888-937-6266 or 644-8321), 916 Rte. 108, Jeffersonville. 6 lovely rooms (2 share bath) in a Victorian overlooking the mountains. Outdoor spa, horseback riding. The owners also operate Smugglers Notch Canoe Touring(see below) and offer packages. www.mannsview.com $$-$$$

(6) Smugglers' Notch Resort (800-451-8752 or 644-8851), Rte. 108, Smugglers' Notch 05464. Self-contained ski/summer resort village consistently wins top ranking for family programs. Restaurants, pools, water slides, tennis school/courts, canoe and fishing trips. www.smuggs.com $$-$$$

(6) Sterling Ridge Suites & Cabins (800-347-8266 or 644-8265), 1073 Junction Hill Rd., Jeffersonville 05464. Inn on 80 acres overlooking the mountains has

8 guest rooms (4 with private bath) and 8 1- 2-and 3-bedroom housekeeping log cabins with fireplaces. Hot tub, outdoor pool, canoes and mountain bikes. www.vermont-cabins.com $-$$$

(9)(R) Black Lantern Inn (800-255-8661 or 326-4507), Rte.118, Montgomery 05470. 1803 National Historic Register inn has 8 antiques-filled guest rooms, and 7 1- and 3-bedroom suites with fireplaces, whirlpool tubs, and queen beds. The candlelit restaurant ($$) serves entrees such as Black Angus filet mignon stuffed with chevre and roasted shallots, and duck with dried cherry and bourbon sauce. www.blacklantern.com $$

(9) The Inn on Trout River (800-338-7049 or 326-4391), 241 Main St., Montgomery Center 05471. 100+-year-old lumber baron's estate on the banks of the Trout River has 10 guest rooms and 1 suite. Outdoor sauna. Restaurant specializes in heart healthy dishes. www.troutinn.com $$

(10) Hazen's Notch B & B and Cross-Country Ski & Hiking Center (326-4708), Rte. 58, Montgomery Center 05471. 3 cozy guest rooms (one with private bath) in a small farmhouse overlooking the mountains. $

(13)(R) Village House Inn (755-6722), Rte. 14, Albany 05820. 8 charming guest rooms in a lovingly-restored village Victorian. The dining room ($$), with porch seating, offers specialties such as Cajun chicken and veal Oscar. Desserts are homemade. D Fri. & Sat. $-$$

(14) Craftsbury B & B (586-2206), Craftsbury Common 05827. 1860s farmhouse has 6 guest rooms with shared baths, and a warm, inviting atmosphere that makes families feel right at home. The property abuts that of the Craftsbury Outdoor Center. www.scenesofvermont.com/craftsburybb $

(14) Craftsbury Outdoor Center (800-729-7751 or 586-7767), Box 31, Craftsbury Common 05827. 140-

acre resort offers a variety of lodging options and outdoor activities; private beach, rowing, canoeing. FAP. www.craftsbury.com

(14)(R) The Inn on the Common (800-521-2233 or 586-9619), Craftsbury Common 05827. Elegant accommodations in 3 buildings (some with fireplaces and canopy beds). Cocktails at 7:00, and 5-course, candlelight dinners (with an excellent wine list), with entrees such as sauteed breast of duck or oven roasted rack of lamb (non-guests: $40 prix fixe). Solar heated pool, and tennis court. Pets welcome with prior notice. www.innonthecommon.com $$$

(15) Highland Lodge (533-2647), Caspian Lake, Greensboro 05841. 1860s inn overlooking the lake has 11 rooms and 11 cottages (4 open in winter). Comfortable common rooms; restaurant, beach, boats, trails. Summer programs for kids. Open late May-mid-Oct. and mid- Dec.- mid-March. MAP. www.highlandlodge.com $$$

(15) Lakeview Inn B & B (533-2291), Main St., Greensboro. The inn, first opened as a boarding house in 1872, has been completely restored with 12 antiques-filled guest rooms. Screened porch overlooks mountains. www.hcr.net/lakeview $$

(16) Brick House Guests (472-5512), Box 128, Brick House Rd., East Hardwick 05836. 1840 Victorian nestled amid an extensive herb and flower nursery (see Activities below) has 1 guest room and 1 apartment that sleeps 3-4 and overlooks the gardens. www.antiqueplants.com $$

(17) Kahagon (472-6446), Nichols Pond Rd., Woodbury 05843. This 300-acre retreat that bills itself as "The Secret Place" truly is. There are 3 rooms with shared bath in the 1870s farmhouse and 7 modern lakefront housekeeping lodges that sleep 2-10. Dinner is served Thurs. -Sat. Canoes, windsurfers and rowboats, and a stable near by. $-$$

Restaurants

(3) Michael's on the Hill (244-7476), 4182 Stowe-Waterbury Rd., Waterbury. Fine Swiss cuisine in an 1820 farmhouse, with Swiss-born chef Michael turning out dishes such as a Gouda cheese tart appetizer, and entrees such as skillet chicken with buttermilk Vidalia onion rings or "Michael's veal" with mushrooms and a white wine cream sauce. D, closed Tues. $$$

(3) Mist Grill (244-2233), 95 Stowe St., Waterbury. Housed in an 1807 gristmill, the bistro has quickly become "the" place for homemade breakfast goodies, creative luncheon fare, and solid, New England comfort food at dinner. Sun. night supper, with a choice of 4 entrees, is served family style. Closed Mon. $-$$

(4) Blue Moon Cafe (253-7006), 35 School St., Stowe. Contemporary American dishes inspired by Asia, the Mediterranean and South America are elegantly served in a bistro environment. Appetizers include Maine crab cakes and vegetable nori rolls; entrees might include braised local rabbit or pepper seared yellowfin tuna wit caramelized shallots. D. $$-$$$

(4) Chelsea Grill (253-3075), Mountain Rd., Stowe. One of the town's hottest new restaurants serves "refined country comfort foods," with dishes such as butternut squash ravioli and grilled rack of lamb with roasted peppers and goat cheese. Extensive wine list. L Fri.-Sun., D nightly. $$

(4) Cliff House (253-3500), summit of Mount Mansfield. Salads, stews, crepes, sandwiches, and a cheese-lover's "Mountain foundue experience." You can buy a one-way ticket and walk off your meal if you wish. Early July - mid-Oct., 11-3. $-$$

(6) Jana's Cupboard (644-5454), junction of rtes. 15 and 108, Jeffersonville. Good burgers, homemade soups and breads, daily specials, and huge cremees. Outdoor deck. B on weekends, L, D . $

(9) The Belfry (326-4400), Rte. 242, Montgomery-Jay Peak. Popular with the apres-ski crowd, this is the place for grilled lamb chops and steaks, salads, burgers, and live music. No reservations; you might have to wait. D. $-$$

Attractions

(2) Camp Meade Victory Museum and Lodging (223-5537), Rte. 2, Middlesex. $

(3) Ben & Jerry's Ice Cream (244-8687), Rte. 100, Waterbury. Tours, tastings, and a gift shop. Adm.

(3) Cold Hollow Cider Mill (800-327-7537), Rte. 100, Waterbury Center.

(3) Waterbury Center State Park (244-1226), Old River Rd., Waterbury.

(4) Stowe Mountain Resort (253-3000), Mountain Rd., Stowe: Alpine Slide and Skate Park, Mid-June-Labor Day, daily, after Labor Day-Columbus Day, weekends; The Gondola, mid-June-mid-Oct.; the Toll Road, mid-May-mid-Oct.

(4) Smugglers' Notch State Park Campground (253-4014), 7248 Mountain Rd., Stowe. CCC-built campground at the base of Mt. Mansfield. $

(4) Vermont Ski Museum (253-9911), 1 S. Main St., Stowe. Ski technology and history, period clothing, local history, and special exhibits. Closed Tues. $

(6) Mary & Alden Bryan Memorial Art Gallery (644-5100), Main St., Jeffersonville. May-Oct. Donations.

(9) Jay Peak Ski and Summer Resort (800-451-4449 outside Vt; 988-2611), Rte. 242, Jay. Gondola rides; mountain bike park. $

(10) Hazen's Notch Association and Outdoor Education Center (326-4789), Rte. 58, Montgomery Center.

(10) Hazen's Notch Natural Area (241-3693), Rte. 58, Montgomery Center.

(15) Barr Hill Nature Preserve (229-4425), Greensboro. Property of The Nature Conservancy of Vermont, 27 State St., Montpelier.

Activities and Shopping

(3) Cabot Annex Store (244-6334), 2653 Waterbury-Stowe Rd., Rte. 100, Waterbury. Vt. wines, microbrews, specialty foods, and lots of samples.

(3) Vermont Clay Studio & Gallery (244-1126), Rte. 100, Waterbury Center.

(3) Ziemke Glass Blowing Studio (244-6126), Rte. 100, Waterbury Center.

(4) The Fly Rod Shop (800-535-9763), Rte. 100S, Stowe. Free fishing maps and lessons (Wed. afternoon and Sat. morning), fly rod and reel rental, fishing and hunting licenses; guide service.

(4) Little River Hotglass Studio (253-0889), 593 Moscow Rd., Moscow. Original pieces by Michael Trimpol include perfume bottles and paperweights. Thurs.-Mon.

(4) Moscow Tea House (253-2955), Moscow Rd., Moscow, serves tea and pastries Thurs.-Sun. noon-5.

(4) Mountain Sports and Bike Shop (800-682-4534 or 253-7919), Mountain Rd., Stowe. Mountain bike, in-line skate, and baby jogger rentals; river trips.

(4) Peterson Brook Farm (253-9052), Edson Hill Rd., Stowe. Guided trail rides for all abilities.

(4) Stowe Soaring/Whitcomb Aviation (1-800-898-7845), Rte. 100, Morrisville. Glider and airplane rides.

(4) Topnotch Stables (253-8585), Rte. 108, across from Topnotch Resort, Stowe. Carriage and trail rides.

(4) Umiak Outfitters (253-2317), Rte. 100, Lower Village, Stowe.   Kayaks and canoe sales and rentals; sea kayaking instruction; guided river trips.

(6) Green River Canoe (644-8336), Rt. 15 (in back of Jana's Restaurant), Jeffersonville. Canoe rental/ shuttle on the Lamoille River.

(6) Northern Vermont Llama Treks (644-2257). Treks from Smuggler's Notch Resort into the surrounding hills. Lunch provided.

(6) 1829 House Antiques (644-2912), Rte.15 E, Jeffersonville. 35+ dealers display their wares on two floors of rambling old barn.

(6)(L) Smugglers Notch Canoe Touring at the Mannsview Inn (800-937-6266), Rte. 108, Jeffersonville. Guided and self-guided trips on the Lamoille River.

(6) Smugglers' Notch Antique Center (644-8321), Rte. 108 (next to the Mannsview Inn), Jeffersonville. 30+ dealers. May 1 - Oct., daily; weekends Nov. - April.

(6) Vermont Horse Park (644-5347), Rte.108 (across from Smugglers' Notch Resort) Smugglers' Notch. Guided trail and pony rides. Hay and sleigh rides.

(7) A Clever Twist (644-2844), Lapland Rd., Waterville. Hidden treasure of a shop jam-packed with antiques, gift baskets and collectibles.

(7) Miller's Family Farm, Rte. 109, Jeffersonville. Corn maze, fishing, farm tours.

(7) Ledge Maple Farm (644-5404), Nelson and Patricia Slack, Waterville.

(R) Kilgore's Store (326-3058), Main St., Montgomery Center. Old-time soda fountain, homemade soups and sandwiches, picnic supplies, crafts, and antiques.

(14) Catamount Boat Rentals (586-6942 or 586-7542). 16 ft. aqua patio pontoon boats, 14 ft. Smoker Craft salmon boats, canoes and kayaks.

(14) Music Box (586-7533), 147 Creek Rd., Craftsbury. Live music includes picking, traditional songs and dulcimer.

(14)(L) Craftsbury Outdoor Center (800-729-7751 or 586-7767), Box 31, Craftsbury Common 05827.

(15) The Miller's Thumb (800-680-7886 or 533-2960), 4 Main St., Greensboro. Antiques, Italian pottery, Vermont crafts, furniture, and clothing in historic grist mill overlooking Caspian Brook.

(15)(L) Vermont Daylilies (533-7155), Barr Hill Rd., Greensboro. More than 400 varieties of field grown daylilies; antique shop; Greensboro House B & B.

(15) Willey's Store (533-2621), Greensboro Village.

(16) The Galaxy Bookshop (472-5533), Main St., Hardwick.

(16) Perennial Pleasures Nursery and Tea Garden (472-5104), Brick House, East Hardwick. More than 900 varieties of flowering plants, ornamental trees and shrubs, and medical, culinary and aromatic herbs. Tea is served in the garden or greenhouse daily, except Mon. from 12:30-4:30 in season.

(18) Legare Farm Market (454-7784), Rte. 14, East Calais.

(18) Grand View Winery (442-3636), Max Gray Rd., East Calais.

Danforth's Sugarhouse (800-887-9536 or 229-9536), Rte. 2, East Montpelier.

Not on the Drive

Butternut Mountain Farm (635-2329), Main St., Johnson. Maple syrup and products, Vermont crafts.

Fishing NEK (586-2273). Bruce Bartlett offers his 20+ years of expertise in fly fishing, spin casting and instruction. Equipment rental.

The Forget-Me-Not Shop (635-2335), 942-B Route 15 W, Johnson. Famous label off price clothing, jewelry & accessories.

Johnson Woolen Mills (635-7185), Main St., Johnson. The 150+-year-old mill has a retail store and a "seconds" room. Don't leave Vermont without a pair of their trademark green woolen work pants and red plaid jacket. Closed Sun.

Vermont Maple Outlet (644-5482), Rte. 15 between Jeffersonville and Cambridge. Maple syrup and products, local cheeses, specialty foods, and crafts.

Drive 12

St. Johnsbury Shires

61 miles

Art and science find charming provincial homes in St. Johnsbury, a town that literally weighs heavily in American industrial history. Starting in "St. Jay" this drive strikes south for the Connecticut River at Barnet, then winds west to tiny Peacham, gem in an Arcadian shire. A zigzag route completes the loop, with stops at an expansive state forest and one of the cheese making capitals of America.

1) **St. Johnsbury**, shire town of Caledonia County, gateway to the Northeast Kingdom, and the largest community in northeastern Vermont, lies at the confluence of the Passumpsic, Moose, and Sleepers rivers. It was named for Hector St. Jean de Crevecoeur, the French emigré commentator on early American life and first popularizer of the "melting pot" idea, and is the only St. Johnsbury in the world.

Although the city was first settled in 1786, its history really began in 1830, when Thaddeus Fairbanks filed for a patent on his revolutionary lever scale. Over the next 40 years St. Johnsbury's population tripled, as Fairbanks Scales were shipped to the four corners of the globe. Long the city's first family, the philanthropic Fairbanks clan contributed to the building of many of the city's grandest structures, including the

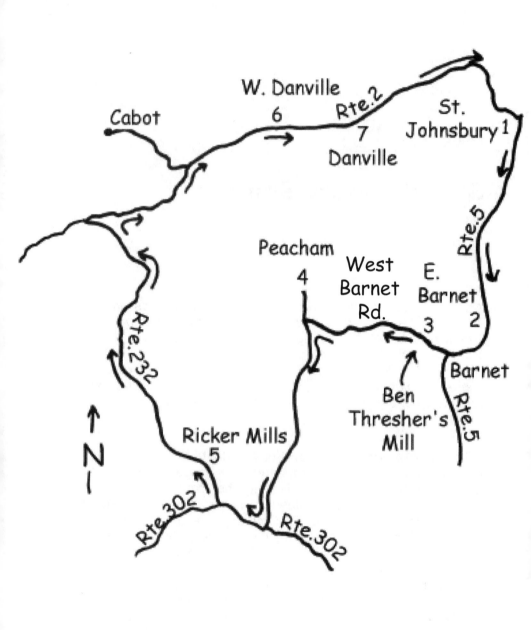

handsome, Second Empire **St. Johnsbury Athenaeum**, one of only fifteen libraries in the nation to be declared a National Historic Landmark. Horace Fairbanks intended the Athenaeum not only as a place of study, but of visual delight: a substantial rear wing of the building houses an art gallery whose collection, mostly landscapes and still lifes, has been kept unchanged as a precise record of the artistic tastes of a century and a quarter ago. But there's more than historic interest here: the splendid Eastlake-style gallery's centerpiece is Albert Bierstadt's 10 ft. x 15 foot "The Domes of the Yosemite," a landmark work of the Hudson River School.

Fairbanks money also made possible the St. Johnsbury Academy, an unusual but highly regarded hybrid of private preparatory school and public (for St. Jay and a couple of surrounding towns) public high school; and the handsome Richardson Romanesque **Fairbanks Museum and Planetarium**, a great gallimaufry of ethnographic and natural history exhibits from what our great-grandparents would have called "quaint foreign lands." Museums like this were how people saw the world before the Discovery Channel: here are more than 4,500 stuffed birds, mammals and reptiles, as well as old toys, weapons, fossils, and general exotica. The planetarium is tiny, and the presentations can be a bit amateurish, but it does offer accurate star shows. Also quite accurate -- everyone hopes -- are the weather reports issued each day from the meteorological center in the basement of the museum and broadcast throughout the state on Vermont Public Radio.

Catamount Film and Arts, a nonprofit organization which has served the Northeast Kingdom and northern New Hampshire for more than 25 years, stages performances through the north country. Throughout the year, at its St. Jay headquarters, the organization hosts regional film premiers, foreign and independent films, and a Sunday jazz series. It also exhibits the work of local artists in its galleries. On summer Monday evenings, band concerts are performed in Town Hall Park.

In the 1960s, Fairbanks Scale became a division of a conglomerate which threatened to move the company south -- until townspeople raised enough money to subsidize the building of a new plant on the outskirts of town. No such remedy was able to preserve the city's turn-of-the-century stature as a rail center, home of the St. Johnsbury & Lake Champlain Railroad, nicknamed by some wags "Slow, Jerky & Late Coming. " But downtown St. Jay still has the look of an old railroad town, its sturdy brick business blocks paralleling tracks that still see Canadian Pacific freight traffic. The passenger station? It's now a Chinese restaurant. On Railroad St., the **Moose River Trading Company**, purveyors of great-camp Adirondack furniture and accouterments, will make your house look like the kind of place where the butler has to chase away raccoons.

On the outskirts, **Maple Grove Farms**, the oldest and largest maple sugaring operation in the country, earns St. Johnsbury the title of "Maple Center of the World." There's a guided tour of the factory, a museum, and a fine gift shop.

If Stephen Huneck has his way, the city could also become known as "Dog Haven of the World." The artist and dog lover, known for the whimsical canines that populate his prints and bizarre furniture designs, has created **Dog Mountain**, an art center/sculpture garden where dogs and their humans can soak up a little culture, and then retreat for meditation to a chapel complete with stained glass windows done in dog themes. Turn onto Spaulding Rd. off Rte. 2 across from the Fairbanks plant and follow signs. If you're in Woodstock (see Drive #5), be sure to visit his studio on Central St.

2) Head south out of St. Johnsbury on Rte. 5, along the Passumpsic River, to **East Barnet**, site of the **Fifteen-Mile Falls Dam**, where Moore Station, the largest conventional hydroelectric facility in New England, created the 3,500-acre **Moore Reservoir**, one of the north country's larger bodies of water. (East Barnet is the turn-off for Lower Waterford: see Drive 8) Continue to **Barnet**. The **Goodwillie House**, which now houses the Barnet Historical Society, was built in 1790 by a Scottish pastor (see Drive 8) and was a stop on the Underground Railroad during the Civil War.

Today,   Barnet is providing sanctuary for yet another group of immigrants and their spiritual compatriots -- it's home to two Buddhist centers (see Drive 8).

(3) At Barnet, turn right onto West Barnet Rd. and watch on the right for **Ben Thresher's Mill**, a woodworking mill which was powered by a water turbine from the 1840s until it ceased operation in the late 1970s. When visitors suggested that electric motors would double the output of Ben's machines, he would smile and say "Nope! I don't need to double my output. I guess I'll just stick to water power and what I know. It's always done the job." Laurance S. Rockefeller purchased the mill in 1978 with the intention of moving it to the Billings Farm and Museum in Woodstock, but plans changed, and the mill was given back to Mr. Thresher, who died just a few years ago. A preservation group is now restoring the mill, and is working to get the machinery up and running ... using diesel power.

In 1759 Lord Jeffrey Amherst sent men with provisions from the fort in Charleston, New Hampshire to meet with Rogers' Rangers at the confluence of the Passumpsic and Connecticut Rivers. The Rangers had just completed their successful expedition against the St. Francis Indians in Quebec, and their supplies were depleted. While waiting for Rogers, Amherst's party heard rifle fire and, fearing Indians, fled back downstream with the supplies before the Rangers arrived exhausted and famished. Rogers and several of his men built a raft and floated down the Connecticut to the fort, and returned with a rescue party for those who had not starved in the meantime.

(4) Continue through West Barnet, then turn right at the Bayley-Hazen Country Store in South Peacham and bear right (north) to continue into **Peacham**. The face of the tiny village is familiar to travelers in rural New England: the sharp white steeple of a 1790s Congregational church; a country store; a clutch of houses born of that early nineteenth-century New England architecture that makes poetry out of trim practicality; and for a backdrop, a rumpled quilt of meadows and woods. The features fit a hundred Vermont communities, but only in the sparest handful do they come together as perfectly as in Peacham. It is one of the most photographed villages in the state, and Hollywood

Side Trip

At the little white church in West Barnet, turn left onto Garland Hill Rd. to visit the 409-acre, glacially-scoured Harvey's Lake, a popular destination for rainbow trout fishermen, particularly just after "ice out." The lake also provides good fishing for lake trout and yellow perch. The folks at Harvey's Lake Cabins & Campground, Vermont's oldest private campground, invite you to stop by for a cup of coffee or a cold drink, and/ or picnic on their beach. Back in the early 1920s, there was a summer camp where some of the lakeshore vacation homes now stand. One of the young campers, who had come all the way from France, must have enjoyed the water. His name was Jacques Cousteau.

has shot three movies here. The **Peacham Store** was the setting for the most recent, 1996's *The Spitfire Grill*.

Peacham has earned a reputation as a refuge for the literati: a glass case in the town's library displays books by local authors, several of whose names are recognizable to the world at large. But the same library often features a homier touch -- a half-finished jigsaw puzzle, scattered across a side table as a sort of ongoing community project.

Peacham became a permanent settlement in 1776 and grew rapidly when the Bayley-Hazen Military Road was finished in 1779, providing easy access for pioneers. The tiny town's list of accomplishments and native sons far exceeds its size: the first newspaper in Caledonia County, The Green Mountain Patriot, was published here in 1798. Abolitionist Thaddeus Stevens was raised here, as was one-time *Harper's Weekly* editor George Harvey and Flora Temple, the first horse in the world to trot a mile in less than 2.20 minutes.

Backtrack south to the Bayley-Hazen General Store in South Peacham, but continue straight at the intersection and take the Danville-Groton Rd. to the intersection with Rte. 302. Turn right (west) onto Rte. 302 toward **Groton**, the birthplace of William Scott, the soldier President Lincoln saved from the firing squad following his court-martial for falling asleep at his sentry post (Scott died in combat seven months later, when the Vermont Volunteers attacked the Confederates at Lee's Mills.)

(5) Turn right (north) on Rte. 232 toward **Ricker Mills**, the source of the Wells River, and once the site of the oldest continuously operating stationary sawmill in America. The Old Lake House, which stood just beyond the mill, served as a lumberjacks' boardinghouse and was a haunt of a mid-nineteenth century British-born bank robber named "Bristol Bill Darlington," who was captured here in 1850. While he was being sentenced in a courtroom in St. Johnsbury, Bill stabbed the prosecutor to death.

Ricker Mills marks the beginning of the popular **Groton State Forest**. This 26,154-acre preserve (the second largest contiguous landholding owned by the state) encompasses four primitive campgrounds and **Boulder Beach**, a day use area with a beach, bathhouse, and snack bar on three-mile-long Lake Groton. There are several easy and rewarding hiking trails in the forest: Groton Nature Trail is a fairly level 1/2-mile self-guided loop through terrain that reveals considerable evidence of glacial activity. A bit farther up Rte. 232 is the head of Owl's Head Trail, another easy half-mile hike through mixed hardwoods up CCC-built steps to an octagonal stone fire tower at the top of 1,958-foot Owl's Head Mountain. At the summit there are fine views of surrounding ponds and mountains. Big Deer Mountain Trail, which begins at New Discovery State Park Campground, is a fairly easy 3.4-mile hike through a red pine plantation to the summit of Big Deer Mountain, with views of Peacham Pond, Peacham Bog and the White Mountains. Secluded and undeveloped Kettle Pond and the more built-up Peacham Pond are wonderful spots for canoeing. The Forest's Peacham Bog is one of two documented "raised" bogs in Vermont. **Seyon Fly-Fishing Area** on Noyes Pond is exclusively for fly anglers.

Just before the intersection with Rte. 2, there are excellent views of Camel's Hump to the west. At the intersection turn right (east) on Rte. 2, which follows Molly's Brook past **Molly's Falls Pond**; both are named for the wife of a fondly-remembered Indian named Joe (see Joe's Pond, below). The route also takes you past **Goodrich's Sugarhouse**, which has been making maple syrup for more than 150 years. (To get to **Rainbow Sweets Bakery and Cafe**, turn left (west) off Rte. 232 onto Rte. 2 to Marshfield).

Side Trip

To visit Cabot, home of Cabot Creamery, turn left (west) off Rte. 232 onto Rte. 2 . Along with Ben & Jerry's ice cream and artist Woody Jackson's ubiquitous representations of black-and-white Holstein-Friesian cows, Cabot Creamery is one of the main vehicles for promoting Vermont's international image as a dairy state. You may be thousands of miles away from Vermont, and find your airline flight attendant handing you a mini-pack of Cabot cheddar to wash down with your tiny bottle of Chardonnay. The creamery tour tells the story of how milk becomes cheese, and there's a shop where you can stock up on sharp, mild, flavored, extra-aged, and many other varieties of cheddar.

Cabot was also the birthplace of Zerah Colburn, a childhood genius with numbers: on July 29, 1813, while on a tour to London (his father was exhibiting him as a world wonder), he was asked by the Duke of Cambridge how many seconds had elapsed since the beginning of the Christian era. Zerah replied promptly (and correctly): 57,234,384,000.

(6) Continue to **West Danville**, home of **Joe's Pond**, named for an Indian guide who, with his wife, Molly, befriended early pioneers and lived on an island in the pond. According to one account, "Old Joe had no passion for war himself, but he was a great whig and rejoiced in the defeat of the British whom he could never forgive the slaughter and dispersion of his tribe [the St. Francis] in Nova Scotia ..." His refusal to ever again set foot in Canada was so adamant that he is alleged on one occasion to have given up the pursuit of a moose that slipped across the border. "Good Bye, Mr. Moose" was his reported valedictory to the beast, who was unwittingly seeking asylum under the British Crown. Joe reasonably believed that this

sort of loyalty deserved compensation: learning that George Washington was going to be visiting upstate New York, Joe and Molly went to see him and returned with a letter granting them a pension of $70 a year. Joe is buried at the Ox-Bow Cemetery in Newbury (see Drive 8). Each spring, his namesake pond is the site of an annual ice-out contest, in which competitors guess which spring day will see the ice disappear. Information and tickets are sold at the 200-plus-year-old **Hastings Store** at the junction of Rte. 2 and Rte. 15.

(7) Continue on Rte. 2 to **Danville**, a handsome town along the slope of a broad plateau overlooking New Hampshire's White Mountains. Once a retreat for hay fever sufferers, Danville is the national headquarters for the **American Society of Dowser**s, founded in 1961. Stop in to learn how to find water using a forked stick or other rudimentary device.

Side Trip

At Hastings Store, ask owners Jane or Garey Larrabee for directions to Stoddard Swamp, an 11,000+-year-old, 12-acre cedar bog whose many varieties of flora and fauna include numerous species of orchids.

Danville's most famous native son, Thaddeus Stevens, was born in 1792. "The Great Commoner," whose goal was to disenfranchise former slave owners and who helped engineer the impeachment of President Andrew Johnson, was described by historian Samuel Eliot Morison as "a sour and angry Congressman who really loved Negroes." Stevens also loved his mother. In his will he left funds for planting roses or "other cheerful flowers" at her grave in Peacham.

Side Trip

If you're passing through Danville on the last Sunday of a month between May and September, consider a jog north out of the center of town to North Danville. The congregation of the 1832 Old North Church conducts a lamplight service at 7:30 P.M.

In 1840, Englishman Benjamin Greenbanks opened one of New England's biggest woolen mills along Joes Brook. An 1885 fire razed the mill and a nearby covered bridge. The mill was never rebuilt, but the bridge was replaced a year later. It's the Greenbanks Hollow Bridge; ask in town for directions.

Return to St. Johnsbury on Rte. 2.

Information

Northeast Kingdom Chamber of Commerce (800-639-6379 or 748-3678), 357 Western Ave., St. Johnsbury 05819. www.nekchamber.com

Lodgings

Note: there are a number of motels in and around downtown St. Johnsbury; contact the Chamber for a listing.

(1) Aime's Motel (800-504-6663 or 748-3194), Jct. rtes. 2/18, St. Johnsbury 05819. 16 simple but comfortable units alongside a stream. Pets welcome. May-Oct. $

(1) Albro Nichols House (751-8434), 7 Boynton Ave., St. Johnsbury. 3 cozy rooms with private or shared bath in an in-town, 1846 Federal farmhouse just off Main St. near Arnold Park. $-$$

(1) Fairbanks Inn (748-5666), 32 Western Ave., St. Johnsbury 05819. 46 nicely decorated units and 1 suite, within walking distance of town. Heated pool. Continental breakfast. www.vermonter.com/ fairbanks/ $$-$$$

(3) Harvey's Lake Cabins & Campground (633-2213), RR l, Box 26 E, West Barnet 05821. Fully furnished housekeeping cottages (5 overlooking lake) for 2-4 people. Weekly rates. Mid-May-mid-Oct. $-$$

(3) The Old Homestead (877-653-4663 or 633-4016),1573 Rte. 5, Barnet. C. 1850 village Colonial has 4 rooms (2 with shared bath): the White Mountain Room has a private screened porch and mountain views. The owner, also a musician, hosts chamber music parties and rehearsal retreats at the B&B. www.theoldhomestead.com $-$$

(4) Ha'Penny Gourmet (800-471-7658 or 592-3310), Peacham. 4 cozy guest rooms share 2 baths above the Peacham Store. Dinner by reservation. $$

(6) Indian Joe Court (684-3430), Rte. 2, Joes Pond, Danville 05873. Basic cabins and housekeeping cabins overlooking the pond. Private beach, boat rental. May 15-Oct. 15. $-$$

(7) Broadview Farm (748-9902), 2627 McDowell Rd., Danville 05828. Shingle-style country mansion on 200+ acres overlooking the mountains. 4 antique-filled guest rooms with private or shared bath. Walking trails and gardens. June-Oct. $-$$

(7) Emergo Farm B&B (888-383-1185 or 684-2215), 261 Webster Hill, Danville 05828. The fifth generation of Websters welcome guests in the farmhouse of their 200-acre "Dairy of Distinction." Rooms with shared bath and a 2-bedroom apartment with full kitchen and bath. And "there is no charge for helping with the farm chores." $-$$

(7) Sherryland (684-3354), 760 Brainard St., Danville. Working farm-25 Devon cattle in big red barn. Nothing is fancy at Sherryland, including the prices. Caroline Sherry's simply furnished 19-room farmhouse on a working dairy farm has a wraparound porch. 5 rooms share one bath. TV in den. $

Restaurants

(1) Anthony's Restaurant (748-3613), 50 Railroad St., St. Johnsbury. Solid American fare, daily specials, hamburgers and homemade potato chips at this casual family restaurant. B, L, D.

(1) Cucina di Gerardo (748-6772), 1216 Railroad St., St. Johnsbury. Housed in an old creamery; fine Italian veal, chicken, fish and and pasta specialties share the limelight with excellent pizza. D (closed Sun. and Mon.) off-season. $-$$

(1) St. Jay Diner (748-9751), Memorial Drive, Rte. 5 N, St. Johnsbury. Solid diner fare. B, L, D. $

(5) Rainbow Sweets Bakery and Cafe (426-3531), Rte. 2, Marshfield. A small restaurant with a big reputation serving dishes such as gnocchi, spanakopita, pizza, and great homemade desserts. B, L; D Fri. and Sat. Closed Tues. $

(5) The Creamery (684-3616), Hill St., Danville. Homemade soups, fish and chicken, fresh ground hamburgers, and freshly baked pies. Lighter fare ($) in the pub. L Tues.-Fri., D. Tues.-Sat. $$

(5)(L) Danville B & B (684-3484), Danville Village. 3 hearty meals a day served in a casual, homey atmosphere Mon.-Sat. from May through Oct.; and Fri. and Sat. the rest of the year. The $9.95 Saturday night buffet is popular. $-$$

Attractions

(1) The St. Johnsbury Athenaeum (748-8291), 1171 Main St., St. Johnsbury. Closed Sun.

(1) Fairbanks Museum & Planetarium (748-2372), Main St., St. Johnsbury. Daily July-Aug.; weekends Sept.-June. $

(1) Maple Grove Farms of Vermont (800-525-2540 or 748-5141), 1052 Portland St., St. Johnsbury. Mon.-Fri. except holidays; gift shop and sugar house open daily May-Oct. $ tour.

(1) Methodist Episcopal Church, Central St.,
St. Johnsbury, houses the memorial window,
"Annunciation to the Shepherds" by Louis C. Tiffany.

(1) Stephen Huneck's Dog Mountain (800-449-2580
or 748-2700), Spaulding Rd., St. Johnsbury. June-Oct.
daily; other times by appointment.

(2) Fifteen Miles Falls, Visitor center off Rte. 135,
Littleton, New Hampshire. Memorial Day weekend-
Labor Day, Thurs. - Mon.

(3) Ben Thresher's Mill. West Barnet Rd.,Barnet.
Saturdays in summer, 10-4.

(5) Groton State Forest: Boulder Beach (584-3823)
day use area. Seyon Fly-Fishing Area (584-3829) has
a boat rental. For camping information: Department of
Forests, Parks and Recreation at 241-3655.

(6) Cabot Creamery Visitors' Center (800-837-4261
or 229-9361), Cabot. Short tour and video; gift shop.
June-Oct.; call for cheese-making days. $ tour.

(7) Danville Morgan Horse Farm (684-2251), Joes
Brook Rd., Danville. 9:30 A.M.-3:30 P.M.

(7) American Society of Dowsers (684-3417), 84
Brainerd St., Danville. Supplies, books, occasional
weekend workshops, tools. Mon.-Fri.

(7) Old North Church (748-9350), North Danville.

Activities and Shopping

(1) American Society of Dowsers Bookstore (800-711-
9497), 430 Railroad St., St. Johnsbury. Books, tools,
supplies, and information. Tues.-Sat.

(1) Caplan's Army Store (748-3236), 457 Railroad St.,
St. Johnsbury. Hiking equipment, sportswear, and
clothing.

(1) Catamount Film and Arts (800-757-5559 or 748-2600), 139 Eastern Ave., St. Johnsbury.

(1) Moose River Lake & Lodge Store (748-2423), 69 Railroad St., St. Johnsbury. Rustic furnishings, pack baskets, fishing creels, moose antlers, old taxidermy, wines, vintage canoes, and lots more.

(1) Northeast Kingdom Artisans Guild (748-0158), 101 Railroad St., St. Johnsbury. Co-operative shop for Northeast Kingdom artists. Closed Sun.

(2) Samedhi Cushions (800-331-7751 or 633-4440), Church St., Barnet. Retail store for Karme-Choling Buddhist Meditation Center sells meditation cushions, incense, Asian art, and handicrafts.

(3) Harvey's Lake Cabins & Campground (633-2213), RR l, Box 26 E, West Barnet. Beach; canoe, rowboat, paddle boat and bicycle rental.

(4) Peacham Store (592-3310), Peacham. Gourmet snacks, homemade soups and sandwiches, local crafts and lots of country treasures.

(4) The Peacham Corner Guild (592-3332), next to the Peacham Store. Small antiques, hand crafts, and specialty foods. June-Oct.

(6) Hastings Store (684-3398), jct. Rte. 15 and Rte. 2, West Danville. Groceries, post office, and library.

(6) Injun Joe Motor Court (684-3430), Rte. 2, West Danville. Rowboat rental.

(7) Farr's Antiques (684-3333), Peacham Rd., Danville. Three floors of antiques in an old-fashioned country store.

(7) Goodrich's Sugarhouse (563-9917), Cabot. Modern and antique equipment displays. Tours. Mar.-Dec.

Drive 13

Northern Vermont Lakes

74 miles

This is the country where the rivers really do flow north, as in the Howard Frank Mosher novel set nearby. The Black, the Barton, the Clyde, and a slew of lesser streams all empty into the international waters of Lake Memphremagog, where this drive begins in the old logging capital of Newport. East and south of Newport a scattering of smaller yet grandly scenic lakes mark an ice-age glacier's passage and retreat: Seymour, Echo, Willoughby and Crystal all summon visions of a long summer with nothing to do but fish, swim, and sit on the porch. The route winds back to Newport via an immense monument to learning, and a marshy refuge teeming with birds.

(1) Begin in **Newport**, Vermont's northernmost city, situated along a sloping promontory at the southern end of Lake Memphremagog. The Algonquin and Abenaki Indians who first lived in this area gave the lake its name, which translates as "beautiful waters." Only five of the thirty-three miles of the lake are in the U.S. The northern end, which splits into east and west forks, extends as far north as Magog, Quebec, and summer weekends bring many French-speaking boaters to Newport's downtown marina. The island-dotted lake is 350 feet deep in places, and teems with lake, brown and rainbow trout, landlocked salmon, pickerel, walleye, northern pike, large- and smallmouth bass, perch, smelt, bullheads ... and

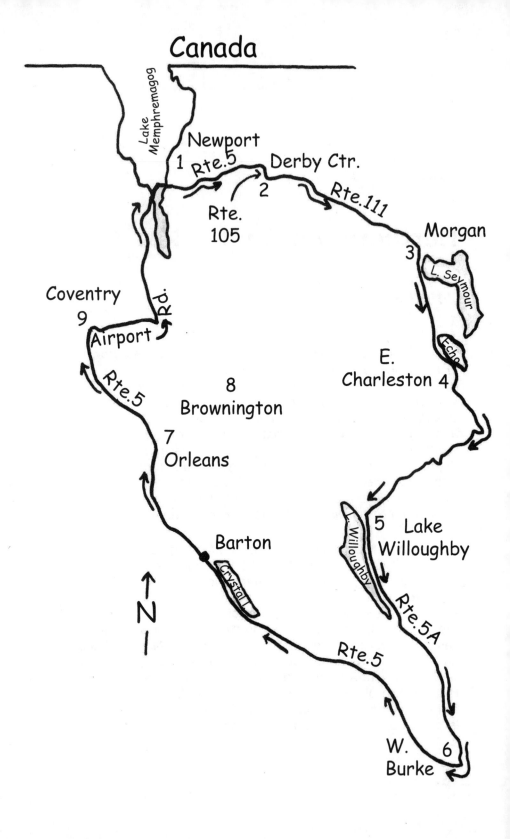

the requisite monster that no one ever really sees, in this case bearing the obvious and unlovely name Memphre. Heavily wooded mountains, most notably 3,360' Owl's Head (named for an Indian chief), hem in the shoreline north of town.

The first documented white visitors to the southern shores of Lake Memphremagog were Rogers' Rangers, returning from their successful raid against the Quebec home base of the St. Francis Indians in 1759 (In *Northwest Passage*, Hollywood's version of this epic French and Indian War adventure based on Kenneth Roberts' fine novel of the same title, Spencer Tracy played the redoubtable Major Rogers).

During the nineteenth century, vast surrounding forests and good railroad connections made Newport an important lumber town. Its firm of Prouty and Miller was one of the biggest timber companies in the east, and Lake Memphremagog's South Bay was choked with logs awaiting the sawmills. The railroads also made Newport a resort destination, bringing passengers from Boston to the now-vanished, 400-room Memphremagog House and its hot springs spa.

For a great view of the lake, drive up Prospect Hill to St. Mary, Star of the Sea Roman Catholic Church, a twin-towered harbinger of the monolithic granite churches that dot the landscape of Quebec. After heading back downtown, park and take a stroll down Main Street, the best place to gauge the progress Newport has made in its transition from a forest products economy to one based on tourism and other post-industrial pursuits. It hasn't been an entirely smooth ride -- you'll probably see an empty storefront or two -- but all in all the old lakeshore city has picked itself up quite handily, and now boasts an assortment of Main Street outlet shops.

Just a block away, the once-tatty waterfront has become a focus for civic improvements. The docks at the handsome Gateway Center are a fine place for a stroll, especially on a summer's day when you can wallow in sailboat envy to your heart's content. If the farther vistas of Lake Memphremagog are more tempting, hop aboard **Newport's Princess**, a little replica stern wheeler (OK, the paddle wheel isn't really functional) that offers brunch, cocktail, dinner and moonlight cruises. And in late July, the city's Summerfest pulls downtown and the lakefront together with fiddlers, fireworks, an antique boat show, and a torchlight canoe parade.

Free concerts are held at the bandstand in Gardner Park on Wednesday evenings throughout the summer. The park is also the site of a Farmers' Market on summer Wednesdays and Saturdays. Prouty Beach, named for the late Vermont senator and Newport native Winston Prouty, is just east of the city. It has a swimming beach, picnic area, and campground.

In 1996, at the behest of local citizens, Citizens Utilities removed the 100-foot- long, 20-foot-high concrete Dam #11 that for forty years had prevented salmon from swimming freely between Lake Memphremagog and the Clyde River, where they spawn. The salmon are back once again, and the best time to catch them is usually the first week of October.

Back on our main route, heading north and east out of Newport on Rte. 5, watch for the red **Miss Newport Diner** on the left side of the road. A 1946 gem out of the famous Worcester Lunch Car Company of Worcester, Massachusetts, the Miss Newport features snazzy floor tiles and a pink formica ceiling. Depending on your tobacco stance, it also features either sweet solace or outright toxicity. A few years ago, the management transformed the little eatery into a "Smoking and Social Club" to get around new state regulations that made smoking verboten in restaurants. A membership card is available to anyone over 18, for a $1.00 fee.

Side Trip

Before beginning this drive's clockwise route out of Newport, birders might want to consider a detour in the other direction. Just south of downtown, via Rte. 5, is South Bay Wildlife Management Area. This 1,559-acre marsh at Lake Memphremagog's southern end is a nesting area for osprey and black terns, and also harbors bald eagles, great blue and green herons, American bitterns, and painted and snapping turtles. To reach the public access point, turn left off Rte. 5 onto Airport Road.

(2) Continue on Rte. 5 to the intersection with Rte. 105 in **Derby Center**, putting Newport's last few strip malls and the modest studios of quaintly-named WMOO Radio behind you. Those aren't cows, though, grazing behind the fence at the intersection. In 1992, dairy farmer Doug Nelson decided to diversify, and began raising American elk, also known as wapiti, which were long ago native to this area. Today his herd at **Cow Town Elk Ranch** numbers more than seventy. Visitors are welcome, and the best time to stop by is at 4:00 PM, when Doug brings his herd into the front pasture to feed. If you're visiting in fall, don't miss the "rut" -- the elks' mating season.

(3) At the T intersection by the elk farm, turn right off Rte. 5 onto Rte. 5A/105, and then left (east) onto Rte. 111. That's Lake Salem off to your right; as the lake disappears from view, a lovely roller-coaster stretch of Rte. 111 cuts through pretty dairy country on its way to the tiny settlement of Morgan and **Seymour Lake**, one of the largest bodies of water lying entirely within Vermont's boundaries. The lake is popular among anglers seeking lake trout and landlocked salmon. That would be one of the trout, weighing in at twenty-five pounds, in the picture hanging above the post office window in the Morgan store; he's posing with the fellow who caught him in 1956. If you want to try for a twenty-six-pounder, there's a boat rental east on Rte. 111 in **Morgan Center**, right near a little bathing beach for those content merely to swim with the fishes.

Side Trip

If you head north (instead of south, our direction) on Rte. 5, you'll soon reach Derby Line, on the U.S.-Canada border. And we do mean on the border. At the recently-restored, late nineteenth-century Haskell Opera House, the audience sits in the U.S., and the stage is in Canada. (There's a program of plays, concerts and musicals from mid-April to mid-Oct.). Downstairs, in the town library, you can cross the international border by walking from one room to another.

(4) Unless you're ready for a fishing excursion or a dip, however, turn right at the store onto East Charleston Road. Continue as

the road turns into Echo Lake Road, then Echo Pond Road, and finally West Echo Lake Road as it hugs the shore of Echo Lake (bear right at each fork). At the stop sign in **East Charleston**, turn left onto Rte. 105. The tiny village, originally named Navy by Revolutionary naval officer (and grantee of the town) Commodore Whipple, once boasted a thriving lumber mill.

(5) About 1 mile out of East Charleston, turn right onto Hudson Road, then, at approximately 1/4 mile, left onto Westmore Road. Bear right as the road turns into Hinton Road, then Hinton Ridge Road, and climbs up out of the woods until spread directly below you is beautiful, fjord-like **Lake Willoughby**, set between the steep slopes of Mount Pisgah (east shore) and Mount Hor (west shore, set further back). The 1,692-acre lake was formed more than 12,000 years ago, when glaciers gouged a trough in the underlying granite, and with a maximum depth of 312 feet it is the deepest in the Northeast Kingdom. The cold waters provide some of the best fishing in the region -- again, the top species are landlocked salmon and lake trout; many fine specimens of the latter are taken through the ice.

At the stop sign where Hinton Ridge Road ends at the lake, turn left onto Rte. 5A to continue this drive and/or to head towards **Willoughby State Forest** (see below). To get to the small public beach at the northern end of the lake and/or the **WilloughVale Inn**, turn right at the stop sign.

The sheer cliffs of Mts. Pisgah and Hor have been designated a National Natural Landmark, and lie within the 7,300-acre Willoughby State Forest. The forest, much of which was planted with Norway and white spruce and red and white pine by the CCC during the 1930s, offers hiking, cross country skiing, and snowmobile trails. Six cold-water ponds within its boundaries are stocked annually with brook and rainbow trout.

For superb views of the area, and possibly a glimpse of some of the cliffs' resident peregrine falcons, plan a hike up **Mount Pisgah**. The trailhead for the moderately difficult 3 1/2-mile route to the summit is on the left side of Rte. 5A, just past the southern tip of the lake; there's a parking lot on the right. (An interesting footnote: the original "south" trail up the mountain has been in use almost 200 years.) The falcons returned here in 1985, after a thirty-year hiatus. They come back each spring, nest during the summer, and generally leave by August. The best time to view them is in the early morning and late afternoon.

Although the summit of **Mount Hor** is wooded, there are splendid views from several vantage points on the cliffs. To reach the trailhead, continue through the parking area for Mount Pisgah, and up a gravel road at the right side of the parking area. Bear right at the fork to the parking area, and follow the blue-blazed trail. Total hiking distance is 3.5 mi., and the rating is easy to moderate. For the best views, follow the East Branch Trail to the East Lookout Trail to Prospect Rock (if you're there in late August, stop and pick some of the plump raspberries that grow along the way).

(6) Continue south on Rte. 5A, past the turnoff for Newark through **West Burke**. (The Burkes were named for British statesman Edmund Burke, the British parliamentarian who though renowned as a conservative was sympathetic to the American colonists.) At the intersection of Rte. 5A and Rte. 5, turn north on Rte. 5 toward **Barton** and continue alongside the Sutton River to lovely, glacially-formed **Crystal Lake**. To get to **Crystal Lake State Park**, continue into Barton and turn north on Rte. 16: The entrance is just ahead on the right. The water here is sparkling clean, the views superb, the beach sandy, and, unlike many other Vermont lakes, the bottom is clear of sticks and weeds.

Just north of West Burke, there's a left turn for Newark. Don't confuse this Newark with the one that has the airport. All Newark, Vermont has in common with Newark, New Jersey is the name ... but therein lies a tale. It seems there is an informal association of Newarks the world over -- Newark, England; Newark, California; Newark, Delaware; and several other Newarks great and small. Every year, representatives from all the Newarks gather at a different host Newark. The honor of playing host fell to our Newark a few years back, and we would love to have seen the reaction of cosmopolitan Newarkites to this hamlet of some 300 souls.

The fair-sized and rather plain town of Barton, at the north end of the lake, was once a thriving industrial community. During the heyday of passenger rail service, six trains a day delivered fun seekers to Barton on their way to Crystal Lake and Lake Willoughby. But industry has left, the trains stopped arriving, and today Barton is at its liveliest in early August when it hosts the Orleans County Fair at the fairgrounds on the outskirts of town. The old fashioned soda fountain in The Marketplace is a fun place for a light lunch or coffee.

Side Trip

Take Rte. 16 south a few miles to Glover to visit Labour of Love Public Gardens, Antiques, Crafts where more than 400 varieties of hardy perennials are in bloom from April until frost. Visitors are invited to picnic by the river and visit the restored 1880s Greek Revival home, filled with antiques and a hand weaving studio; guest accommodations are available.

Continue south approximately 1 1/2 more miles and turn onto Rte. 122 to the home of the Bread and Puppet Theater. The huge puppets on display here are the creation of Peter Schumann, and are a common sight at political and social rallies throughout New England.

(7) Continue north on Rte. 5 alongside the Barton River to **Orleans**, where the Barton and Willoughby Rivers merge on their way north to Lake Memphremagog. At the intersection of Rte. 5 and Rte. 58, turn right and continue into town. Turn right onto Church Street and then left onto Brownington Street toward Brownington.

If you're visiting between the last week of April and the second week in May, stop at **Willoughby Falls Wildlife Management Area**, just 1/10- mile after the Brownington turn, to look for rainbow trout struggling upstream over the raging Willoughby Falls on their way to spawn in the clean gravel beds of the Willoughby River and its feeder streams. The annual "rainbow run" begins downstream -- in this case, to the north -- at Lake Memphremagog.)

(8) For many visitors, tiny **Brownington Village**, has the feel of a rural Shangri-La. It's hard to imagine that the sleepy

hill town surrounded by farmlands and distant mountains was a thriving community on the main stage route between Boston and Montreal in the early part of the nineteenth century. But the handsome homes and public edifices built in the village's heyday -- now the National Register of Historic Places Historic District -- are a testament to past glories.

One, the **Old Stone House Museum**, is a monument to the determination and hard work of Alexander Twilight, who built the four-story granite structure in 1836 to serve as both a dormitory and classroom for his academy, the only high school in Orleans County for much of the remainder of the century. To this day, Twilight and his building are somewhat shrouded in mystery. There is some question whether he is, as Middlebury College claims, the first African-American graduate of an American college (it is believed that his father was black). No one is sure where he got the funds to build the massive structure, or how he transported the Canadian shield granite rocks south to Brownington. The building now houses the eighteenth- and nineteenth-century collection of the Orleans County Historical Society, which sheds light not only on Twilight and his impressive academy, but on all the vanished bustle of what has become a gorgeous backwater. Twilight's Greek Revival home, directly across the road from the museum, serves as a visitor center and headquarters.

Before you head back to Orleans, climb to the deck of the observatory in the meadow behind the church for a wonderful view of the distant hills. A walking tour booklet is available at the museum.

(9) Back in Orleans, continue north on Rte. 5 through rolling farmland to **Coventry**. To visit **Barton River Marsh**, one of New England's most pristine large, shallow freshwater marshes, turn right onto Airport Road and bear left at Coventry Station, three miles east of Coventry. Birding is a prime activity at this 500-acre area, which encompasses cedar-red maple swamp forest, bulrushes, cattails, pond lilies, and duckweed. (Note: this is part of the **South Bay Wildlife Management Area** mentioned in the Newport section above).

Continue on Airport Road back to Rte. 5 and Newport.

Information

Vermont's North Country Chamber of Commerce (800-635-4643 or 334-7782), the Causeway, Newport 05855. www.vtnorthcountry.com

Northeast Kingdom Travel and Tourism Association (888-884-8001 in US, or 525-4386), P.O Box 465, Barton 05822. www.travelthekingdom.com

Lodging

(1) Newport City Motel (800-338-6558 or 334-6558), 974 East Main St., Newport 05855. Well-kept inn close to town has 64 nicely-appointed rooms, an indoor pool, hot tub, and fitness center. www.vermonter.com/ncm $-$$

(3) Seymour Lake Lodge (895-2752), 28 Valley Rd., Morgan 05853. Waterfront lodge has 6 rooms with private and shared baths, including a 2-room suite that sleeps 4 and has a TV and fridge. Guests have kitchen privileges and free use of canoes, kayaks, and rowboats. Powerboats ($). Pets welcome. www.seymourlakelodge.com $-$$

(5) Trail's End Cottages (525-4132), Lake Willoughby. 4 cottages near Mount Pisgah; canoe available. Property manager, Carol Anne's Rentals, also has private houses for rent on the lake.

(5)(R) WilloughVale Inn (800-594-9102 or 525-4123), Rte. 5A, Westmore 05860. One of the area's finest accommodations has 8 rooms with bath in the inn and 4 lakefront housekeeping cottages with screened porches, fireplaces, and private docks. Small pets allowed in cottages. The restaurant ($$) serves dishes such as a baked brie appetizer for 2, and entrees such as roast duck and scallop and pesto linguine. Canoe and kayak rental. www.willoughvale.com $$ -$$$

(6) Crystal Lake B&B (525-4607), 202 Lakeside Lane, Barton 05822. Lakefront lodging. Lakeside loft apartment. Deck. Boat and canoe rental. May-Nov.www.crystallakebb.com $

(6) Pinecrest Motel & Cabins (525-3472), Rte. 5N, Barton. 10 tidy riverside cabins (5 housekeeping) and 5 motel rooms. Pool. Pets welcome. $

(9)(R) Heermansmith Farm Inn (754-8866), Coventry Village. An unpretentious country inn with 7 small but pleasant guest rooms and one of the region's finest restaurants. Dinner ($$), served by candle and kerosene light, might include a Swiss, crab and potato strudel appetizer, and entree of the house special roast duck. D; closed Tues. $-$$

Restaurants

(1) East Side Landing (334-2340), 25 Lake St., Newport. Good food, ample portions, and a festive atmosphere make this one of the area's most popular spots for solid American fare. Outdoor deck, tie-up service; gifts, antiques and VT products. B Sat. & Sun.; L, D $

(1) Lago Trattoria (334-8222), 95 Main St., Newport. The city's newest restaurant offers a large selection of well-prepared Italian dishes in a sophisticated yet casual setting. Try the caramelized sweet onion with sausage and the ricotta-stuffed ravioli. Homemade pizza. L Fri., D Tues.-Sun. $-$$

(1) Miss Newport Diner (334-7742), 985 East Main St., Newport.5 A.M.-1:30 P.M. Mon.-Fri., until 11:30 A.M. Sat. and Sun. $

(1) Newport Natural Foods & Bakery (334-2626), 66 Main St., Newport. Homemade breads and entrees prepared for lunch daily. $

(2) Abbie Lane Restaurant (334-3090), 501 Pleasant St., Newport. Creative European and new American fare elegantly presented in this chef-owned bistro. Early dining specials. D; closed Mon.

(6) B & W Snack Bar, Rte. 5, Barton. Open summer and fall for snacks, cremees, and french fries. $

(10) Martha's Diner (754-6800), Rte. 5 & 14, Coventry. Classic diner fare in a classic diner. B, L. $

Attractions

(1) Newport's Princess (334-6617), East Side Marina, Lake St., Newport. Mid-May-late Oct. Reservations recommended, especially during foliage season. $

(1) South Bay Wildlife Management Area (748-8787), Coventry St., Newport.

(1)(R) Cow Town Elk Ranch (766-5068), jct. Rtes. 5/ 105, Derby Center. Gift shop, restaurant specializing in beef.

(2) Haskell Opera House and Library (819-876-2020), Derby Line. Late April-mid-Oct.

(6) Crystal Lake State Park (525-6205), Rte. 16N, Barton. Memorial Day-Labor Day. Snack bar; changing room, picnic area. $

(8) Old Stone House Museum (754-2022), Brownington Village. Mid-May-June and Sept.-Oct. 15, Fri.-Tues. 11-5; daily in July and Aug. $

Activities and Shopping

(1) Bogner Haus Factory Outlet (334-0135), 150 Main St., Newport. Men's and women's outdoor and golf wear at discount prices.

(1) Great Outdoors of Newport (334-0135), 177 Main St., Newport. Boat, kayak, canoe, x-c ski, and snowshoe rental.

(1) Newport Boat Rentals & Marine Services (334-5911), Farrants Point, Newport. Canoe, rowboat, pontoon and runabout rentals.

(3) Fishing/Hiking Guide (895-4209), Vermont Sportsman Lodge, Rte. 111, Morgan Center. Bob Beaupre offers a fishing and hiking guide service.

(3) Tradewinds General Store (895-2975), Rte. 111, Morgan Center. Canoe rentals.

(6)(L) Crystal Lake B&B, 202 Lakeside Lane, Barton. Boat and canoe rental.

(6) The Marketplace, Post Office Square, Barton. Fountain, sundries and gifts.

(6)(L) Labour of Love Public Gardens, Antiques and Crafts (525-6695), Rte.16, Glover Village. Gardens open daily; antique shop open Thurs.-Sat.

(6) Lake Parker Country Store (800-893-6985 or 525-6985), West Glover. Gourmet sandwiches, homemade desserts, VT products, and a terrific wine selection.

(6) Sugarmill Farm Maple Museum (800-668-7978), Rte. 16, Barton. Sugarhouse, exhibits.

Drive 14

Heart of the Northeast Kingdom

98 miles

The Northeast Kingdom, Governor George Aiken named it, and here at its northeasternmost it most resembles a sovereign forest fastness. Drive north from St. Johnsbury and Lyndonville to a proving-ground for American Olympic skiers, then leave civilization behind as the drive presses north towards the wilderness outpost of Island Pond. Due east through nearly unbroken forest lies the valley of the Connecticut River, barely beginning a drive to the sea that splits New England in two. Follow the river south, then plunge back into the deep woods towards a clutch of Vermont's smallest and most rustic settlements and the eerie silence of a vast, primordial bog.

(1) Head north out of St. Johnsbury on Rte. 5 (see Drive 12 for city tour and information). There are five covered bridges in the **Lyndon/Lyndonville** area, including several which we'll pass on this drive. Pick up a walking tour brochure of the bridges at the Lyndonville Information Booth or at the town's Cobleigh Library, 14 Depot Street.

In **Lyndon**, the General William Cahoon House was the first two-story house built in town, and is the oldest house still

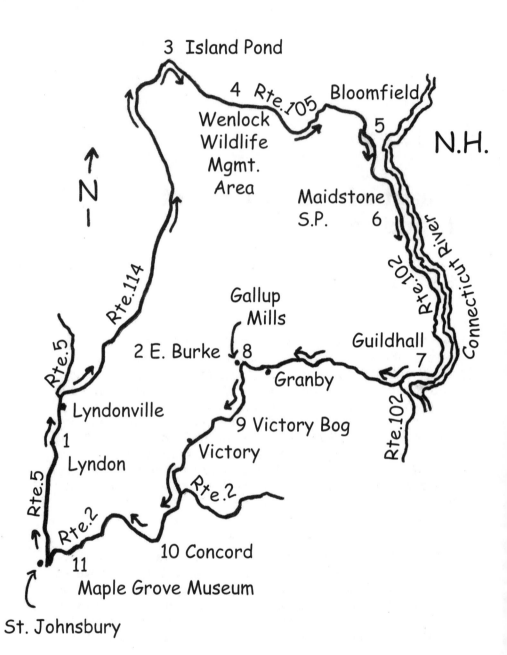

3 Island Pond

4 Rte.105   Bloomfield

Wenlock
Wildlife
Mgmt.
Area

5

N.H.

Maidstone
S.P.   6

N

Rte.114

Gallup
Mills

Rte.5

2 E. Burke 8   Guildhall

Granby   7

Lyndonville

9 Victory Bog

1

Victory

Lyndon

Rte.2

Rte.5

Rte.102

Connecticut River

Rte.102

Rte.2

10 Concord

11

Maple Grove Museum

St. Johnsbury

standing in the community. To drive by it, turn right a quarter-mile past the I-91 overpass onto Red Village Road and look for the house on the left just past the Pines Nursing Home.

Back on Rte. 5, as you follow what passes in Caledonia County for suburban sprawl on your way into Lyndonville, watch for the **Miss Lyndonville Diner** on the right. Although not a diner in the true architectural sense, it serves up classic roadside fare, including breakfasts hefty enough to stoke a Northeast Kingdom logger, and fresh strawberry pie in season. On the left, **Trout River Brewing Company** makes all-natural, unfiltered ales and lagers using traditional methods and will be glad to let you taste the wares ($.50 for samples). They have a tasting room, retail store, and, on Fri. and Sat. nights, serve what some consider the best pizza in the north country.

During the 1860s, Lyndonville was the headquarters and terminus of the Passumpsic Division of the Boston & Maine Railroad, and its days of prosperity, though long past, are still evident in the handsome Victorian architecture along Depot Street. Today the town is home to enterprises as diverse as Lyndon State College, home of an appropriately-sited degree program in meteorology; and the Dairy Association Company, manufacturers of Bag Balm, the ointment in the little green tin which was developed in 1899 as a soothing unguent for cows' udders and is now used to soothe the chapped hands and dry skin of humans, many of whom have never had an actual bovine encounter. Lyndonville Cutting Tools, a successor to Lyndonville Tap & Die, continues the town's legacy as a tool manufacturing center. And on the intellectual front, don't miss **Green Mountain Books**, which has a terrific selection of new and used Vermont titles.

As you continue north on Rte. 5 , watch for the town green and bandstand. One of the region's oldest musical ensembles, the Lyndonville Band, plays here on Wednesday evenings in the summer. Gerald Aubin, who plays the baritone horn and the double-billed euphonium, has been with the band since 1929.

The covered Sanborn Bridge spans the East Branch of the Passumpsic River just south of the intersection of Rte. 5 and Rte. 114. The open-sided bridge, built in 1867 to a design called the Paddleford truss, is on the property of the

Lynburke Motel. It was moved here from another Lyndonville location in 1960, when it was threatened with demolition.

(2) Veer right onto Rte. 114 and follow signs for Burke Mountain and Island Pond. Did you notice the Darling Apartments in downtown Lyndonville? Just ahead is Darling Hill Road, the turnoff for the **Wildflower Inn**. Darling is a big name in these parts: native son Elmer A. Darling built "Burklyn" (still a private home) on the side of Burke Mountain, and, in 1933, donated the 1,726 acres of land (now 1,998 acres), including the mountain itself, to the state for what is now **Darling State Park**.

Stay on Rte. 114 past Darling Hill Road, keeping an eye out on the right for the 1865 queenpost Randall Bridge, which crosses the East Branch of the Passumpsic River next to Old Burrington Road. Rte. 114 continues to follow the East Branch into the tidy but unpretentious little ski town of **East Burke**, headquarters of Kingdom Trails, a 100-mi.-long (50 mi. in winter) playground for non-motorized vehicles which has been cobbled together from logging, fire, and scenic country roads. Much of the network crosses private property, so it's extremely important that users obey the rules. Day member ($5 adults) and annual member ($20) passes are on sale at the Village Sports Shop in Lyndonville and East Burke Sports.

After stocking up on provisions (including homemade pizza and sandwiches) and local crafts at **Bailey's & Burke**, be sure to stop in at the library, donated by Mr. Darling. Among its collection of historical oddments is a copy of one of the last official documents signed by Abraham Lincoln. It isn't exactly the Gettysburg Address: "Allow the bearer, A.B. Darling [Elmer's uncle] to pass to, and visit Mobile, if, and when that city shall be in our possession. A. Lincoln. April 13, 1865." The president was shot the next day.

Just north out of town on Rte. 114 is the turn-off for Darling State Park (and the **Old Cutter Inn**), which encompasses **Burke Mountain Ski Area**. A steep, paved road winds past the ski slopes to the summit of 3,267 ft. Burke Mountain; the views of adjacent Kirby Mountain, Lake Willoughby, and beyond the Canadian border are worth the drive on a clear day. Nearby Burke Mountain Academy -- considered to be one of the premier skiing-oriented secondary schools in the country -- is a training ground for Olympic hopefuls.

As you plunge deeper into the heart of the Northeast Kingdom, still following along the East Branch of the Passumpsic River, the mountains give way to more expansive views. You're now in moose country: keep an eye out for "licks" -- areas where salt used on roads in winter has run off into surrounding bogs. Moose love the taste and often come to these spots to get their dose of salt, generally in the early morning hours. Moose antlers add a decorative touch to many a home here. You'll note several mounted on garages, next to satellite dishes (if there's no dish, that means the antlers themselves are tuned to pick up the Outdoor Life Channel).

(3) At the junction of routes 114 and 105 , bear right and continue east on Rte. 105 to **Island Pond**. The town that bills itself as "Vermont's last frontier" really does have the feel of an outpost at the edge of a vast wilderness. In winter it adds yet another sobriquet: "Snowmobile Capital of Vermont." This is no idle boast. The Gervais family, former owners of the **Lakefront Motel**, have worked hard and successfully over the past ten years to make the town a mecca for snowmobilers. On a fine winter's day, when the Kingdom's forests glisten and the trails are firm and white, there often seem to be as many snow machines as cars in town. Their riders stop for gas and provisions, and often to spend the night. In more than a few cases, that's one night among many: an Island Pond motel clerk recently remarked that he has seen a marked increase in the number of snowmobilers cruising coast to coast. That's right: from Washington State to Maine or perhaps even the Canadian Maritime provinces, on an interstate highway system that melts in the spring.

Founded in 1781, Island Pond takes its name from the two-mile by one-mile body of water -- really a small lake -- at the southern end of the village. (Visitors are delighted to find that because the "pond" is shallow, the water warms up early on and swimming can be delightful even in June.) Back in the golden age of train travel, the town was a major division point on the Grand Trunk railroad between Portland, Maine and Montreal. The first trains from those cities met here -- it's actually the halfway point on the route -- on July 18, 1854, thus opening a long-dreamed-of avenue of transportation between the Quebec metropolis and Maine's ice-free port. Nowadays only freight trains (and, in autumn, the luxury excursion trains of the Acadian Railway) rumble through Island Pond, although the tracks still loom large along Main Street.

In the early morning hours of June 22, 1984, a cadre of Vermont state police officers and social workers invaded Island Pond. One hundred and ten adults and 112 children -- all members of the Northeast Kingdom Community Church, a religious group which modeled itself on a first-century Christian sect -- were rounded up and bused twenty miles to the city of Newport. The authorities were responding to reports that the children, home-schooled within the group, were being physically abused -- i.e., disciplined according to a rigorous "spare the rod, spoil the child" philosophy. The state asked for a 72-hour blanket detention to allow time to question the children. District Judge Frank Mahady, however, ruled that "in our society people are not pieces of evidence" and the cases were dismissed for lack of evidence. The Community continues to reside in Island Pond, and has opened up numerous retail businesses, selling everything from shoes to Vermont crafts, throughout the state.

Before heading out of town, stop in and take a look at the 100+-year-old **Clyde River Hotel**. "The snowmobilers love my old hotel," says the owner, and it's easy to see why: rambling and snug, it's the lodging you'd expect to find at Vermont's last frontier. If you aren't spending the night, and plan to meander slowly back to St. Johnsbury, it's a good idea to do as the snowmobilers do and stock up on lunch supplies at one of the local markets: there are very few places to shop between here and St. Jay.

Pristine, 152-acre **Brighton State Park**, the Northeast Kingdom's most northerly state park, occupies a spit of land between Island Pond and secluded Spectacle Pond. It's a great place for launching a canoe exploration of the area. There's a swimming beach, nature trails, and boat rentals.

(4) Head east out of Island Pond on Rte. 105. Approximately seven miles out of town, watch for **Wenlock Wildlife Management Area**. This 1,993-acre tract of land lies at the southern edge of the Nulhegan River drainage basin, and much of the land is flat wetlands and spruce-fir forests. The area is part of a 6,000-acre softwood basin that is the state's largest deer wintering area. It's also home to several uncommon bird species, including the black-backed three-toed woodpecker and the boreal chickadee; and is home to Vermont's only breeding population of the threatened spruce grouse. It's also prime moose territory, and home to the shy and reclusive black bear. The river is a good place to fish for native brook trout, and is stocked with brown trout.

(5) Continue east on Rte. 105 to the junction of Rte. 102 in **Bloomfield**, where, on December 30, 1933, New England recorded its lowest temperature: -50 degrees F. (The record was challenged by a Maine reading during the winter of 1998-99, but much to Bloomfield's relief it was later discovered that the Mainer's thermometer was on the fritz.) If you continue straight across the bridge, which spans the Connecticut River, you'll be in New Hampshire. To continue this drive, turn right on Rte. 102 and follow the river as it meanders south from its source at the First Connecticut Lake near the Quebec-New Hampshire border. It's a long way from here to Long Island Sound, but that's where this stripling stream is headed.

(6) A few miles south is the turn-off (the entrance is 3.8 mi. from here) for the gorgeously remote **Maidstone State Park**, in Maidstone State Forest. The centerpiece of the park is the pristine, three-mile-long glacially-formed Maidstone Lake, home to nesting common loons At dusk, full-voiced in their plaintive wail or eldritch laugh, these birds are the soul of the North Woods. The lake is also home to lake trout up to twenty-five pounds, landlocked salmon, and rainbow and brook trout. The surrounding forests, in which spruce and fir stands alternate with mixed northern hardwoods, harbors a wide variety of wildlife, including white-tailed deer, river otter, snowshoe hare, fisher, great horned owls, broad-winged hawks, and red fox. Jack-in-the-pulpit, bloodroot and trillium blossom each spring.

(7) Back on Rte. 102, continue south to the pretty little village of **Guildhall** (pronounced "Gilhall"), seat of Essex County government and one of the earliest towns to be settled in this part of Vermont (1764). Ten years earlier, Captain Peter Powers had discovered the falls that were to power some of the town's first industries, including a gristmill and hat factory. In 1795, those primal settlers built the eponymous **Guild Hall**, today the town hall. The elegant Community Church on the green was built in 1844.   Just behind the church, the North Burying Ground, laid out by the selectmen in 1797, recalls the settlement's history through two centuries of epitaphs. The Guildhall bridge is a popular launching spot for canoeists: the 23-mile stretch of Connecticut River between here and Gilman, Vermont flows south through woods and pastures, over a Class II rapids, past an old dam, and under a covered bridge.

(8) A few miles south of town, watch for the right-hand turn onto Granby Road for **Granby** (the sign is only readable from the south, so don't be surprised if you have to do a bit of backtracking for course correction). The dirt road, a thoroughfare for lumber trucks, winds through the woods for nine miles past isolated dwellings before reaching tiny Granby, home of one of the last one-room schoolhouses in Vermont. This was one of the last three towns in Vermont to get electricity -- in the same year that Alan Shephard rocketed into space. Victory and Jamaica were the other two.

The next bump in the road is the hamlet of **Gallup Mills**, part of the town of **Victory**. Improbable as it seems today, this minuscule settlement was once the site of one of the region's most important sawmills, built when the Northeast Kingdom's virgin forest was first felled, and was a stop on the St. Johnsbury and Lake Champlain Railroad. The unique "license plate" house on the left side of the road was the home of Orien Dunn, featured in Scott E. Hastings, Jr.'s fine book, *The Last Yankees*, who for many years practiced the arcane trade of boring pump logs -- the wooden pipes that carried water from the pump or water tub at the house to wherever it was needed on the farm. Until 1961, remember, water pumping and a lot of other activities in Victory were performed by hand, and kerosene lit house and barn.

(9) Just out of Gallup Mills, turn left onto River Road to **Victory Bog** and the **Victory Basin Wildlife Management Area**, a glacially-formed, 4,970-acre northern ecosystem made up of lowland spruce-fir forests, upland hardwoods, sedge meadows, alder swales, and true bog, watered by the Moose River. The best way to explore the area is by canoe or on foot along its hiking trails and logging roads. The area's residents include river otter, moose, American bittern, saw-whet and great-horned owls, and ruffed grouse. Rare pitcher plants are among the bog flora. There are several parking areas along the road.

(10) In North Concord, turn right (west) at the intersection with Rte. 2 and head to **Concord**. A roadside marker commemorates the site of the first American normal school (the old name for a teachers' academy) in nearby East Concord. In 1823 Samuel Read Hall was offered $300 a year (plus $4 to ring the bell) as the town's church missionary. Deploring the quality of teaching he had seen in the hills, he expanded his duties and founded his pioneer normal school. His methods included practice teaching, along with study of his *Lectures on School Keeping*, America's first real manual for teachers. He told his students: "it is your work to take these children as you find them and to train them with reference to their duties as citizens of a free country, as members of society, and as moral agents, under the government of the Great Creator." The school itself was located some 2 1/2 miles south of here, at Concord Corner.

(11) Stop in at the venerable **Farmer's Daughter Gift Barn** and browse through their huge selection of Vermont products, handicrafts, and maple products. There's lots of free fudge, cheese and syrup samples.

A bit further west, on the outskirts of **St. Johnsbury** (see Drive 12), is a marker honoring the site where the first American Platform Scale was manufactured. For a first-hand look at maple syrup making, stop at **Maple Grove Farms & Museum**, the oldest and largest maple products factory in the country. They have a factory tour, museum, and gift shop.

Information

Burke Area Chamber of Commerce (626-4124), P.O. Box 347, E. Burke 05832. www.burkevermont.com

Island Pond Chamber of Commerce (723-6300), The Historic Railroad Station, Island Pond 05846. www.islandpond.com

Lyndon Area Chamber of Commerce (626-9696), 51 Depot St., P.O. Box 886, Lyndonville 05851. Information booth: Broad St. across from Lyndonville Savings Bank, Memorial Day-Labor Day. www.lyndonvermont.com

Northeast Kingdom Chamber of Commerce (800-639-6379 or 748-3678), 357 Western Ave., St. Johnsbury 05819. www.vermontnekchamber.org

Vermont Association of Snow Travelers (VAST) (802-229-0005), 41 Granger Rd., Berlin (Barre) 05641. Snowmobiling information for the Northeast Kingdom. www.vtvast.org

Lodgings

(1) Branch Brook B & B (800-572-7712 or 626-8316), P.O. Box 217, South Wheelock Rd., Lyndon 05849. 5 nicely decorated rooms (3 with private bath) in a lovely 1850s home. $-$$

(2)(R) Inn at Mountain Farm (626-9924), Box 355, East Burke 05832. The 440-acre retreat has 12 antiques-filled guest rooms in a handsome Georgian colonial. Dinner, served Fri.-Sun., ($$-$$$) includes a variety of entrees, such as duck confit, Tuscan chicken stew, and grilled filet mignon with wild mushrooms. www.innmtview.com $$

(2)(R) Old Cutter Inn (800-295-1943 or 626-5152), Pinkham Rd., E. Burke. 9 guest rooms and a 2-bedroom suite with fireplace. Heated outdoor pool.

The Swiss owner-chef serves traditional dishes, including rahmschnitzel, rack of lamb, and rosti potato cake. Dinner ($$) Thurs.-Tues.; Sun. brunch by reservation. Tavern menu. www.pbpub.com/cutter ($)

(2) The Village Inn (626-3161), Rte. 114, East Burke. 1845 village home has 5 spacious guest rooms with private baths, a kitchen for guests' use, gardens, and a picnic area by a trout brook. Pets by arrangement. www.villageinnofeastburke.com $

(2)(R) The Wildflower Inn (800-627-8310 or 626-8310), Darling Hill Rd., Lyndonville 05851. 500-acre resort offers a variety of accommodations, including a 3-room family suite; one with hot tub and 2 baths; and a renovated 1-room schoolhouse. Heated outdoor pool, tennis, hiking and mountain bike trails. Supervised children's activities. The restaurant ($$), overlooking the mountains, serves creative fish and meat dishes, as well as traditional favorites such as beef stew. www.wildflowerinn.com $$

(3)(R) Clyde River Hotel (723-5663), Cross St., Island Pond 05846. 15 simple rooms (6 with private bath), and 3 efficiencies. www.islandpond.com/clyde-river-hotel $

(3) Lakefront Inn & Motel (723-6507), Cross St., Island Pond 05846. Modern, lakefront motel has 20 rooms, suites and efficiency units (some with lake views); boat rental. www.thelakefrontinn.com $-$$

(7) Guildhall B & B (800-987-8240 or 676-3720), Box 129, Rte. 102, Guildhall 05905. 1811 colonial in village has 3 guest rooms with shared bath. $

Restaurants

(1) Miss Lyndonville Diner (626-9890), Rte. 5, North Lyndonville. B, L, D. $

(2) River Garden Cafe (626-3514), Rte. 114, East Burke. Creative and eclectic fare served in a casual environment; lovely seasonal patio and porch. L, D, and Sun. brunch. Closed Mon. and Tues. $-$$

(3) Friendly's Pizza (723-4616), Cross St., Island Pond. Pizza, subs, Greek salads and daily specials. Lunch and dinner. $

(3) Jennifer's (723-6135), Cross St., Island Pond. Steaks and seafood. Three meals daily. Sat. is prime rib night. Kids' menu. $-$$

Attractions

(2) Darling State Park/Burke Mountain (800-541-5480 or 626-3305), East Burke 05832.

(2) East Burke Library, East Burke.

(2) Kingdom Trail Association (626-0737), Box 204, E. Burke 05832.

(3) Brighton State Park (723-4360). Late May-mid Oct. $

(3) Lady of the Lake (723-6649), Island Pond. 1-hour narrated cruise on Island Pond. Mid-May-mid-Sept. $

(4) Wenlock Wildlife Management Area (751-0100 or 748-8787), Vermont Fish & Wildlife, 184 Portland St., St. Johnsbury.

(6) Maidstone State Park (676-3930) RD, Box 455, Guildhall 05905. Camping, picnicking, grills, fireplaces, sandy beach, boat rentals. Late May-Labor Day. $

(7) Essex County Courthouse, Guildhall. Original Ethan Allen furniture.

(9) Victory Basin Wildlife Management Area (748-8787), Vermont Dept. of Fish & Wildlife, 184 Portland St., St. Johnsbury.

(11) Maple Grove Farms & Museum (748-5141), 167 Portland St., St. Johnsbury.

Activities and Shopping

(1) Green Mountain Books & Prints (626-5051), 100 Broad St., Lyndonville. 50,000 volumes includes used and new books, rare and first editions, as well as remainders (especially art books) Closed Sun.

(1) Village Sport Shop (800-464-4315 or 626-8448), Rte. 5, 511 Broad St., Lyndonville. Bikes, canoes, pedal boats, kayaks, and roller blades for rent. USGS maps, retail supplies. Kingdom Trail passes.

(2) Bailey's & Burke General Store (626-3666), Rte. 114, East Burke. Turn-of-the-century general store: deli, bakery, handicrafts, handmade baskets.

(2) East Burke Sports (626-1188), Rte. 114, East Burke. Hiking and biking maps, mountain bike, canoe, and ski rentals. Repair shop. Kingdom Trail passes.

(2)(R) Trout River Brewing Co., (626-9396), Rte. 5, Lyndonville. Samples for $.50. Store/tap room 11-6; pizza Fri. 5-8:30 and Sat. 4:30-8:30. Open Wed.-Sat.

(2) Rohan Farm (467-3701), Darling Hill Rd., East Burke. Trails rides for experienced riders.

(3) Northern Wildlife Taxidermy and Sports (723-6659), Rte. 105, Island Pond. Canoe and rowboat rentals by the half and full day.

(11) Farmer's Daughter Gift Barn (748-3994), Rte. 2, St. Johnsbury.

A SAMPLING OF ANNUAL VERMONT EVENTS

May
Vermont City Marathon (863-8412), Burlington. 26.2 mile course through downtown; Sports and Fitness Exposition and buffet dinner. Entry fee. www.vcm.org

June
Burlington Discover Jazz Festival (863-5966). Six days of concerts, dances, street parties, musical cruises, and jams at venues throughout the city. www.discoverjazz.com

Ethan Allen Days (362-2100), Ethan Allen Homestead, Burlington. Vermont's history is brought to life with reenactments, music, crafters, and an old-fashioned barn dance. Free. www.ethanallendays.com

Kids Maritime Festival, Lake Champlain Maritime Museum (475-2022), Vergennes. Tours, live music, arts & crafts, and exploring. www.lcmm.org

Strolling of the Heifers (877-VTSBEST), Brattleboro. Vermont's Running of the Bulls honors small farmers. Parade and heifer ball (admission to ball).

Vermont History Expo (479-8500), Tunbridge. Historical societies throughout the state host exhibits, a Heritage Parade and Box Lunch auction, children's activities, and encampments. www.vermonthistory.org/expo

Vermont Quilt Festival (485-7092), Norwich University, Northfield. More than 400 quilts are displayed; merchants' mall, workshops, and an ice cream social. www.vqf.org

July

19th-Century Croquet Tournament (765-4021), Strafford Common, Strafford. An old-fashioned tournament with 19th-century attire and modern-day rules. www.morrillhomestead.org

Stoweflake Hot Air Balloon Festival (800-253-2232), Stowe. Twenty-five balloons launch at 6:30 a.m. and 6:30 p.m. on Friday and Saturday; there's live music, a beer garden, and a children's corner. www.stoweflake.com

Vermont Mozart Festival (862-7352). A three-week festival in July and August of chamber and orchestral music at indoor and outdoor locations throughout the state. www.vtmozart.com

Windsor Heritage Days (674-5910), Windsor. "Turn back the clock in time" to July 8, 1777, when the state of Vermont was born. Period costumes, reenactments, music, parades, and arts and crafts.

August

Vermont Festival of the Arts (800-517-4247), Waitsfield, Warren and Fayston. 17-day festival includes music, dance, theater, visual arts, exhibits, open galleries, food, and

hands-on children's events. Some admission.
www.vermontartfest.com

Vermont State Fair (775-5200), Rutland.
Late August-early September event includes
agricultural events, live music, and food.
www.vermontstatefair.net

September

Fine Wine and Food Festival (652-4500),
Shelburne. Featuring specialty wines and food
products. Live music, auction. www.flynncenter.org

New World Festival at Chandler (728-9878 or
728-9133), Randolph. Celtic and French Canadian
music and dance. www.NewWorld Festival.com

Old Fashioned Harvest Festival (899-3369),
Underhill. Parade, entertainment, flea market,
artisans, and children's activities. Free.

Plymouth Cheese & Harvest Festival (672-
3773), President Calvin Coolidge State Historic
Site, Plymouth Notch. Historic farm and craft
demonstrations, wagon rides, sheep shearing,
children's games. Free. www.historicvermont.org

Tunbridge World's Fair (800-889-5555),
Tunbridge. 130+-year-old fair includes agricultural
exhibits, sheep dog trials, antique tractor pulls,
and entertainment. www.tunbridgefair.com

Vermont Regiment Civil War Expo (476-3580),
Tunbridge. Day-long civil war reenactment includes
sharpshooters, displays, and torchlight parade.

October

Applefest (372-5566), South Hero. Two-day Champlain Islands festival features crafts, cider pressing contests, a petting zoo, entertainment, and a flea market. Free.

New England Bach Festival (257-4526), Marboro/Brattleboro. Week-long performances include vocal soloists, musicians, the Blanch Moyse chorale and more, hosted by the Brattleboro Music Center. www.bmcvt.org

Vermont Sheep and Wool Festival (446-3325), Essex Junction. Live animal displays, crafts, shearing and sheepdog trials, and vendors. www.vermontsheep.org

December

First Night Burlington (863-6005 or 800-639-9252). New Year's Eve from 2 p.m. to midnight, incorporating performing arts events at venues throughout the city. Buy a button for admission to all events. www.firstnightburlington.com

January

Stowe Winter Carnival (253-7321 or 800-247-8693). Competitions, ice carving contest, snow golf, kids events, chicken pie supper, parade and fireworks. www.stowewintercarnival.com